LONDON WALKS®

LONDON
STORIES

Discover the City's Hidden Gems with
the Original Walking Company

David Tucker & The Guides

Published by Virgin Books 2009
8 10 9 7

General editor Stephen Barnett

London Walks® is the registered trademark of the London Walks Ltd
www.walks.com

Drawings by Pete Scully
Maps by Nick Turzynski
With thanks to Rick Steves for his Foreword

First published in Great Britain in 2009 by
Virgin Books
Random House, 20 Vauxhall Bridge Road,
London SW1V 2SA

www.virginbooks.com
www.randomhouse.co.uk

Addresses for companies within The Random House Group Limited can be found at:
www.randomhouse.co.uk/offices.htm

The Random House Group Limited Reg. No. 954009

A CIP catalogue record for this book
is available from the British Library

ISBN 9780753515051

Typeset by Palimpsest Book Production Limited,
Grangemouth, Stirlingshire

The Random House Group Limited supports The Forest Stewardship Council® (FSC®), the leading international forest-certification organisation. Our books carrying the FSC label are printed on FSC®-certified paper. FSC is the only forest-certification scheme supported by the leading environmental organisations, including Greenpeace. Our paper procurement policy can be found at www.randomhouse.co.uk/environment

Printed and bound in Great Britain by Clays Ltd, St Ives plc

For Mary (Poppins):
'Practically perfect', she made it home . . .

Contents

FOREWORD

By Rick Steves, author of *Europe Through the Back Door* and thirty other European travel guidebooks

The best way to see a city is not just on foot . . . but on foot with a good guide. A local person who lives in a great city can shine a light on its soul. Where I come from, you can wander lanes and parks, and gaze at balconies and street signs, and there's little to say. But in a city like London, movers and shakers of Western Civilisation walked the cobbles, sipped beer in snugs, and shaped our past.

London lends itself to walks as well as any city in Europe. It's a city of towns and villages which grew together while maintaining their personality quirks. It's a city still roamed by the spirits of Romans and the proud Celts they put down. It's a city that inspired literary greats. It's a city that stood up to a battering in the darkness of the Second World War and refused to break. And, it's a city that confounds tourists without a guide.

For twenty years, as a visiting and curious and sometimes overwhelmed traveller, I have enjoyed David Tucker and his band of London guides. Each has a passion that carbonates the slice of London they share. And they have helped me appreciate the many facets of their city.

Now, with this collection of essays, these guides take their gift to travellers and amplify it so that we can all, wherever we are, sit back and enjoy a little slice of one of our world's great cities.

INTRODUCTION

DAVID TUCKER

London still has – thank heavens – some 2,000 gas lamps. And even in the 1980s there was still one gas-lamp lighter at work! His beat was the Temple area, part of the lawyers' quarter. He made his rounds every evening at dusk. He carried a long pole – his lighter. With it he'd reach up and catch and open a turncock of sorts. That would release the gas. Then he'd turn the implement in his fingers and apply a lighted taper to the newly released gas, which blossomed into flame. Then he'd be around again, first thing in the morning, implement in hand, to extinguish the flame. Purely by chance I happened to be in the Temple area that day in the mid-1980s when the work crews were going through there, fitting out each of the gas lamps with a timer, a clock, which would do the job automatically. I was strangely moved. The thought being: a hundred years ago there would have been hundreds if not thousands of gas-lamp lighters in London, earning their livelihoods, supporting their families. And here we were – in the middle of the ninth decade of the twentieth century – and it had come down to one last gas-lamp lighter. He was the last of the Mohicans. And he was about to be made extinct.

We don't have gas-lamp lighters any more – but we do still have gas-lamp clock winders. They wind the clocks – and adjust the lighting-up and extinguishing times – for London's remaining gas lamps. And there's one gas lamp in London where we – the public – can be, however momentarily, a gas-lamp lighter. We can turn it on and off. But you'll have to go on Angela's walk to find it!

Now all of this is by way of saying that London Walks® guides are, after a fashion, latter-day gas-lamp lighters. Picture it: the lamplighter's figure moving along a London street in the gloaming and one by one the street lamps coming out like stars. And you think there's no romance to London? So that's what we do – light things up for people. Both out on the streets of London when we're guiding, and here, in these pages.

Local knowledge, knowing where to go when – you can't beat it. How did the thirteenth-century poet Rumi put it? 'Whoever travels without a guide needs two hundred years for a two-day journey.'

WHERE TO READ THIS

No question about it: the *wonderful* Café in the Crypt at St Martin-in-the-Fields, the old church in Trafalgar Square.

London Walks® is the oldest urban-walking tour company in the world. It is by common consent the best urban-walking tour company in the world.

A great walk is accretional in the sense that a guide's understanding of a neighbourhood grows, develops, gets richer and richer over time. It takes years – this is England, after all – but in time a guide will become part of the furniture of a given neighbourhood, will become accepted and trusted by the locals. And that's when the 'magic' really starts to happen. Because the locals will then open up to the guide, sharing fascinating titbits with him or her about the neighbourhood. It's that sort of connectedness that sets London Walks® apart.

When it came to thinking about a book based on all the accrued knowledge and feel for the city, we wanted something different from the bog-standard walking-tour guidebook. What we wanted was it to be a great read. In short, we wanted it to be an armchair read as well as a useful on-the-street guide. This is why each chapter has a little 'side bar' suggesting where you might read that particular section. The idea being – for readers who are in London at any rate – you can read the chapter while seated comfortably in, say, the Founders Arms or in front of the great fourth-floor windows of Tate Modern with their wonderful panoramic view out over the Thames and across to the City skyline (those are the two recommended reading 'spots' for my chapter on the Thames that opens the book), and then go out and do some exploring on your own. The French have the word for this sort of thing: *flânerie*. We wanted the London Walks® book to be one that would allow for some flâneuring. Read and then explore on your own. Flâneuring allows for happy accidents, for discoveries.

We also wanted the guides' individual voices to come through. London Walks® is like a symphony orchestra: a team of great people that works together brilliantly. But within that orchestra every guide is also a solo and we wanted a range of voices, because that is London Walks®, the result of a richness – and indeed collegiality – you get when you have a team of seventy or so world-class guides simultaneously tilling their own rows *and* working together.

And we wanted the thing to shine with intelligence. Another contributing factor to London Walks®' reputation is the intellectual audacity of the guides. Some of that, of course, is attested to by their professional qualifications, the guides comprising authors, a barrister, a physician, a roll-call of award-winning Blue Badge guides (not to mention Chief Examiner of the Blue Badge course), PhDs, distinguished London historians, archaeologists, journalists, broadcasters and more. And they are experts in the tours they lead. As the *New York Times* unerringly put it many years ago, 'London Walks® puts you into the hands of an expert on the particular area and topic of a tour.' That's what we've done on the pavement for nearly half a century. And it's what we've done here on the page. Among the contributions, our 'Jack the Ripper' chapter by the distinguished criminologist (and London Walks®' Ripper guide *extraordinaire*) Donald Rumbelow, who is, as *The Jack the Ripper A to Z* put it, 'internationally recognised as the leading authority on the Ripper'. Then there is the gifted actor Shaughan Seymour – 'the best ghost walks guide in London' – who has of course contributed a haunted London story; distinguished barrister Tom Hooper MBE on London and its history in law; cutting-edge journalist Adam Scott and Fleet Street; leading London archaeologist Kevin Flude and Roman London; and 'One-man London gazetteer' and renowned London historian Ed Glinert and his Soho chapter. And so on. Regrettably the remarkable resource the guides comprise can be represented only in part in this book – it just isn't possible to include contributions from the full complement of guides – but a superb representation it is.

When you're marinated in the cask the way our guides are, inevitably London becomes part of you. There's an exceptionally pretty little row of white cottages in Hampstead. You look at them with their splendidly colourful doors – red, green, yellow, pink – and you think for a moment you're on a Greek island. Anyway, in front of one of them there's a low iron gate and the vegetation – the tree – beside it has grown round some of the bars in that gate. It has literally ingested them. Iron bars and tree have become one. Well, that's a pretty good metaphor for London Walks® guides and their material.

I also want to acknowledge the origins of this book, in the shape of Steve Barnett. The book's concept was his, as was the idea of *stories* within a framework of chapters. Together we hit on the notion of a structure of paired stories (well, five stories in the case of the chapter on London's villages, and the chapters on the Thames and Dickens stand alone) in order to better explain the city and its history. London is so big, and so deep – Henry James spoke of its 'inconceivable immensity' – that it can be difficult to conceptualise.

What it all adds up to is that *London Stories* is a different kind of guidebook. Some of the information is well known – the landmarks and signposts along the road of London's history – but there is much that will be new to readers. And, of course, it's all in the telling, which is what London Walks®' guides do best.

London for me – and for my colleagues – is an enchanted forest. It's full of wondrous strange music and echoes, past and present. In short, my London is also Chaucer's London and Shakespeare's London and Donne's London and Pepys's London and Dickens's London and Boudicca's London and Mrs Pankhurst's London and Churchill's London and John Lennon's London and so on. And that's the London – those are the *Londons* – that we explore on our walks. And in these pages.

THAMESIS

DAVID TUCKER

The best way to see London is to hear it: The Thames, Londinium, Lundenwic, Lundenburgh, Thames Street, Fleet Street, the Strand, Shipwright's Lane, Holborn, Strand Bridge, Queenhithe, Paul's Wharf, Bankside, Walbrook, Mill Bank, Horseferry, Chelsea, Putney, Stepney, Hackney, Battersea, Bermondsey, Thorney, Eastbourne, Westbourne, Kilburn, Tyburn, Marylebone, Moorfields, Greenwich Palace, Palace of Westminster, Whitehall Palace, Custom House Stairs, Swan Stairs, Fishmongers' Hall . . . The common denominator? The Thames.

The Mississippi drains a continent. Small beer, really. The Thames drains time itself.

It's entirely appropriate that Greenwich – London's 'harbour town' – should be the birthplace of time. And that time's lighthouse – Big Ben, the most famous clock in the world – could be mistaken for a ship's lantern high up in a mast.

The Thames. London. Notice the sequence. It's the correct one. The travel agents' brochures speak of the Thames as 'London's river'. Close but no cigar. It's the other way round. London is the Thames' town. No Thames, no London; it's as simple as that. The Thames was here before London. The Thames is the reason London is where it is. The Thames *made* London.

Look at the 1572 Braun and Hogenberg map of London.* Many of those same streets are there today, nearly four-and-a-half centuries later. To the south of St Paul's – towards the river – there are only three streets running east to west. The other axis – the north–south axis – is a different story. There are fifteen or so north–south streets, a ratio of 5:1. What that tells us is that it wasn't so desperately important to be able to go east or west. And in any case, for that you had London's largest – and most important – street: the river Thames. What was vitally important was to be able to go north or south. And it's not the compass points that are important here. What's important is what lay to the south: the river Thames. London is orientated to its river.

The point is underlined – in every way – by Thames Street. It's the biggest and most important of the east–west *land* streets between the river and the cathedral. It's closest to the river. It *accompanies* the river. And, yes, it's still with us. You can walk it. It's been rechristened Upper Thames Street and Lower Thames Street, but it's essentially the same street.

OK, let's go down to the river; get into the slipstream of history. If you

---

*You can see it at http://historic-cities.huji.ac.il/british_isles/london/maps/braun_hogenberg_I_A.html

lend an ear, what can you *see*? Let's start with the name itself – Thames. It's the second oldest place name in this country ('Kent' pipped it to the post). We don't know with any certainty where the name comes from or what, precisely, it means. Various explanations have flowed down to us from the 'dark backward and abysm of time', dark being the *mot juste* – because whether it's Celtic or even older (Sanskrit is a possibility), *tame* or *teme*, the core of the name, is said to mean 'dark'. It's the very adjective you'd use to describe the Thames today.

Indeed, it's the very adjective that sounds the keynote of one of the most spellbinding overtures in English literature: the great opening scene of Conrad's *Heart of Darkness*. On a cruising yawl lying at anchor in the Thames – 'the flood had made . . . the sea-reach of the Thames stretched before us' – a group of friends are taking their ease, chatting aimlessly in the fading light. Then they fall silent, as if, in the gloaming, they've sensed a presence far more deeply interfused: 'the spirit of the past was all about them'. Cue Marlowe, the tale's 'narrator'. Quietly, chillingly, he remarks: '. . . and this also has been one of the dark places of the earth'.

He's talking about the Roman era and what it must have been like for the commander of a trireme – or a young Roman citizen, 'in a toga' – to come up this river. 'Imagine him here – the very end of the world, a sea the colour of lead, a sky the colour of smoke . . . sand-banks, marshes, forests, savages', knowing that in coming up these waters he had crossed a frontier, was heading into a wilderness, heading into a place where civilisation's remit didn't reach, heading into the unknown.

WHERE TO READ THIS

Level 4 of Tate Modern has stunning views out over the river to St Paul's (and the City skyline in general). Or for a riverside (as opposed to elevated) vantage point, the Founders Arms, the modern pub just along from Tate Modern, has a superb riverside terrace, not to mention good food and beer!

What we do know is that the 'dark one' wasn't always here. Three quarters of a million years ago its course lay several miles to the north, through the 'Vale of St Albans'. The 'event' that redirected the Thames – diverted it to its present location – was a glacier, a 'sheet' of ice a mile high. Was that important? Well, it bears repeating – no Thames, no London. So the most important event in London's history took place 750,000 years ago.

And if that's not enough *forever* for you, try this for size: just about every London street is 40 to 70 million years old. That's how long ago London's clay was laid down, the clay that for centuries has been quarried for the bricks that are the bass line of London's domestic architecture. Indeed, the Thames foreshore is red with the stuff to this day – in the shape of discarded mediaeval roof tiles.

Shall we get that timeline into perspective? There are 3.2 million houses in London. An average-size London house – 2 to 3 bedrooms, semi-detached – will run to about 8,000 bricks. That's 25 billion bricks in London. One way to keep track of 70 million years is to make a brick a day. At that rate you'll have enough bricks for London – all 25 billion of them – in 70 million years!

Clay's the stuff for bricks, but it won't do for the foundations of a city. The problem is, it doesn't drain. We're not talking damp – we're talking a swamp. So how did London come up out of the ooze? It's the Thames to the rescue again, in the shape of its deltas – the four stepped gravel terraces it laid down over the eons. Gravel terraces that drained. Gravel terraces that were covered with lighter woodland and so were easier to clear. Gravel terraces that made London habitable for human beings instead of swamp birds.

Some of that pre-history is frozen in the amber of London place names: Chelsea, Putney, Stepney, Hackney, Thorney. The suffix '-ney', with a long 'e', is Anglo-Saxon and means 'the rising ground up above the surrounding wetlands'.

All right, it's taken aeons, but the London table is just about set for human beings. We know that hunter-gatherers ranged through here thousands of years ago. We know this because they left a couple of flint hand axes behind. One was found at King's Cross, another under Leadenhall Street.

And – incredibly – there's a Bronze Age bridge whose wooden posts are still (just) visible at low tide. It's a few yards upstream from today's Vauxhall Bridge, right by the mouth of the Effra, one of the Thames' many tributaries.

Which brings us to AD 43, Year Zero for London. Say hello to the Romans, and hello to London, or Londinium as the Romans called it.

Those three – the when, who and what – are just the warm-up acts. It's the other two – the why and where – that are shiver-up-the-spine stuff, like the tingle you get when you realise that this was the *only* spot the entire 215-mile length of the Thames where everything – *everything* – came together to make possible what was to become the great world city. As Noel Coward might have put it, this little bit of all right was *all right!*

So what was it about this spot – 51.36N (latitude) and 00.05W (longitude) – that caught the eye of the finest urban planners the world has ever known?

'All time is eternally present' said T S Eliot (*Four Quartets*). Both the present and the future are 'contained in time past'. He might have been talking about London – and Rome. Time future is contained in time past because history is a continuum – one thing leads to another. And because history rests on geography and geography shapes, geography is destiny. Indeed, the smaller the number of people involved and the less developed their technology, the more importance geography assumes. In other words, the natural advantages and disadvantages of 51.36N and 00.05W counted for everything in AD 43 precisely because there were just a few thousand Romans involved and they were wielding first-century technology.

The Romans put Londinium where they did for several interlocking military, maritime, geological and commercial reasons. The most important of those reasons were the military and maritime ones, and the evidence is still there for us to see today. The past is contained in the present.

Take and hold was the order of the day, and of the centuries, and that meant high ground – it could be defended. It was classic military doctrine, so, like Rome, Londinium was built on hills. St Paul's crowns Ludgate Hill, the westernmost of the two hills of London.

They put Londinium where they did because on the south flank was the Thames, which provided a natural defensive barrier to one side that doubled as a broad highway sweeping down to the Channel. Almost directly across the Channel was the mouth of the Rhine – and, into the bargain, the mouths of the Meuse, the Elbe, the Scheldt, the Somme, the Seine and the Weser, arteries taking them into the heart of the continent. (The reason the mouth of the Rhine is directly across from the mouth of Thames is that 9,000 years ago, when Britain wasn't an island, when the land bridge was still there, the Thames was the principal tributary to the Rhine.)

The Romans put Londinium where they did because on the west side was a second river, the Fleet River. The very word 'fleet' is derived from the Anglo-Saxon for 'moving water'. Our English word 'float' shares that same Anglo-Saxon root. The Fleet provided the Romans with a natural defensive barrier to the west and, into the bargain, a natural harbour. It's still there, of course – it's well-nigh impossible to get rid of a river. It's just that today the Fleet's been culverted and is part of London's storm overflow sewer system. At low tide you can see that outflow opening from Platform 8 of Blackfriars railway station.

And make no mistake, the Fleet was no tiddler. Take a look at New Bridge Street at Blackfriars. It's a very wide street by London standards. And the reason? The time-honoured London principle of the sanctity of the 'building line'. London bricks and mortar (or London stones) have their 'hour' upon the London stage but the building line – where the buildings stand in relation to the street – is all but sacrosanct. In short, New Bridge Street is as wide as it is because it's more or less a perfect 'echo' of the Fleet River. Indeed, in the Middle Ages, Londoners were grousing (and dowsing) for the good old days when ten or twelve ships could sail *abreast* up the Fleet to Fleet Bridge or even to Oldbourne (Holborn) Bridge – in other words, to today's Ludgate Circus or Holborn Viaduct. What was causing the arteriosclerosis of the river at that time was the proliferation of wharves, the diversion of water to the mills of the Temple and everybody using the Fleet as a liquid tip.

They put it where they did because to the third side – the east – was a third stream. It was just a brook – Sir Thomas More Street runs along its line today – but it would have provided a barrier of sorts.

To the north – the fourth side – was an area that was marshy, which came to be known as Moorfields. And it, too, had defensive characteristics. Sloshing through a swamp and simultaneously storming a city are mutually incompatible activities.

They put London where they did because between the two hills was a fourth stream – the Walbrook, London's third most important river. The Walbrook initially provided the Romans with a source of fresh water – and subsequently with a sewer. Location, location, location. Running down through the middle of the city, the Walbrook offered up the perfect marriage of position and function.

Quays were another key. They were a key because of the architecture of Roman ships. That Roman citizen white-knuckling his toga would have come up this river in a primitive but big ocean-going, deep-draft vessel. To get deep-draft ships alongside and off-loaded you have to have quays. And quays needed fairly steep vertical banks. Sure enough, London met that requirement. At Billingsgate, right by Customs House, was where those first Roman wharves were sited, compliments of the steep vertical banks there. Further upstream – where Embankment station is today – the foreshore was a long, gently sloping affair, perfect for the Anglo-Saxons' shallow-draft, flat-bottomed boats, but utterly wrong for Roman ships.

The Romans put Londinium where they did because, directly over the river, perfectly placed, there was a narrow tongue of gravel stretching back from the shoreline. It was like striking gold, because most of that foreshore was a low-lying marsh, a series of mudflat islands. That tongue of gravel was what was needed for the bridge pier on the far shore of the Thames.

And so we come to the birds. Ancient mariners knew that the presence of birds meant land wasn't far off. Roman augurs foretold the future by 'reading' the flight of birds – or examining their entrails. Take a look at the 'aviary' high up on the piers of Blackfriars Bridge. By aviary I mean the carved stone birds cresting the top of those bridge supports. On the downstream side of the bridge they're sea birds. On the upstream side they're freshwater birds. Those birds – and how they are positioned – crystallise the matter for us. They're on their respective sides of the bridge because this was the point at which the tide played itself out.

And that was the linchpin, because as good as Roman engineering was, it was not capable of sinking bridge piles in a powerfully tidal river. Today the difference between the flood tide and the ebb tide is seven metres. If you want to think horizontally, in Roman times, not very much further downstream, at ebb tide the river was 300 metres across, at flood tide 1,000 metres.

Indeed, it's so powerful you can see it. Look at the direction of the flotsam when the tide is coming in – you're watching water flow uphill. Or look at the Southwark 'beach' by Blackfriars Bridge at ebb tide. You can walk on the riverbed four-fifths of the way out to that first bridge pier – a fair distance. At flood tide it'd be a long – and dangerous – swim to get out there.

Want some figures? Today, midstream at Blackfriars Bridge, the Thames is about four metres deep at low tide; at flood tide she's eleven metres deep. Two millennia ago it was a different story – the tide ended here. Today the Thames is tidal for seventy miles – fifty miles from the estuary to London and then another twenty miles to Teddington. But 2,000 years ago it played itself out here. Roman engineers could sink those bridge piles! And that, taken together with all those other geographical factors – the two hills, the vertical banks, the natural harbour, the Walbrook – is why London is where it is.

Not to put too fine a point on it, if God himself had drawn up the plans for London he could hardly have done a better job of it than chance, Mother Nature and Father Geography. Though he might have done something about the weather!

The Thames is liquid history

The Odyssey – that was some trip. It took Ulysses ten years – ten years of shock and awe: the witch-goddess Circe (who turned his sailors into swine); Sirens; Lotus-Eaters; Cyclops; Polyphemus . . . Well, you get the idea.

Our odyssey takes rather longer: 2,000 years. It's made of the same stuff, though; it's just that there's a lot more of it. I'm talking about the history of London, and the way the Thames is the thread along which so much of that history is strung.

We can start with General Plautius and his legions in AD 43, in other words with the Claudian invasion, the birth pangs of London. That Roman force – disciplined and far better armed – would have shocked and awed the native Britons.

But it was no 'cakewalk'. The locals were brave, beautiful, and blue.*

---

*Not with cold, with woad. And beautiful? In Rome, the Britons were much prized as slaves because of their beauty.

'Armed' with local knowledge and fighting for their homes, they gave the Romans fits, served up some shock and awe in the other direction. Plautius' hard-pressed army crossed the Thames at a ford and dug in. We're not sure which ford, but it might have been at Westminster – at Thorney Island. Plautius sent to Rome for help, for a 'surge'. Help came in the shape of the Emperor Claudius himself and the Praetorian Guard . . . and the Elephant brigade. It worked. Claudius got his 'Mission Accomplished' Triumph. And the Romans got on with it.

Well, it wasn't quite mission accomplished, it never is. Eighteen years later, Boudicca* – Queen of the Iceni – staged her famous revolt. The Iceni wanted to collaborate with the Romans. Boudicca's husband, the king, left half of his all to the Romans. It wasn't enough. The Romans seized the lot. Boudicca's daughters were raped. Boudicca was publicly flogged. Big mistake. She raised a huge force. Sacked Colchester, Verulamium and Londinium. Massacred the inhabitants, up to 60,000 Londoners. It was worse than the bare figures, grim as they are, suggest. Boudicca didn't just dispatch the inhabitants; she worked up to it. The young native women who'd taken up with Romans had their breasts sliced off and crammed into their mouths. She crucified many of those first Londoners. Finally, she put the city to the torch. It was the first great fire of London. London's history is underfoot, like geological strata. The beginning of London is about twenty feet down. Just above AD 43 there's a tell-tale layer of red ash: Boudicca's handiwork.

And the Thames connections – apart from the wonderful 'chariot of ire' statue of her on Westminster Bridge? (London cabbies – eschewing political correctness – say it's a statue of the first woman driver: she's not holding the reins, she's indicating left and her horses are going left and right.) We're not sure where Victory fought Victory**, but it may have

---

*The Celtic root of her name means Victory.
**The Roman legion that defeated her

been up Hampstead way. Facing defeat, Boudicca tried to get to the Thames – to steal a boat and escape. She made her way to the Fleet River, knowing it would lead her Thamesward, but the Romans caught up with her where King's Cross Railway Station is today – caught up with her and did for her. She's buried beneath Platform 7: that's the legend.

Name-wise there have been five Londons. Londinium was Roman. Ditto Augusta. Londonwic (or Lundenwich) was early Anglo-Saxon; Lundenburgh late Anglo-Saxon. Finally – London.

Londonwic and Lundenburgh were in different places! For early Anglo-Saxon London – Londonwic – head for Covent Garden. Late Anglo-Saxon London – Lundenburgh – was back in the Roman city. The reason Londonwic was west was because of the *fit* between Anglo-Saxon vessels and the foreshore. Everything comes back to the Thames – it's the fount, the river of London's life. Anglo-Saxon vessels were flat-bottomed, shallow-draft affairs and upstream, approximately where Embankment station stands, the foreshore was long and gently sloping. Perfect for a river market, for dragging flat-bottomed vessels ashore. You can *hear* it. The place name *wich* means village/market/port.

And late Anglo-Saxon London – why was Lundenburgh back in the Roman city? To answer the question we head to the ninth century and join some Lundenwicers on a riverside stroll. Then we see it, the most terrifying sight we'll ever see: 160* long ships arrowing toward us, carrying scores of the world's most fearsome males. Say hello to the Vikings and their idea of a pleasure cruise. Their *modus operandi*? Ride the flood tide to Greenwich Reach, tie up, wait for the next tidal cycle. And up they'd come. The world's finest mariners, they didn't just cross the North Sea – they crossed the Atlantic. They could make twenty knots (an hour) with the wind. Five knots *against* the current of a river. They reached Lundenwich,

---

*Why the precise figure? It's representative of course but it's based on a citation in the *Anglo Saxon Chronicles*.

Up close – the Thames

Two piquant Thames details.

First, Queen Mary's Steps behind the Ministry of Defence, near the Horse Guards Avenue end. Sweeping, elegant and graceful – not that that should come as any surprise, given that they were built by Sir Christopher Wren – they're a rare surviving fragment of the old Tudor Whitehall Palace complex, which burned down in 1698. They're a graphic reminder of how much wider the river was before it was embanked, and that everybody – royals included – travelled by river.

Second, if you stand in Victoria Tower Gardens, for example, and look across the river you can see, at regular intervals, lions' heads, mooring rings through their mouths, set high up in the Embankment wall. It's the London pride. In every sense. Before we had the Thames barrier, London coppers were told that if they were walking a beat along the Embankment they should check on the lions. *Because when the lions drink, London's in danger.* Of flooding. No question about it, water levels that high meant that the authorities needed to be alerted at once and the appropriate actions taken – sewers closed off, and so on.

ramrodded their ships up that long, gently sloping foreshore, disembarked and did what Vikings did: raped, pillaged, plundered and murdered.

Enter the first great English king, Alfred, wondering: 'do we really need these periodic visits from over the whale road?' The answer to that rhetorical question was, of course, a resounding, 'no'. Ergo Alfred's decision to up stakes and head back to Londinium with its long-ship-unfriendly steep banks and its wall. One hundred and fifty years after the Romans founded Londinium they'd walled it, fortified it. Why change the name to Lundenburgh? *Burgh* – as in Edinburgh, for example – means fortified place.

Indeed, Southwark – just over the river from Lundenburgh – also answers to the name *The Borough*. It's the same word. The narrowed Thames here was a natural choke-point on the invasion road. Fortify both sides of the river and you could squeeze off an attempted invasion. Those two place names – *Lundenburgh* and *The Borough* – bear stark witness to the single most important *fact* of London's existence a millennium ago.

They did come again, of course, those 'north men'. They just didn't come from the quarter Alfred had feared. Which brings us to 1066 – the year of four kings and Haley's Comet. The year of the Norman Big Bang – and everything 'downstream' from the Conquest, most conspicuously of all of course – apart from the language we're intercoursing in right now – the Tower of London, *the* most important mediaeval fortress in Europe. There it is, looking implacably – stonily – down on the Thames and down on London. The noun – *Tower* – and adverb – *down* – crystallise the matter. Tower is French. And as for *down*, the point is that the White Tower – the centrum, the oldest part – is ninety feet tall, thirteen feet thick at the base. And that's not English stone – it's French, from Caen in Normandy. Let that sink in. You can feel the massy, oppressive, psychological weight of that stone – how it will have borne down on the conquered: the Anglo-Saxons. If you bring stone from over the ocean, you're coming to stay.

There's another linguistic measure of that. The Anglo-Saxons built in wood. Indeed, the Anglo-Saxon word for *wood* was cognate with the Anglo-Saxon verb *to build*. Building ninety foot high walls out of stone brought from over the ocean was something profoundly alien and oppressive. The other side of that linguistic coin is that the 'power' words in English – castle, judge, government, law, duke, minister, army – are French. It's yet another measure – another outcropping – of that past. Get properly inside your language and you're face to face with two stark truths: in Faulkner's words, the dead past isn't dead – it isn't even past; and history hurts.

Castles are the architectural equivalent of a mailed fist. The Normans slammed another one down at the southwestern corner of the city, beside the Fleet River. Baynard's Castle to guard the upstream approach. The Normans knew that the Thames was London's front door and back door.

The way to take care of business was to take care of those two approaches.

It's no wonder that shock and awe is stamped onto language as well as architecture. Consider the most famous London – and Thames – episode ever. There would have been very old Londoners alive in 1066 who could remember what happened half a century earlier. How could they not? We remember it – indeed, sing it, incant it – 1,000 years later.

And the tale?* Yet another Viking horde had pitched up. They were on the threshold – on London Bridge, overnighting, dreaming of pillage, plunder, rape, murder. On the morrow they were going to come down on London like the proverbial wolf on the fold. It would be yet another 'cakewalk', because London didn't have an army and couldn't defend itself.

It did have an ally, though – another Scandinavian, a Norweyan as they might have said then. Olaf. He had a plan. In the dead of night, Olaf and some Londoners crept down to the river armed with heavy ropes. The sheer desperation of it! They rowed out to the bridge and tied the ropes to its supports. And waited. The timing was everything. They waited until the tide turned, then they rowed downstream. They rowed for their lives and the lives of their families, and the life of their city.

It worked. The current, the ebb tide, and those straining ropes did the trick. The supports gave way and London Bridge came down, spilling the Viking horde into the Thames and to their deaths.

The happy outcome was the London purim. No wonder it branded itself on the English-speaking psyche: London Bridge is falling down. And that's by way of introducing old London's *signature*: 'London Bridge', the most famous bridge in the world. It came along two centuries later and spanned 600 years of London's history. It must have seemed eternal – no wonder Londoners regarded it as one of the wonders of the world. Picture it: houses, shops, two chapels, a drawbridge, a water-wheel,

---

*Tale being the *mot juste* – the episode is, as they say, shrouded in legend.

traitors' heads – slubbering, maculate, *leering* – from stakes atop the gatehouse roof. There were nineteen arches so close together they created a weir – the water level downstream was several feet lower – which, when it was cold enough, trapped ice floes. Whereupon the Thames seized up – froze over. Shocking, and pretty awesome. So, yes, 'frost fairs' are also part of the story.

When old London Bridge came down in 1831 that put paid to it, because the river-pinching arches went with it. And here's another brush-stroke: old London Bridge was the reason London had to have two harbours. The most famous was the London Pool – just downstream from London Bridge. In its day it was a forest of masts – you could skip from wooden deck to wooden deck. The Pool's little sister, Queenhithe, was just upstream, the bridge's narrow arches being the bottle neck. You could only get tiny skiffs through them. The 'Pool', which handled the downstream 'traffic', explains why Customs House is where it is. Queenhithe – you can still see its outline, where the shoreline pulls sharply inland like an opened drawer between the Millennium Bridge and Southwark Bridge – was for upriver traffic.

And when you're looking for Queenhithe – *hithe** means harbour, incidentally – you might as well also get Hensa (and indeed some Mediaeval Thames history) into focus. Hensa's headquarters – known as the Steelyard – stood where Cannon Street Railway Station stands today. Chances are you haven't heard of Hensa – unless you're German. You should have done. Hensa was to mediaeval Europe what the seven big oil company giants are to our day. When London's population was 50,000, Hensa was operating 75,000 vessels and had 300,000 men working for it. Hensa, short for the Hanseatic League, was seven north German cities which had joined forces. They controlled the mouth of every north- and west-flowing river on the continent. Impressive? I'd say

---

*It's an old Anglo-Saxon word.

so, particularly when you bear in mind that it's only with the coming of the railway in the nineteenth century that rivers are finally superseded as arteries of communication and transportation. You control all the rivers that drain a continent into the Atlantic Ocean and you're the carburettor of a continent's economic activity.

Hensa also had a monopoly on salted herring. If you don't believe me, how do you think you got here – DNA-wise, I mean? How did your north European ancestors survive those harsh, barren winters in pre-refrigeration days? That's right – salted herring. It was northern Europe's food staple. There's nothing cheaper than table salt today. But it's worth remembering that the words salt and salary are cognate. Roman legionnaires were often paid in salt, because salt acted as a preservative of flesh. Salt meant you had something to eat in those desperate weeks before spring lambing.

There was a black market in salted herring, but if you bought on the black market you'd often be cheated. *Bait and switch.* The top layers were fine – everything below was rotten. The Easterlings, as Londoners called the Hensa folk (Germany being to the east), had a 24-carat reputation for honest dealing. They never cheated. Their name became a byword. People would say, 'look it's a can't miss – as good a deal as you'd get from the Easterlings'. Over time the word Easterling becomes sterling, the name of our currency. So you actually have heard of Hensa, you just didn't know it. You're carrying that history around with you – those pound coins in your pocket represent several centuries of not just Thames and London history, but European history.

As for Tudor London and its history, the Thames is its amniotic fluid. Its waters bore Elizabeth I on her coronation day and the day of her funeral. Think of her knighting Drake on the deck of the *Golden Hinde* down in Deptford. Think of Christopher Marlowe stabbed in the eye – dying in a brawl in a riverside tavern in Deptford. Think of Shakespeare and the Burbages and their fellow players dismantling 'The Theatre' in Shoreditch in 1599, transporting the timbers across the Thames, re-erecting them on the Bankside, renaming that 'new' theatre The Globe. Overhear that foreign visitor back then, exclaiming, 'the world affords no finer sight, take land and sea together, than to come up the Thames from Gravesend, shoot the bridge at high tide and go along to Westminster, surveying the grand palaces fringing the north bank.' One of those palaces – well, its eighteenth-century descendant – survives to this day: Somerset House. As does that wonderful shipwreck from the past – the watergate to York House.

More than any other century, the seventeenth is studded with pivots on which London's history turns. Many of them are Thames connected, including the Great Plague and Great Fire (1665–6). The plague because fleas were the vector of the bacillus – fleas on *rattus rattus* (the black rat) that came ashore from Thames-moored ships that had come from infected overseas ports. The Great Fire because what kicked it into overdrive was when it burned down to the wharves and their barrels of pitch for caulking – tarring – the wooden walls of ships. That turned a run-of-the-mill London fire into a firestorm – it was like tossing a lighted match into a bucket of petrol. The statistics – 13,200 houses, 87 churches, 44 livery halls destroyed – are impressive. But statistics always have a built-in buffer – codifying, safe on the page, they're at a 'remove' from the actual event. If you really want to *see* the fire – feel on your face the blast from its suddenly opened furnace door – you have to take to the Thames, as Londoners did to escape the infernal region that their city had become. Think of the Thames acquiring a couple of new tributaries in the shape of molten rivers of lead flowing down to it from the conflagration of old St Paul's cathedral. Those lava flows of lead had been, just hours earlier, the cathedral roof. Or think of a Westminster schoolboy – two miles upstream – reading Terence at night by the light of the fire. Or his counterparts at Eton, twenty-one miles away, picking up leaves of books that fluttered down on the school grounds – leaves of books that had been squirreled away in St Paul's crypt.

Speaking of conflagrations, what the Dutch fleet did a year later in 1667 – coming up the Thames and torching the English fleet at Gravesend – cut awfully close to the London bone. The shock and awe, fear and trembling in London would have been stark-staring.

Thirty one years later it was a Dutch fleet again – but in rather different circumstances. Instead of being city-wide, the shock and awe would have been lasered into a single frontal lobe: James II's. The Dutchman – William III – was coming, invited by parliament, to take the throne. James had a weather vane – it's still there – erected on the roof of the Banqueting House so he could see which way the wind was blowing, literally and figuratively. He knew that as long as it was blowing from the west he was safe. William's fleet and army couldn't come up the Thames. James' luck held for three months, then one night the weather vane swung round. Clutching the Great Seal of State, James skedaddled down to the Thames to make his getaway. He got away – and so did the Great Seal, though not with him. Sure enough, the clutch was klutzed – James butterfingered it into the river. A fisherman later recovered it.

That Chaplinesque episode took place in the waters that run sweetly by Tate Britain. That stretch is one of the nodal points of London's riverine history. The Tate stands on the site of the old Millbank Prison. A couple of its cells survive – they've been incorporated into the basement of the Morpeth Arms, the pub over the way. *The Locking Piece* – the riverside Henry Moore sculpture – marks the spot where long grey lines of convicts shuffled on board ships that transported them to Australia. It's said the ubiquitous Australian appellation 'pom' is an acronym derived from the iron-bound nomenclature, Prisoner of Millbank.

There's more. Over the river is the headquarters of the Secret Intelligence Service, aka MI6. As its sobriquet – Babylon on Thames – attests, it's a peacock of a building. London architecture doesn't come much more, well, intrepid. John Barry, the James Bond theme composer, once owned the penthouse atop Peninsula Heights, the 60s block over the way from the MI6 building. He sold it to Bernie Ecclestone, the Formula 1 squillionaire, who sold it to Jeffrey Archer. It was there that Thatcherism's most prismatic polyp presided over his notorious shepherd's pie and Krug parties.

Around another bend and we're in the nineteenth century, watching the funeral pyre of the mediaeval Palace of Westminster on that October night in 1834. The cause of the fire? They were burning wooden tally sticks in a furnace in the cellar. The fire got out of control and, apart from Westminster Hall and the Jewel Tower, the old mediaeval palace was no more. Where to build its replacement – should it be relocated? The Duke of Wellington weighed in: 'put it where the old one was'. He wasn't being sentimental: 'You mustn't locate parliament where the London mob can surround it'.

Or watching Joseph Bazalgette, creator of the Embankment and London's 'modern' sewer system, and his army of labourers transform the river – and transform London – out of all recognition. There's a statue of Bazalgette on the Embankment. The Latin inscription reads, 'he put the river in chains'. Putting it that way is perhaps at variance with *our* ecological sensibilities – but his achievement stands at the forefront of all of London's civil engineering feats, let alone its health benefits.

And the twentieth century? Let's talk about a flight path and five bridges. The Thames was the flight path – the Luftwaffe used it as a navigational aid. On a moonlit night all they had to do was cross the channel. Down below, the moonlit Thames looked like a ribbon of tin foil leading them up to target-rich London: shipping, docks, road bridges, railway bridges, railway stations, power stations, light industry, the seat of government.

And the five bridges? Look closely at the piers of Tower Bridge. Near the waterline you can see big iron rings for attaching anti-U-boat nets. Of no military consequence of course, but imagine the propaganda triumph of a U-boat surfacing by the Palace of Westminster and gunning down Big Ben in seconds.

The other four bridges 'nest' in Waterloo Bridge, like Russian dolls. There's today's bridge – Waterloo Bridge. But Waterloo Bridge is also the 'Ladies' Bridge'. That was its early sobriquet, because the late 1930s and early 1940s workforce that built it was female. Men were in uniform.

The third bridge is the one today's Waterloo Bridge replaced. By John Rennie, the master bridge builder, it was the most beautiful bridge in Europe.

Lastly, there is 'the temporary bridge'. The Rennie bridge was so rickety they closed it to traffic while the ladies were abuilding. To hold the fort they erected a temporary bridge – the kind of steel structure that army engineers specialise in. When the Ladies' Bridge was finished in 1942 the temporary affair was dismantled. Out of sight, out of mind. Well, not quite out of mind. Some people were exercising some forethought. Come June 1944 the Allies' command of the skies was total. Apart from the Remachen Bridge, the bridges over the Rhine were kaput. And the Remachen was crippled. Out of its mothballs came the temporary 'Waterloo Bridge'. It was shifted across the channel and overland to the Rhine, where it was re-erected. Across 'Waterloo Bridge' rumbled most of the allied armour that knifed into Nazi Germany. It was the bridge too near for what was left of the Wehrmacht. So, yes, four bridges. Seen with a certain amount of awe – because one of them was the most beautiful bridge in Europe and another was the dagger plunged into the heart of Nazi Germany.

And here's some natural history that should awe and will certainly come as a shock. The Thames is probably the cleanest urban waterway in the world. Its 'resurrection' has been an astonishing success story. Thirty-five years ago it was biologically dead. Today it has 250 species of plants and 120 species of fish. Dolphins and seals frequent the Thames. The salmon's come back. The Thames *looks* dirty. It's always going to look dirty because it's tidal. But fill a glass with Thames water and wait twenty minutes. The silt will settle and that water will be as clear and nearly as clean as tap water. If you move to London and drink tap water, in about three months' time you'll be sixty-six per cent Thames water. The human body is two-thirds water – so every Londoner, past and present, is (or was) a walking Thames aquarium!

Let's end with London's Millennium landmarks – the Eye, the Millennium Bridge and the Dome, all of them on the river. There was no conscious decision taken about the Thames somehow linking them. But the pull of the river will have been subliminal, instinctive, deep-seated – and irresistible. Because the Thames is the force and the fuse that runs through London and its history. Fuse is the right word. The Thames *fuses* London *and* its history *and* its people. It's at once protean and eternal. It's uniquely *hic et nunc* and omnipresent. It simultaneously keeps to its watercourse and is ubiquitous. It links every Londoner to every other Londoner – 200-day-old Isobella to 2,000-year-old Semponius Sempronianus.*

The Eye is a wheel – a wheel by a river. Perhaps a ship's paddle-wheel. But let's drill down deeper. Transport-wise, the first technological breakthrough was a vessel. The door of the old ICI building – it's the most astonishing door in London – on Millbank shows, amongst other things, some Bronze Age people dragging a log down to a river. They're going to turn it into a vessel. So: boat first, then wheel. Wheels go round and surveying the Thames and its London history you could say, what goes by comes by. An example? Think of the Walbrook providing the Romans with a perfectly positioned sewer. Today there's a crane and waste containers there. The crane loads the containers onto barges and a tug takes them downstream. Waste disposal, the same activity that took place there 2,000 years ago. The outward form's changed, the essence hasn't.

---

*Semponius Sempronianus was a Roman centurion who lived and died in Londinium nearly 2,000 years ago.

And the Millennium Bridge? A bridge connects. London, like Budapest, is two cities divided by a river. The bridge conjoins those two cities. It also connects past and present. Anybody crossing the Millennium Bridge must necessarily be put in mind of London's ancient 'signature' – the world's most famous bridge, London Bridge. And the people who walked across it – Chaucer and Shakespeare and Christopher Wren and Sir Isaac Newton and Charles Dickens. So you're here and now – in twenty-first-century London crossing the Thames via a twenty-first-century London bridge – but you're also in some very special company. They're here too.

And the much derided Dome? 'An albino tortoise undergoing a serious acupuncture treatment'. Think again. Resembling half a satellite, that dome – nature's most perfect form – reminds us of the way London and all it stood for, all its ideas, all its energy and astonishing creativity, seeded all winds, went round the world. Went round the world from here – from this river, this fuse. And there's every reason to believe that while the outward form has changed – London no longer sends sailing ships to the four corners of the globe – the essentials will carry on. In the beginning was the word . . . The 'word from London' ('This is London' in Edward R Murrow's *and* the BBC World Service's signature line) will still go forth. So a huge satellite by the Thames couldn't be more apt, couldn't be a more perfect union.

Tale of
Two Cities

THE FAMOUS
SQUARE MILE

JUDY PULLEY

Greater London today stretches out over 600 or so square miles, but the one square mile of the City of London is where its story begins. From Holborn, south to the river, and from the west end of Fleet Street to the Tower of London, the boundaries of the Square Mile are often marked by statues of silver dragons. They are part of the City's coat of arms, the crest containing the red cross of St George and the short sword of St Paul. Every street sign in the City bears this symbol, leaving you in no doubt as to where you are.

Any exploration of London should start here at its early heart – where the Roman invaders established the City called Londinium almost 2,000 years ago in about AD 50.

Stand in Guildhall Yard off Gresham Street and beneath your feet is the elliptical arena of the amphitheatre, today marked by a curved slate line. Imagine the roar of the crowd as 6,000 gathered to watch animal and human combat. On the lower floor of the nearby Guildhall art gallery, part of the southeast wall can be seen and the remains of a small room where gladiators lit a candle and offered a prayer before entering the arena. Emerge from Tower Hill underground station and you are confronted by a vast expanse of Roman city wall. Very few sections now survive but this imposing barrier enclosed the City from AD 200, keeping citizens safe from potential outside threats. City streets today still bear the name of its gates – Aldgate, Newgate, Ludgate. Near to Bank station, beneath a street called Walbrook, runs the freshwater stream of that name around which grew up the original small Roman settlement of timber houses often likened to a Wild West frontier post, but which eventually became the fifth largest city in the western Roman empire with a population of 30,000.

Traces of this City – nine metres below the streets today (with all subsequent layers of history sandwiched between) – are continually being unearthed by the archaeologists who move in when a City office building is demolished for redevelopment.

We know the site of the main public baths at the junction of Queen Victoria Street and Huggin Hill – apparently the Romans tried to encourage the unwashed locals they found here to take up this custom. The basilica, where justice was administered, and the vast forum or marketplace both lie beneath the splendidly ornate Leadenhall Market built in 1881. Built around the forum and the wharves of the river port, by AD 60 the City, as the historian Tacitus tells us, was 'filled with traders and was a great centre of commerce'.

WHERE TO READ THIS

A perfect place would be on one of the stone benches in Guildhall Yard off Gresham Street: under your feet, the slate circle marking out the Roman amphitheatre, to one side the ancient fifteenth-century Guildhall and to the other, Sir Christopher Wren's church of St Lawrence Jewry, completed after the Great Fire and so named because nearby was an area of Jewish settlement before the community was expelled from England in 1290.

Trade is still the nature of the City of London today, but in its role as a leading financial centre, trade is now in invisible commodities. Banking, international insurance, foreign exchange markets and derivatives have replaced Roman imports of olive oil, wine, fish sauce, jewellery and pottery, and exports of tin, hides and hunting dogs. Reference in the media to 'The Square Mile' or 'The City' means just one thing – the world of shares and investments, interest rates and hedge funds.

Gradually throughout the latter part of the third century, the Romans began to withdraw. The rule of Rome officially ended in 410 with the Emperor Honorius relinquishing all responsibility for the defence of Britannia. The once grand City became a ghost town and fell into disrepair. The next group of invaders, Saxons from northwest Europe who were not city dwellers, set up small village settlements to the west, which by the 600s had grown into a town known as Lundenwic in the area of today's Covent Garden.

It wasn't until the ninth century that the old walled City, much of which had by this time been levelled, started to be resettled. Much of the present street pattern and layout can be traced to this period in the reign of King Alfred. Around this time the City began to establish the foundations of a unique form of government – the first independent local authority. Formed long before a government at Westminster, it is often referred to as the 'Grandmother of Parliaments' and many of its ancient traditions, surviving into the twenty-first century, have their origins over 900 years ago.

Aldermen (or 'eldermen') administered the City from the eleventh century. Eventually the aldermen began to summon 'wise and discreet' citizens for consultation and from 1376, they became known as the Court of Common Council, which with its twenty-five aldermen still exists today as the 'town council' of the City of London.

In 1067, one year after the Norman Conquest, William I granted the City self-government by charter. This hugely important document still survives today in the archives of Guildhall library – a tiny piece of parchment (15cm by 4cm), with just four lines written on it. William is not known as the Conqueror here in the City because no conquest as such actually took place. The City agreed to accept him and, in return, he agreed to them keeping their ancient rights and privileges, again confirmed in Magna Carta in 1215.

The oldest ceremonial office is that of sheriff – the shire-reeve or port-reeve – originally the King's representative within the City. However, in 1199 King John granted the City the right to elect its own sheriffs, a significant move and transfer of power. Two are still appointed each year, attending the Lord Mayor of the City of London on official duties and being present at sessions of the Central Criminal Court at Old Bailey.

The office of Mayor – later to be known as Lord Mayor – was created in 1189, Henry FitzAilwyn being the first to take office. He held the job for twenty-five years, unlike present-day Lord Mayors for whom one year of hectic ceremonial activity is quite enough. The Lord Mayor's official residence, Mansion House, is a grand eighteenth-century town palace completed in 1752, which stands opposite the Bank of England. In the pediment over the columned entrance, a carving entitled 'The

Dignity and Opulence of the Great City' echoes the confidence of the age in which it was built, where a female figure representing the City tramples Envy underfoot.

A fair and goodly house

Every fourth Thursday at 1 p.m., the Court of Common Council, presided over by the Lord Mayor in his velvet robes and chain of office, meet in Guildhall off Gresham Street. Within this ancient stone building the City has been governed, sheriffs and Lord Mayors elected, and kings and princes entertained since 1428, when builder John Croxton replaced the earlier thirteenth-century hall, changing 'an old and little cottage' into 'a fair and goodly house'.

The interior is decorated with the coats of arms and banners of the City of London's livery companies of which there are over a hundred. These have their origins in medieval guilds, which existed throughout Europe where groups of traders living and working in the same areas began to make provision for regulating competition, controlling stand-ards and training apprentices. Members paid to belong, the name 'guild' deriving from the Saxon word 'guilden' – to pay. Guild members were also required to swear an oath of allegiance on the Bible to the livery company. Masters of the companies wore distinctive clothing and badges or 'livery', and hence in the City they became known as livery companies.

The oldest in origin is the Worshipful Company of Weavers, founded in 1155. Others include the Fishmongers, Grocers, Skinners (who controlled the fur trade), Salters, Wax Chandlers (makers of beeswax candles), Apothecaries and Goldsmiths. Many have their homes in sumptuous halls in the City – the Fishmongers on the north side of London Bridge, the Apothecaries in Blackfriars Lane off Queen Victoria Street – though sadly their buildings are not open to the public. Their powers over their trades declined during the eighteenth century and today their role is largely charitable, raising millions for good causes and supporting education through grants and scholarships. New companies are still being created and in recent years, World Traders, Tax Advisers and Hackney Carriage Drivers (the famous London taxi drivers) have all joined the ranks of more ancient trades. Livery companies are also involved in the election of the Lord Mayor every year.

Looking up at the steeply pitched roof of Guildhall, it is hard to believe that it dates only from 1953. Several roofs have topped the high stone walls, two being destroyed in disasters which devastated this particular area of London – the Great Fire of 1666 and the bombing during the Blitz in the Second World War.

Medieval London with its narrow streets of wooden and thatched-roof houses had always been vulnerable to flames. William Fitzstephen, one of the first London historians, comments in the early twelfth century that the only things wrong with the City were 'the immoderate drinking of fools and the frequency of fires'. For decades Londoners had a fear of what might happen in that year of 1666 – the year of the three 6s, the sign of the 'Beast' – and many prophesied disaster. On the night of 2 September 1666, a fire began in the baker's shop of Thomas Farynor in Pudding Lane, named after the slang term for animal intestines, one of the City's meat markets being situated in Eastcheap just to the north.

The blaze spread rapidly; the Lord Mayor was alerted but dismissed the problem, saying it was so minor that 'a woman could piss it out'. Four days later 13,000 houses, 87 churches and 44 livery company halls lay in ruins. The diarist John Evelyn describes the fire at its height: 'the stones . . . flew like grenades, the lead melting down the streets in a stream and the pavements of them glowing in a fiery redness and neither horse nor man was able to tread on them'.

At least 100,000 citizens were now homeless, living rough in the fields around London, and although amazingly only eight people are recorded as having lost their lives, the number must, in reality, have been higher.

Within ten days, several plans for reconstruction were submitted to King Charles II, the most ambitious being that of Christopher Wren, a mathematician, scientist, architect and Professor of Astronomy at All Souls College Oxford. His desire was to sweep away all traces of the overcrowded medieval City and rebuild wide straight elegant streets and open piazzas. Seen as ultimately too impractical to implement, the authorities rejected most of Wren's project and rebuilt on the old street lines.

Wren did, however, reshape the City skyline. He was given the post of Surveyor General and the task of overseeing the design of fifty-one new churches and of St Paul's Cathedral.

There have been five cathedrals dedicated to St Paul on the site since 604, several of which were destroyed by fires. The church always referred to as Old St Paul's was actually begun in 1087 and finally completed in 1310. Built on a vast scale in the Gothic style, it was in fact taller and longer than the present-day cathedral with an extraordinary spire, the highest in England, estimated to be at least 143 metres high, but the spire was struck by lightning in 1561 and had to be removed. Old St Paul's, already thought by many to be in danger of collapse, was damaged beyond repair in 1666.

Wren's cathedral was completed in 1710, taking thirty-five years to construct – too long, in the eyes of many at the time. Its innovative design incorporated a dome, then something unfamiliar to Londoners. Visitors today can climb the 530 steps to the Golden Gallery encircling the highest point of the dome on the outside, for exceptional views across the City.

Up close – the City

The Lord Mayor's official residence, Mansion House, is a grand eighteenth-century town palace completed in 1752, which stands opposite the Bank of England. In the pediment over the columned entrance, a carving entitled 'The Dignity and Opulence of the Great City' echoes the confidence of the age in which it was built. In it, a female figure representing the City tramples Envy underfoot. Its basement once housed cells. Emmeline Pankhurst, leader of the suffragette movement in the early twentieth century, was once held there.

Commerce and coffee

Throughout the seventeenth century, as a new City emerged from the ashes of the fire, the financial institutions, which still have their home within the Square Mile, came into being.

Coffee was at the heart of it all and in an age where there is now a coffee shop on every corner, it is hard to imagine a time before 1652 when no one in London had tasted it.

In St Michael's Alley off Cornhill, Daniel Edwards, who had discovered the potent beverage during his travels in the eastern Mediterranean, set up his servant Pasqua Rosee in business.

The venture was an immediate success. London merchants, told that coffee 'closes the orifices of the stomach, helpeth digestion and quickeneth the spirits, making the heart lightsome', flocked to try it out. Coffee houses grew in number: in the seventeenth and eighteenth centuries there were probably almost as many as there are today. City merchants found them convenient places in which to meet and negotiate, and eventually different houses became specialised in particular areas of trade. Opened in the 1680s, Edward Lloyd's coffee house in Great Tower Street focused on marine insurance, leading to the founding of Lloyd's of London, the world's foremost insurance market. Jonathan's in Change Alley off Lombard Street was where the Stock Exchange had its origins. In Lloyd's today, about twenty staff attired in blue tailcoats who act as concierges in the building are still called 'waiters' in reference to the days of serving coffee.

The Bank of England, established in 1694 to raise money to wage war against France, issued handwritten bank notes as receipts for money deposited there – a system introduced by goldsmiths a century earlier. Today its impressive home in Threadneedle Street is a building of two halves: the lower solid screen wall with only six windows, designed by John Soane in the late 1700s; and above it, Herbert Baker's 1930s extension where a row of male statues hold keys and chains to represent security and strength.

Throughout the nineteenth century, the Victorian Square Mile was the powerhouse of the Empire, controlling trade and managing the enormous wealth of the largest city in the largest empire the world had ever known. Complexes of warehouses around the Tower of London, Fenchurch Street and Houndsditch were the storehouses for the goods arriving into the docks further to the east – spices and tea, ivory and feathers, fragrant oils and exotic woods – while the great shipping companies' headquarters were situated in and around Leadenhall Street. Goods as well as invisible commodities continued to be traded well into the twentieth century: fur auction houses of the Hudson Bay Company near Mansion House station, the Coal Exchange in Lower Thames Street opposite Billingsgate Fish Market, the Corn Exchange in Mark Lane near the Tower – all now disappeared. The City was a sombre and serious place of business. Men in a uniform of bowler hats and pinstriped suits carrying rolled umbrellas and briefcases travelled in from the suburbs to work – by 9 p.m. the City was a deserted ghost town.

By the end of the 1930s, with Britain preparing for war, the City authorities realised the businesses of the City would be a prime target together with the docks. In the Blitz of 1940 and 1941, two-thirds of the City of London was destroyed as firefighters fought in vain to extinguish the results of the hail of incendiary bombs. Many of the interiors of Wren's churches were destroyed, though often their solid walls, picturesque towers and steeples survived. Sir Winston Churchill sent a message to the City authorities: 'At all costs, St Paul's must be saved'. A volunteer force – St Paul's Watch – patrolled the roof, often in complete darkness, searching for incendiary bombs that had lodged in corners and crevices. It is thanks to their bravery that the dome of Wren's great cathedral still dominates the skyline of the City, although today's soaring modern buildings threaten to obscure it.

Views of St Paul's from some strategic points around London are still protected by a policy introduced in the 1930s called St Paul's Heights, however, competition from areas such as Canary Wharf where many financial companies have relocated, now means City offices are getting ever higher and more imaginative, changing the whole scale and character of the Square Mile. The trend began twenty years ago when Richard Rogers designed Lloyd's extraordinary stainless-steel refinery-like offices in Leadenhall Street. Nearby is the more recent Swiss Re building in St Mary Axe – the rounded bullet-shaped 'Gherkin' – which has now become as much a London icon as Tower Bridge. Within the next few years, even higher towers are set to rise, mostly located on the City's eastern side and some which have already acquired nicknames – the Leadenhall Building (the 'Cheesegrater') opposite Lloyd's, the Pinnacle (the 'Helter Skelter') in Bishopsgate and 20 Fenchurch Street (the 'Walkie Talkie').

The Square Mile of the City of London has throughout history constantly changed and reinvented itself and it is the contrasts and juxtapositions of styles and time existing at every street corner that make this small City within a city so unique.

THE CITY AT NIGHT

PETER GLANCY

Apart from the obligatory trip to St Paul's, glowing in its wonderful tercentenary cleaning, and the less obligatory visit to the Museum of London, few tourists spend much time in the City. The more daring may pop into a Wren church or two, or even, for the positively adventurous, the Bank of England Museum, but generally visitors steer clear. Their loss! There is much to see in the City and the most exciting time to take it all in is at night. This may seem perverse, as everything will be closed, but then that is all to the good. The bankers and City workers are making their way home. The City is slowly emptying and is yours to enjoy in peace.

The Royal Exchange and the Old Lady of Threadneedle Street

Stand in the open space before the Royal Exchange after, say, seven o'clock in the evening and you will feel the life force draining away as the City workers pour down into the Underground, hop on to the buses, flag down a taxi or pop into a watering hole for a last snifter before winding off home. As the buildings start to light up they take on a sort of majesty (even an indifferent building can look impressive illuminated) and somehow the hard reality of the present bleeds away to reveal the magic of the past. And what a past! Empty alleys seem to carry this history more potently at night when they've ceased to carry the bankers. After all, this City is 2,000 years old!

Of course there has been fire, Blitz and general bloody-minded messing about, but there are treasures to find. Take the Royal Exchange itself (a wonderful cleaning job), which goes back to the days of Good Queen Bess. A City merchant Thomas Gresham, having travelled on the continent and seen the great trading Bourses of Europe, was dismayed to find business in London carried out on the streets. He created the Exchange here paying for the enterprise out of his own pocket and the Queen opened it, naming it 'the Royal Exchange'. (Look at the portico to find her name on the left.) Of course, the building went down in the Great Fire of 1666 when all the statues of the kings and queens were shattered, leaving just Gresham's statue intact. The new building lasted a century and a half before also burning down in the not-so-great fire of 1838. It was so cold that day that the water in the city's pipes froze and the building was completely lost. So what we see today is the third building, by William Tite, and I suspect it may be the best of them all. Look up to see Victoria's name on the right; she opened it in 1844. It's open in the evening so do wander in, it's quite spectacular! Pop round the back, too, and you'll find two wonderful old gas lamps fizzing into life. Nothing at night brings back the past like gas lighting, and we've held on to around 2,000 of these old lamps.

WHERE TO READ THIS

The City pubs at night are maybe a little noisy and vibrant to get to grips with reading. But for a spectacular place to settle try the magnificent mid-nineteenth-century neoclassical interior of the Royal Exchange. Or for a cosier read, and a wonderful choice of wines, try the Olde Wine Shades just off Cannon Street down the hill on Martin Lane. The cellars here used to be connected to the river and were reputedly used by smugglers.

West of this grand facade stands that Old Lady of Threadneedle Street, the Bank of England. This is actually two buildings, like a double-decker bus: one below, one up top. The lower half of 1788 is by that eccentric maverick John Soane, but in the 1920s the decision was taken to mostly demolish the original building and extend the building upwards into a sort of chateau, leaving only Soane's fortress-like curtain wall. The great architectural historian Nikolaus Pevsner wrote that 'the virtual rebuilding of the Bank of England in 1921–37 , in spite of the Second World War, was the worst individual loss suffered by London architecture in the first half of the twentieth century'. I certainly agree, as there is so little left of this magnificent architect, who gave us our first public art gallery (which still delights visitors in Dulwich).

For many years there was a terrific nightly scene at the bank when a Brigade of Guards, known as the Bank Piquet, marched through the streets of the City to pipe and drum. They stopped the traffic as they went. This must have been a glorious night-time scene as they ceremoniously approached the Bank. It continued right up until 1973 when the threat of invasion seemed less likely than in the terrifying days of the Gordon Riots back in 1780. Incidentally, if you are lucky enough to get your hands on a £50 note turn it over for a picture of the first governor of the bank Sir John Houblon, an Huguenot of French descent.

Demolition began on a clutch of seven buildings opposite the Exchange in 1988, their listed-building status and the intercession of the Prince of Wales not being enough to save them from the bulldozers. The Mappin and Webb building was the saddest loss and I remember going down to say a fond farewell the day before demolition began. Now there is the massive, post-modernist, pink hulk of James Stirling's Number One Poultry. The clock tower supports a viewing platform which pops out either side like a pair of tiny ineffectual wings. To the south of this slice of a set for *Miami Vice* stands the Mayor's Nest, or more properly the Mansion House in Mansion House Place. This is the official residence of the Lord Mayor and one of the first buildings to be spectacularly illuminated at night. It's by George Dance and dates to the mid-eighteenth century. Inside there is a Justice Room for when the Lord Mayor acts as the City's Chief Magistrate and there are ten cells for men and (rather like the public loos, ladies) only one for women. Known as the Birdcage, this once housed Emmeline Pankhurst, that formidable campaigner for Votes For Women. On an even more eccentric note it also houses a gold telephone, the millionth to be made, giving it a curious connection with the wonderful church of St Stephen at 39 Walbrook right beside. This church contains the phone that took the first distress call made to the world's first hotline for 'suicidal and despairing people'. The year was 1953, the number was Mansion House 9000 and the organisation was the Samaritans, set up by the remarkable rector Chad Varah, who died in 2007 aged in his nineties. BT awarded the five-millionth London phone line as a free line to the Samaritans and this 1970s set remains in the church, both it and the original black phone presented as precious relics in display cases. Another precious object, sitting under Wren's dome, is the altar in Italian marble, which is a late work by the great Henry Moore. Beautiful as it is, Londoners have cheekily nicknamed it 'the Camembert Cheese'.

A strange night scene that took place outside this church many years ago had its beginnings in Italy. Soaking up the sun, and architecture, on his Grand Tour, Lord Burlington, that arch-Palladian and arbiter of eighteenth-century taste, came across a local enthusing about St Stephen's church. 'To think that you have come all this way and yet you have the most beautiful building in the world in London.' Burlington didn't know the church and immediately on his return to England made a beeline to the City to acquaint himself. Unfortunately it was the middle of the night, but that didn't deter him from knocking up the churchwarden, who was dumbfounded by this madman insisting on his unlocking the door. Burlington explored by torchlight tingling with excitement. Like a child on Christmas morning, he was back at dawn to explore by daylight.

These wonderful buildings survived the Blitz because of a curious, and tragic, twist of fate. What happened? Well take a look down nearby Lombard Street and you'll see another treasure, the church of St Mary Woolnoth (on the corner of Lombard and King William Streets) by Hawksmoor. This stands over the Northern Line underground station, the construction of which saw the destruction of the church's crypt. During the Blitz a bomb fell in front of the Exchange, rolled towards the church and found itself somehow being carried down on the escalator to the platform, where it exploded, killing the people sheltering there and leaving the beautiful buildings above intact, for that night at least. A bitter survival indeed!

Up close – the City at Night

When the bombs rained down on London in the Blitz they not only destroyed but revealed! Many strange sights can be seen in the City that are the result of the destruction. If you decided to pop into the Olde Wine Shades you'll see one of these curiosities. On the side wall is a curious rusting cupboard which puzzles everybody who walks past it. It is, in fact, a safe that was once set into an internal wall and now eccentrically braves the elements.

The narrow lane opposite is St Swithin's Lane; long and thin, it almost seems to suck you down. You'll wonder why you bothered when you reach the bottom and the ugly mass of Cannon Street station faces you, but on the right is something quite astonishing, so remarkable, in fact, that people walk past it without so much as a second glance. But at night it's harder to ignore – a fan of light on the pavement blazing from a grille, behind which is the almost mythical London Stone. In Act 4, Scene 6 of Harry VI (*Henry VI, Part 2*) Shakespeare writes:

London, Cannon Street. Enter Jack Cade and the rest, and strikes his staff on the London stone.

Cade: Now is Mortimer lord of this city. And here, sitting upon London Stone, I charge and command that, of the city's cost, the pissing conduit run nothing but claret wine this first year of our reign. And now henceforward it shall be treason for any that calls me other than Lord Mortimer.

And just to show that he's not joking, when a soldier runs in shouting, 'Jack Cade, Jack Cade,' he has him killed on the spot, announcing, rather unnecessarily, that he won't be doing that again.

Legend says the stone arrived in the city when a magician flew to Earth on it, although it's more likely to be part of a Roman building left lying around. At some point it became embedded in the church of St Swithin that then became known as St Swithin London Stone. The church was destroyed in the Blitz and not restored, so now the Stone is embedded in a rather dull office block. Cannon Street, by the way, gets its odd name from the candlewick makers who lived and worked here. If you look around you might find a plaque or two denoting the Ward of Candlewick, but sadly no longer any candlewick makers.

Where the City truly releases its magic at night-time is in a clutch of buildings that thrillingly display past and present as nowhere else. South of Leadenhall Street between Gracechurch and Lime Street is a building that is impossible not to put a smile on your face and a flash of recognition – Leadenhall Market. When Hagrid sets off with Harry in the first *Harry Potter* film to buy his wand, the journey begins here. The building reminds me of all the great shopping arcades of the northern industrial towns where I hail from. Illuminated at night like some huge film set (it also saw John Wayne scrapping in a late film *Brannigan*), it stands on the site of a medieval market. A document of 1345 stipulated that strangers (non-Londoners) must bring their poultry to Leadenhall and Londoners theirs to Westcheap. Underneath Leadenhall Market is the Roman forum of Londinium. It's thrilling to think that some of that ancient structure lies trapped beneath at a depth of about twenty feet.

Standing cheek by jowl to the Market is something spectacularly different, but equally magical. This is the astonishing Lloyd's Building, 1 Lime Street, a staggering building that is nothing less than sensational when illuminated in blue light at night. It resembles a huge set for *Blade Runner*, or a sort of futuristic fairy-tale castle. I love this building with its exposed pipes like modernist turrets and its lifts hurtling up and down the outside of the building offering ever-changing views of the city. A perfect backdrop to the bizarre chase of giant teddy bears and Emma Peel, times two, in *The Avengers* film. And to think that it all began in a seventeenth-century coffee house! Mr Edward Lloyd's establishment was much frequented by mariners and it was here that the great international insurance market germinated. A great gamble on the part of Lloyd's to commission architect Richard Rogers to create this first great masterpiece of the post-war city, but then if Lloyd's can't take a gamble, who can? As well as a perfectly preserved Adam room from Bowood House there are several rooms preserved from the previous 1920s building, and on the outside Rogers has kept the original entrance, a bizarre yet curiously effective conceit.

But the thrills and spills are not over, for opposite is a building that has become the icon of London in the twenty-first century. At night it blazes with intense light, like a rocket about to shoot off to the moon. Londoners, ignoring its majesty, have nicknamed this 'the Gherkin' or,

even more cheekily, 'the Crystal Phallus'. The official name is the prosaic Number 30 St Mary Axe (pronounced Simmery Axe) and was commissioned by Swiss Re from Norman Foster and Partners. The same team is also responsible for the wonderful building right next to Lloyd's rising like a gleaming, metallic Ayers Rock (the Willis Building) and the Millennium Bridge, proclaimed by Foster 'The Blade of Light' and by Londoners 'The Wobbly Bridge'. But the story is not over and the future holds more excitements.

But amid this riot of Modernism there sit, overshadowed in bulk but not in interest, two medieval churches – the old and the new that makes the city so special. St Andrew Undershaft, also on St Mary Axe, gets its name from the maypole that used to stand outside before being broken up by the Puritans as an idolatrous object. Inside is the tomb of the City's first chronicler, John Stow. His *Survey of London* has almost never been out of print since 1598 and a copy is given every year to a child who's written something wonderful about London. The child also gets a quill pen removed from the hand of Stow's statue in 'The Ceremony of John Stow's Pen', which takes place in early April. The other church is St Helen Bishopsgate on Bishopsgate, so full of monuments it's been christened 'The Westminster Abbey of the City'.

Wandering the City at night is a very special experience. The churches may be closed (unless like Lord Burlington you want to take your chances banging on the door) but the sense of atmosphere is incomparable. The lanes are narrow and dark, but don't worry, they are safe, and you will get lost yet there's always a pub, or better still an old atmospheric wine bar just around the corner. And when it's time to go home you won't be far from a tube station or a bus stop.

Literary
London

Shakespeare's London

SHAUGHAN SEYMOUR

Though not a native Londoner, William Shakespeare made himself in London. And it's the Bankside area on the south side of the Thames that provides us with so many reminders of the man who gave us a world on the stage. It would be pointless to expand upon the theories about the man and his life, instead let's look at what is in evidence.

Bankside and the Bard

We start by London Bridge, on the river's south side, where for the most part of 2,000 years there has been a bridge crossing. Because the Thames was narrowed by Victorian engineers the present structure is far shorter than the one the young Shakespeare would have crossed in the late 1580s – then the bridge was 300 metres long (930 feet) long and an impressive feat of medieval engineering. Nineteen arches built on piers called starlings supported the roadway, and piled above were houses, shops, taverns and watchtowers, with a chapel to St Thomas Becket, patron saint of bridge builders, in the centre. Pilgrims on their way to Canterbury would pay the toll, pause awhile on London Bridge, buy a souvenir badge from one of the shops, have a pint of ale and pay their respects to St Thomas in the chapel. They might also have stood by the parapet and watched as boats tried to steer safely between the piers. Going underneath was known as 'shooting the bridge', rather like shooting the rapids.

We think 1587 was the year that Shakespeare came to London, having attached himself to a group of players when they performed near Stratford-upon-Avon. London was then a teeming place. Today the City from Tower to Fleet Street houses some 9,000 people. In 1600 the population of the same area comprised some 200,000 souls. London was a magnet for ambitious young men, it was a city where careers could be made and fortunes won. Merchant adventurers were ready to stake thousands on the chance of exploiting the resources of the New World. The population of England had increased dramatically due to a series of good harvests, plague had diminished, and there was more leisure time for the masses. Economist Maynard Keynes made the observation that the country was in just the right financial position to afford Shakespeare when he presented himself.

While the City was a pot of gold for many, there were far more who had to make do with the scraps that fell from its table. Across the bridge and south of the City was Bankside, the playground of the early 1600s.

Outside the jurisdiction of the Lord Mayor and Corporation, it was a notorious place, frequented by the young blades of town seeking pleasure in the alehouses, theatres, bull-baiting pits and the 'stews' (the houses of horizontal pleasure). Four theatres were established here: the Globe, the Rose, the Hope and the Swan. The very first theatre in London took the original title 'The Theatre'. Built in Shoreditch in 1576 by James Burbage, a carpenter and travelling player, it stood until 1598, when the freeholder decided to capitalise on the theatre's success by tripling the rent. On the day the lease expired, the company dismantled The Theatre and slid the timbers across the frozen river, where they were used for the Globe, which was to be the venue for the greatest of Shakespeare's plays.

WHERE TO READ THIS

There are benches in the garden of Southwark Cathedral; along Bankside by the Globe; and outside the Anchor Tavern. The Globe theatre has a bar with good riverside views, or you could try the Founders Arms.

Dominating the south bank area was the parish church now known as Southwark Cathedral. In the seventeenth century it was called St Saviour's church, and was the earliest church to be built in London in the Gothic style, succeeding the style of the Norman priory church. Shakespeare is recorded as a communicant at St Saviour's and his youngest brother Edmund lies in the crypt. Not much is known about Edmund but his name appears on some lists of actors at the Globe so we presume his brother helped him secure a job. Records tell us that Edmund died in December 1607, probably a victim of plague. Alongside Edmund lie two contemporaries of Shakespeare – successful playwrights John Fletcher and Henry Massinger, their names inscribed on the floor of the choir.

There are several magnificent memorials in the cathedral and also a small model of the area as it was in the sixteenth century. There is also a memorial figure of Shakespeare, carved in alabaster, above which is the Shakespeare window featuring many of the characters from his plays. Upon occasion a sprig of rosemary is placed in William's hand 'for remembrance' and each 23 April, St George's Day and, it is thought, Shakespeare's birthday, a special service is held in the church, with prominent actors performing scenes from his plays and reading his verse.

The church survived the fires that have destroyed so much of what Shakespeare would have known. Ten years after the Great Fire of 1666, a conflagration south of the City destroyed most of Bankside, but another fragment of a building west of the church is a reminder of the presence of the local landlords, the bishops of Winchester. Their great house built in the early 1300s has its west wall still intact, and the latticework of the rose window is still visible. The bishops owned the estate, which included large tracts of parkland, gardens and fishponds in addition to the palace, the refectory and the dormitories for the priory. As landlords, the bishops received rents from some rather dubious sources. Along the riverside were the four theatres, twenty-four taverns and eighteen brothels, or 'stews', giving rise to local prostitutes being known as 'Winchester Geese'. Shakespeare alludes to this in the First Part of *Henry VI*, when a furious row erupts between Gloucester and Cardinal Beaufort, Bishop of Winchester, with Gloucester calling the bishop a prostitute:

> **Gloucester:** Stand back, thou manifest conspirator . . . thou that giv'st whores indulgences to sin.
> **Winchester:** Gloucester, thou shall answer this before the Pope!
> **Gloucester:** Winchester Goose! I cry a rope, a rope! . . . Out, scarlet hypocrite!

Further west from the palace in the area known as the Liberty of the Clink was the Clink prison, a gaol so notorious, so unsanitary and noisome that the term 'clink' has entered the language. As the river rose at high tide, water would leak in to the prison, resulting in prisoners having to wallow in filthy water for most of the day. The area was home to various shifty characters – pickpockets, cutpurses, a variety of con-merchants or 'coney catchers', and beggars (who were far from destitute), and Shakespeare would have only needed to loiter on street corners in order to pick up a few snatches of conversation. There must have been many a Bardolph or Pistol staggering about, ready to start a quarrel, or a Lancelot Gobbo with his 'blind' father, telling a hard-luck tale. The cast of characters was there for the taking.

The Globe Theatre was in Maiden Lane, a polygonal 22-sided building with a thatched roof. Playgoers would queue up at the entrance and drop their pennies into a box, one penny paid for the Pit, or Yard, two for the gallery, three for a cushion. All the boxes were taken to the 'box office', where the cash was counted. One penny was a tenth of an average worker's daily wage then, so pretty good value considering you might be hearing Shakespeare's words for the first time. Today the new Globe seats 1,500; the original catered for an estimated 3,000. Although on average people were smaller in stature than today, it was still a very crowded auditorium. One gentleman of the period observed at the end of a show at a playhouse, 'One penny was admittance to the Yard – where the stinkards were so glued together with their strong breath, when they came forth, their faces looked as if they had been boiled.'

On the day of a performance of one of his plays, Shakespeare would have made his way backstage into the tiring house, or dressing room, and met his fellow players. If that day's play was *Hamlet* he would have been dressing as the Ghost. Richard Burbage, charismatic tragedian and fellow investor in the theatre, was himself the Prince. The actors' costumes were the most valuable assets for the company and there were strict rules governing their care and use. If an actor wore a costume outside the playhouse he would have to pay a substantial fine and he would also be fined if he damaged one. The costumes were the main spectacle on stage and patrons would remark on the latest designs. Sometimes the previous year's court fashions would be recycled and a cloak of a style that had been worn by an ambassador or duke might make its appearance in *Twelfth Night* or *Julius Caesar*.

Up close – Shakespeare's London

At the bottom of Fish Street Hill, across Lower Thames Street in the City stands St Magnus the Martyr church. In the churchyard are two blocks of stone – one white, one dappled grey. The white block is part of the medieval London Bridge – the grey is from the bridge of 1831.

If you walk a short distance to the west of the Globe you will find Rose Alley. When the remains of the Rose theatre were revealed in 1989 during excavation for a new office block, excitement was intense – archaeologists, actors, locals, churchgoers and journalists swarmed around the site like bees. The shape of the theatre became apparent – a fourteen-sided polygon – and in addition the footings of the theatre uncovered, and coins, manicure pins, money boxes and a gold ring unearthed. After a long campaign fought by actors, archaeologists, playgoers and politicians the design of the office block intended for the site was adapted to preserve and include the Rose.

The Rose was the first theatre to be built in the area in 1587. Philip Henslowe was the entrepreneur who saw his chance. He invested £105 in the building, and was later joined by Edward Alleyn, actor and bene-factor. This was where Marlowe's plays were first performed, the likes of *Dr Faustus*, *Tamburlaine* and *The Jew of Malta*; Shakespeare's *Henry VI, Part 1* and *Titus Andronicus* also premiered here, but the Globe, completed in 1599, proved more successful, and the Rose closed in 1605.

In the next alley, Bear Gardens was a different venture altogether. The Davies Amphitheatre, later known as the Hope, was a ringed area surrounded by benches sufficient to seat a thousand spectators. A bear would be chained to a stake, the chain attached to a collar round the bear's neck. Mastiff dogs were then released, and the fight would begin. People of all ranks loved this brutal spectacle; even Queen Elizabeth, who had a bull- and bear-baiting ring at Whitehall. Bets were placed as to which bear could survive longest or which dog would be the victor. In one instance, it was declared the bear had too much advantage so it had its teeth knocked out and its claws removed to even the odds. The Hope theatre was established in the Bear Garden ring by erecting a stage for the actors to perform. But it lost too much money, the actors were dismissed and the bears brought back.

With an audience made up of merchants, artisans, apprentices, courtiers, country bumpkins and foreign tourists, it would have taken great skill on the part of the playhouse actors to hold their attention. Actors had to have a variety of talents; a good loud speaking voice, and be adept at music, dancing, tumbling and stage fighting. At the Globe, Shakespeare, Burbage and others each held a 12½ per cent stake in the theatre, and the takings were shared out between them and the rest of the company. It was something of a co-operative venture. The Rose and the Hope were local rivals for customers and the output of drama required of the companies was challenging. Sometimes ten plays were put on in as many weeks. Actors were never given the whole script as this would have been too costly, and a complete play could be sold to another company for as much as ten pounds (a labourer's annual salary). The players were given their lines only, with cues marked to indicate the next speech. The plot was broken down on a list backstage to mark exits and entrances, so it must have been fairly chaotic at the opening performance. If there were problems, one could always rely on the comedians to improvise, though this sometimes caused problems as the clowns would go off the script and do their own songs and dances and deliberately ruin other actors' moments with mugging and general upstaging.

Shakespeare understood this only too well. When Hamlet gives notes to the players, he pleads: 'Let your clowns speak no more than is set down for them . . . for there be of them that will themselves laugh, to set on some quantity of barren spectators to laugh too.' And yet, without those 'barren spectators' Shakespeare would have been missing out on a tidy profit, which is why, even in a tragedy, there has to be a clown. If you take *Hamlet*, the gravedigger provides us with mordant wit. In *Lear*, he is the necessary foil for the tragic king, and a clown brings on the fatal asp for Cleopatra.

The theatres were all demolished in the 1640s when the Puritans banned all forms of public pleasure, and the original site of the Globe is now marked with a plaque and some panels giving a short history. Archaeologists have performed 'keyhole' excavations on the site and ascertained that the Globe was a large timber-framed building ninety-nine feet across. They also found some trade tokens – coins that could only be exchanged in the alehouses.

The new Globe stands not on the original site but in a prime position on the Bankside, opposite a splendid view of St Paul's Cathedral. The theatre has proved a huge success, thanks to Sam Wanamaker and all those around the world who raised money, cajoled and persuaded politicians and businesses to sponsor the project. Theatre companies from Africa, Germany, India and Brazil have performed their own versions of the canon here. Fittingly, above the original Globe were painted the words '*Totus Mondus Agit Histrionem*' or 'All the World's a Stage', and truly the new Globe is a theatre for the world.

Above the new theatre's entrance is displayed a huge portrait of Shakespeare, in tribute to his legacy. His plays express for us the range of the human condition. He took the twigs and branches of language and storyline and made these flower as no one had done before, or has done since.

Bloomsbury: The Heart of Literary London

BRIAN HICKS

Bloomsbury is like a well-written play. Yes, you can enjoy it on the superficial level of strolling down its boulevards and into its grand squares, but beneath the facades there are layers. Layers filled with stories. The sediments of history lie here behind every block and under every paving stone. When you walk out of Holborn underground station on a bright summer's day you walk into a manuscript. Glance around at the London planes, their hand-shaped leaves waving to you like so many shades of emerald. These very same trees greeted Virginia Woolf and so many of that group who called themselves the 'Bloomsberries'. Indeed Virginia, who walked up the nearby Southampton Row, described that street as either 'as wet as a seal's back or dappled with red and yellow sunshine'.

Bloomsbury Square

The area of Bloomsbury is supposedly so called because of William Blemonde, who was given the land in the thirteenth century by the King. He built a house or shelter here, the Germanic word for this being 'bergan', eventually becoming the word 'bury'. This develops into 'Blemonde's Bury' and then like some etymological Chinese whisper into 'Bloomsbury'.

The family associated with the development of this green-field site, at a much later stage, are the Wriothesleys (pronounced Ris-ley), who have their own literary link of some importance. Henry Wriothesley was the Third Earl of Southampton and was also a significant patron to William Shakespeare. Shakespeare dedicated some of his sonnets to the Earl. It was his son Thomas Wriothesley, not surprisingly the Fourth Earl of Southampton, who in the late 1660s began his development of Bloomsbury Square. This was referred to by his contemporary the diarist John Evelyn as 'a small town'. Shops were provided for the new inhabitants. The square itself, probably the first in London, was dominated on the north side by Southampton House, later renamed Bedford House when it came into the hands of the Russell family, the Dukes of Bedford. Bloomsbury Square is not far from here, straight up Southampton Row and off to the left, but before you dash to see that, let's have a look at an extraordinary church built for the new inhabitants of the square in 1730.

WHERE TO READ THIS

You have a choice, either venturing in through the elaborately cast gates of culture into the sacred hallows of the British Museum and finding a quiet spot there, or you could do as Marx himself would do at the end of a busy day and pop into the Museum Tavern opposite the Museum in Great Russell Street. Who knows, you may be sitting in the exact same seat where the 'father of communism' sat before you.

St George's Church Bloomsbury rests in between Bloomsbury Way and Little Russell Street. A good view of this church may be had from the junction of New Oxford Street and Museum Street. This church was designed by Nicholas Hawksmoor, a baroque architect and pupil of Sir Christopher Wren. Whether it was in fact laid out along some Satanic superhighway as people such as Peter Ackroyd, in his book

Hawksmoor, have suggested is debatable, but architecturally this church is a recently restored treasure.

The church was built in response to the demands of the 'small town' development. The ladies and gentleman residing in Bloomsbury before its construction had to make their way over to the church of St Giles-in-the-Fields. To get to St Giles they had to brave an area referred to as 'the Rookery'. This area was filled with prostitutes – 'the ladies of negligent virtue' or 'the daughters of pleasure' as they became known. As well as this there were many drunks frequenting the vicinity – because of William III's hatred of the French and his ban on the import of French brandies, 'genever', or gin, had become commonplace. It was cheap, and this area became known as 'Gin Lane' and is depicted in an engraving of that name by William Hogarth (1751), with St George's Church in the background. As well as the drunks and prostitutes there were many thieves here – 'footpads' or 'cutpurses' as they were known. The gentry could not cope with running the gauntlet of these lowlifes each time they wanted to go to church so they petitioned Queen Anne to have their own church built and were granted this privilege under the Fifty Churches Act of 1711.

The oddest feature of this church has to be its steeple. Hawksmoor was 'inspired' in his design of the steeple by one of the seven wonders of the ancient world – in this case the Mausoleum at Halicarnassus. Rather conveniently, large parts of that structure ended up in the British Museum just down Museum Street. The Mausoleum had a stepped pyramid surmounting it, so Hawksmoor took that idea, narrowed it down and formed a stepped 'steeple'. It is truly bizarre and until 1871 it included lions, symbolising England, and unicorns, symbolising Scotland, trying to mount the base of it. After that date they were removed because the stone was becoming unstable. Horace Walpole, who was responsible for a Gothic revival in architecture and literature, saw this church and described it as 'a masterpiece of absurdity'. When I say 'Gothic', in literary terms think here of books like *Frankenstein* and *Dracula*; Walpole himself wrote a Gothic novel entitled *The Castle of Otranto*.

The church was familiar to Charles Dickens, who knew this area well. He lived to the north in Tavistock Square and to the east at 48 Doughty Street, which is now the Charles Dickens Museum. In his *Sketches by Boz*, Boz being Dickens's original pen name, you have 'the Bloomsbury Christening' taking place in this very church. Mr Kitterbell, who lives at 14 Great Russell Street, brings his son here to be christened. Unfortunately Mr Kitterbell invites his uncle, a miserable man with the wonderfully appropriate name of Nicodemus Dumps. Nicodemus hero-worships King Herod because he kills children, and when Nicodemus makes a speech detailing the dangers faced by a young life he reduces all to a state of misery.

Although that christening is fictitious, it was in this same church in 1815 that the writer Anthony Trollope was baptised. His father was a not very successful barrister who suffered from depression and who lived nearby in Malet Street. His mother Frances Trollope wrote over a hundred books, of which remarkably forty were published. I say remarkably, because they weren't particularly good. There is only one of her works referred to regularly today. It was entitled *The Domestic Manners of the Americans*. It was not overly flattering to the people of North America and was considered very irritating by people from that part of the world, but became a bestseller in Britain when published in 1832.

Anthony Trollope joined the post office as a clerk when his father died in 1834. He apparently hated every moment he was there but was 'posted' over to Ireland where he worked as a postal surveyor. Although he didn't actually design the original postbox, it was he who had them introduced as standard around the British Isles (originally they were painted green, not red). To pursue his writing he had to get up at 5.30 a.m. and he tried to write a thousand words per half-hour before he began his working day for the postal service. He wrote two famous series of books. *The Barchester Chronicles*, including *Barchester Towers*, deals with the political infighting of the clergy within Barchester, which is a cross between the real towns of Winchester and Salisbury. His second series of books, *The Pallisers*, includes a book entitled *The Prime Minister*. Indeed Trollope was the favourite author of former Prime Minister John Major, who was a supporter of the move to erect a memorial to Trollope in Poets Corner in Westminster Abbey. Trollope is not buried there, though – in 1882 he was buried in Kensal Green cemetery. Joanna Trollope, writer of among other things *The Rector's Wife*, is a distant relative of Anthony.

In 2006 St George's Church underwent massive restoration. The American philanthropist Paul Mellon had made a bequest of £4.55 million for the refurbishment of this amazing church. Another £12 million has come from the World Monuments Fund, the Heritage Lottery Fund and English Heritage. The big question was, would they have the money to restore the lions and the unicorns back to their precarious positions? I am pleased to report that the answer was yes! And truly magnificent they look as well. As you look at these creatures, the symbols of England and Scotland, do remember when this church was built – 1730. This was at a time of friction between England and Scotland that led to the Jacobite rebellion of Bonnie Prince Charlie in 1745. It always looks to me as if the lion of England is stalking the unicorn of Scotland – you judge for yourself.

You may also notice that next to the church is a hotel, now the Thistle Bloomsbury but previously called The Kingsley. Named after the author Charles Kingsley, who wrote *The Water Babies* and *Westward Ho!*, there is an image of him over the main entrance. The original founders were fond of Kingsley's stand on morality and alcoholic abstinence. It was here that E M Forster used to stay with his mother Lily when Forster was teaching Latin at the Working Men's College in Great Ormond Street. He wrote sections of *A Room with a View* here, not that he was getting much of a view at the time.

The British Museum

If you walk north from the church you will stumble into the great edifice of the British Museum. This internationally famous museum is packed with literary associations. As you stare at the pedimented frontage you are literally looking at the triumph of civilisation. I say literally because that is what is depicted in the pediment. From the crocodile crawling out of the swamp you are drawn to the central figure representing reason.

The museum was effectively founded by a doctor called Hans Sloane in 1753. Hans Sloane came from County Derry in Ireland. He trained as a doctor and became physician to Queen Anne, and later George I and George II. He travelled to the Caribbean with the Duke of Albermarle when he was appointed governor of Jamaica. There he discovered that cocoa mixed with water was prescribed as a curative. He found it 'nauseous and hard of digestion', so he mixed it with milk and sugar. It became, not surprisingly, more popular. It was this recipe for 'Sloane's' milk chocolate that was eventually taken over and marketed by the Cadbury family.

Sloane had begun his passion for collecting when a child and it was while in the Caribbean that his collection expanded enormously. He served the Duchess of Albermarle after the death of her husband and was able to set up a successful medical practice just down the road from the present museum at 4 Bloomsbury Place. He married well and during his lifetime purchased collections amassed by many others. When he died, on 11 January 1753, he offered his vast collection that included 50,000 books and 32,000 medals and medallions as well as flora and fauna, maps and manuscripts to the government for a mere £20,000. I say 'a mere'– but this was when the average annual salary in the country was £5.

His collection was estimated to be worth at least £80,000, so this was still a very generous offer on his part. The collection was bought and shown on this site in a house bought with the help of a national lottery. Montagu House became the base for what was to grow into the British Museum. Over the years many others made donations to this national collection. Edward Harley gave the Harleian collection of books, Robert Cotton gave the Cotton collection of books, King George II gave his 'Kings library' – which was an important move because his library was a deposit library and every copy of a book produced in this country had to be deposited here. So it was the library, based here in the museum, which became the great magnet to the writers in the area.

Up close – Bloomsbury

Today, if you want to see the writing desk used by Jane Austen, if you want to see two copies of the Magna Carta, or the beautifully illuminated Lindisfarne Gospels, or listen to the voice of Virginia Woolf, or see the handwritten songs of the Beatles, it's up to the new British Library at St Pancras you go and to the free exhibition they have there.

By 1855 Montagu House was too small, so it was demolished and Robert and Sydney Smirke built the great structure that stands before you today. In the centre of this building there was a garden, so you could stroll and get fresh air. By 1857 they realised they needed that space as well, so a man called Antonio Panizzi designed a domed reading room to be the heart of the library. It was based upon Hadrian's Pantheon in Rome. All the rest of the garden space became used up by buildings associated with the library and the storage of books.

Then in 1970 it was decided to move the library elsewhere and this was finally done in 1998 when the new British Library was born up at St Pancras.

Now in the normal course of events anyone can go into the old Reading Room. In the past you had to have one of the coveted 'Reader's tickets' and show you were doing research. Charles Dickens acquired his when he was 18 years of age (normally you had to be 21 but he was working as a journalist so he got his early). Oscar Wilde had his reader's ticket withdrawn when the scandal came out about him in 1895 and Sherlock Holmes also had a reader's ticket – well, a fictional one, anyway. (Apparently, in a recent survey, 58 per cent of people asked thought Holmes was real. Presumably it was this same group of whom 25 per cent believed Winston Churchill was a fictional character.)

A few years ago Mikhail Gorbachev was being shown around in the Reading Room and he apparently stopped his tour guide and said, 'This is the birthplace of communism.' Karl Marx was a reader and wrote *Das Kapital* here in rows J–P. Trotsky said he 'gorged himself on books', there were just so many books to read, and Lenin registered as a reader under yet another false name. Under the name of Jakob Richter he would write articles in seat L13 for a magazine called *Iskra*. When he wasn't doing this he would also act as tourist guide and show other exiles around the area. Guides can be a radical lot.

It was the reading room and library which was the draw to many other writers as well, including Rudyard Kipling, Mahatma Gandhi when he was a law student at University College and Inner Temple, George Orwell and George Bernard Shaw. Also H G Wells, Virginia Woolf, Alfred Lord Tennyson, Joseph Conrad, Arnold Bennett, W B Yeats, Thomas Hardy, E M Forster, Agatha Christie, Thomas Carlyle, Algernon Swinburne and Edward Gibbon, to name but a few.

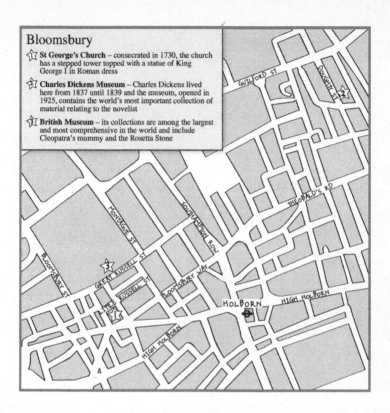

Bloomsbury

☆1 **St George's Church** – consecrated in 1730, the church has a stepped tower topped with a statue of King George I in Roman dress

☆2 **Charles Dickens Museum** – Charles Dickens lived here from 1837 until 1839 and the museum, opened in 1925, contains the world's most important collection of material relating to the novelist

☆3 **British Museum** – its collections are among the largest and most comprehensive in the world and include Cleopatra's mummy and the Rosetta Stone

London's Villages

HIGHGATE VILLAGE

JOHN MAHONEY

Highgate Village stands proudly on London's highest hilltop ridge, elegantly poised between Hampstead Heath and Muswell Hill. There was a hamlet here in the thirteenth century, and in the fourteenth the Bishop of London allowed a road to be built over the hill as the old track around the hill was often impassable in winter. The name 'Highgate' dates from this time, the 'High' an obvious reference and the 'Gate' for the tollgate that was built, now sadly long since dismantled. As with so many of London's constituent villages, a huge amount of history is crammed into a relatively small space, spiced with, in the case of Highgate, exquisite glimpses of the city below.

Because of the cleaner air here – a contrast with the fetid air of the city – many of London's wealthier citizens built their homes high on Highgate Hill. It was a migration that began in the late medieval times, increased through the eighteenth and nineteenth centuries, and continues today with the rich and famous. It's a desirable place to live: handsome houses, good schools, fine views and open spaces.

Clean-air considerations may have been influential but location was more important. Highgate Village sits across the Great North Road, one of the main routes out of the capital. It all started at the entrance to the Bishop of London's hunting park on top of the hill.

The Gatehouse pub, which dominates the high street, is built on the site of the old park's entrance. One of the earliest residents was a hermit who lived on site, and who was charged with the job of maintaining the road's surface using gravel dug from what is now Pond Square, the village centre.

Another important reason for Highgate's growth was that it became the last stop for the drovers taking their animals to London's Smithfield Market. Over the course of a year, thousands of cattle and sheep were driven long distances 'on the hoof', so a chance to pause, graze and fatten up was welcome before the final downhill miles to market. In summer the air would be thick with dust kicked up by the animals; in winter mud was a big problem. In parts of the high street today there are still houses with elevated entrances and steep steps down to the road, to distance the problems of dust and mud.

Naturally the drovers themselves needed places to stay and, of course, to drink. The Gatehouse and the Angel on the high street, and the Wrestlers a bit further on, are among the first five recorded pubs in the village. In all, 49 pubs can be traced back through Highgate's long and thirsty history. In 1841 there were 21 pubs for the 700 men in the village.

Over the years the problems with the road were not just the steep gradients and the waves of four-legged beasts coming down the hill. Because this was the main north–south route there were also traffic problems, in particular those caused by stagecoaches and wagons that ploughed deep ruts in the surface of the road. By 1780 at least eighty coaches a day were passing through the village. The situation eased slightly during the nineteenth century with the construction of a bypass. By 1884 the good burghers of Highgate proudly acquired Europe's first cable tramway on the hill.

WHERE TO READ THIS

Try a seat in Pond Square, at the heart of the village. For a read with refreshments, try the Flask pub. For a read with a view, take a seat in Waterlow Park near the statue of Sir Sydney Waterlow himself – it's one of only two statues in London holding an umbrella!

From the Gatehouse to the Grove

At the top of Highgate High Street stands the Gatehouse. First mentioned in 1634 records, there have been rebuilds and facelifts aplenty since then. Tolls were collected here from 1318, and the tollgate was demolished in 1892 because the arch wasn't high enough to allow loaded haycarts through.

Just beyond the tollgate crossroads is Highgate Public School and chapel. Its royal charter was granted in 1565, in the reign of Elizabeth I. T S Eliot was a schoolmaster here and in 1916 taught the young John Betjeman, later to become poet laureate.

For years the school chapel doubled as Highgate's parish church and was the original burial place for Samuel Taylor Coleridge. In Southwood Lane alongside the chapel lived Mary Kingsley. A distinguished African traveller and scholar, she was the inspiration behind the founding of the Africa Society in 1901, one year after her death. Years later former Prime Minister Harold Wilson sketched out plans for the home-study programme, the 'Open University', on the kitchen table there.

Opposite the Kingsley house is a row of quaint, well-preserved Widows' Almshouses, rebuilt in 1722. Tenants were required to attend church every Sunday; no men were allowed to stay on the premises.

Beyond the Gatehouse, in North Hill, is picturesque Byron Cottage.

The poet A E Housman was the upstairs lodger here when he wrote *A Shropshire Lad*, a poem at one time familiar to every English schoolboy and a copy of which, it's said, found a place in the kitbags of many an English soldier in the 1914–18 war. A little further on is Dickens' House – in fact, his two-week holiday home in 1832, when with sickness in his family, they spent time recovering in Highgate where they could escape the pestilential airs of the city below.

The Grove is Highgate's smartest address. Known locally as 'Quality Walk', it's quintessential Highgate for quintessential Highgate people. Dating from the 1680s, the Grove's six most famous houses were built as three semi-detached dwellings. Former residents include Samuel Taylor Coleridge, the great poet/writer/philosopher. Known as 'The Sage of Highgate', his many works include *Kubla Khan* and, at Wordsworth's suggestion, *The Rime of the Ancient Mariner*.

Other famous residents of the 'big six' were Gladys Cooper, actress and 1914–18 pin-up, Yehudi Menuhin, J B Priestley, Sting, Annie Lennox, playwright John Drinkwater, Robert Donat and the artist and scholar Roger Fry, who did much to introduce Impressionism to the British.

'Witanhurst' at the far end of the Grove is the second largest residence in London after Buckingham Palace. Built by Sir Arthur Crosfield, the soap millionaire, the mansion's private grounds were once famous for tennis. Crosfield's Greek wife was well known as the ultimate tennis enthusiast and the house became a famous venue for the pre-Wimbledon weekend society garden parties that were often attended by the Royal Family.

The estate fronts on to Highgate West Hill, one of London's steepest streets and which in the early days of the motor car was used for testing car engines. A few metres down from Witanhurst is the old Fox and Crown, now no longer a pub. Once, when the young Queen

Victoria was returning from a drive, a wheel came off her carriage and the horses were on the verge of bolting down the hill. It's said that catastrophe was averted by the pub's landlord, who brought the horses under control.

No. 31 Highgate West Hill is the childhood home of Sir John Betjeman. His autobiography *Summoned by Bells* immortalised the bells of St Anne's at the bottom of the hill. Also on West Hill is the former Russian Trade Mission campus, infamous for espionage activities during the Cold War. At one point British security services set up a double-glazing company that won a contract to double-glaze the Mission's windows. Over two years the British workforce proved highly effective at their work, which included much planting of electronic bugging devices!

The elegant spire that can be seen from miles around belongs to St Michael's, Highgate's parish church in nearby South Grove and final resting place for Samuel Taylor Coleridge after his remains were moved from the school chapel. Built in 1832, the spire gets a mention in Dickens's *David Copperfield*.

Sharing the skyline with St Michael's is the BBC communications tower, Highgate's only ugly structure. Built during the early days of television in the 1930s, the tower was built to transmit broadcast signals from down in the city to the main studios at Alexandra Palace. When during the Second World War television was closed down, the tower was adapted to beam signals up at enemy bombers to interfere with their navigation systems and cause them to miss their targets.

The Flask in Highgate West Hill is one of Highgate's most famous and popular pubs. The main building dates from 1767 but there was a pub here as early as 1716. There's nothing better than a Sunday morning walk over Hampstead Heath followed by a well-earned pint at the Flask. The origin of the pub's name is non-alcoholic, however.

It comes from the flasks of special Hampstead spa water brought across the heath for sale in Highgate.

Like most Highgate pubs, the Flask has its ghost and, of course, stories of Dick Turpin, famed as a highwayman but who was in fact more of a deer poacher and horse thief. (His famous ride to York on his horse Black Bess is total fiction.) The Flask's ghost is female and, it's said, causes the temperature to drop noticeably whenever she's in the bar. The Gatehouse's ghost is also female – Mother Marnes – but she won't appear when children or animals are about. At other times, though, you might need to have your wits about you. There are even stories of a chicken ghost in the main Pond Square, the result it's said of an early experiment in refrigeration using snow in 1626.

Highgate's unique custom of 'Swearing on the Horns' is believed to date from the seventeenth century; it may have its origins in entry rituals relating to the Fraternity of Drovers. The ceremony consists of swearing a nonsensical oath – administered, unsurprisingly, by the landlord – in front of a pair of horns. Some even say that men taking the oath got to kiss the prettiest girl in the tavern. More likely it was a way of selling more ale and fleecing even more money from passing travellers. Lord Byron took the oath and famously devoted a verse of *Childe Harold's Pilgrimage* to it.

At the top of Highgate West Hill you arrive at Pond Square, the village's main open space – although 'pondless' for quite a while. The two original ponds were the result of years of gravel extraction. They were drained in 1844. Pond Square is the venue for the annual Highgate Festival.

Overlooking Pond Square is Church House, said to be the inspiration for Steerforth's house in *David Copperfield*. It's next door to the handsome 'Lit & Sci', the Highgate Literary and Scientific Institution. Dating from 1840, its purpose is: 'to improve the mind by the cultivation of science and general literature'.

Up close – Highgate Village

Highgate may be ancient in origin but there's one architecturally world famous building that's relatively modern – Highpoint, a superb example of art deco design. Built by the Russian-born architect Berthold Lubetkin (1901–90), it has the highest penthouse apartment in London and an unrivalled 360-degree view of the city from the roof. It was one of the very first high-rise apartment blocks and is unique in its pioneering, imaginative use of reinforced concrete. Built between 1933 and 1935, it was far ahead of its time and was praised by Le Corbusier, the great French architect, who called it 'the seed of the vertical garden city'. Located on North Hill, just opposite Charles Dickens's house, it is notable for clean lines, maximum light and space, with imaginative but earthy use of natural materials to complement the basic concrete structure. Lubetkin was a committed socialist, convinced that architecture was a tool for social progress.

The High Street and the Hill

No. 44 Highgate High Street, on the corner of Townshend Yard, was once a chemist's shop with a discreet side door, where Samuel Taylor Coleridge would call in regularly to get his supplies of laudanum, a derivative of opium to which he was addicted.

Further on, halfway down the Hill is Lauderdale House, just inside Waterlow Park, built in the sixteenth century in the reign of Queen Elizabeth I by the Master of the Royal Mint. Charles II is said to have used the house for his favourite Nell Gwyn. In a moment of tantrum she is supposed to have threatened to throw their baby out of the window unless the King did something to recognise the boy, whereupon the Merry Monarch is said to have called out: 'Save the Earl of Burford!' Waterlow Park is pretty but unpretentious, except for magnificent views over London. It was given to London as a 'Garden for the Gardenless'.

Highgate's most famous character is Dick Whittington and at the bottom of the hill outside a pub stands the Whittington Stone. Dated 1821, it's the third stone to be placed there and is topped off with the figure of a rather fat cat installed in 1964. It marks the spot where Dick Whittington, according to legend, was told to 'turn again' on hearing the chimes of Bow Bells. Legend says he was a poor boy; the historical record has evidence that he was from a well-to-do Gloucestershire family.

Back to Waterlow Park, which you can walk through to Highgate's greatest glory, the world famous Highgate Cemetery, a magnificent invocation of the Victorian way of death. When burial conditions in London became intolerable in the early nineteenth century, Parliament authorised the creation of private cemeteries in Inner London. Highgate (West) Cemetery opened in 1839 and was extended in 1854 with the opening of the East Cemetery.

No Victorian was more fixated on death than Queen Victoria herself. She mourned Prince Albert for forty years, dressed in black every day and kept their rooms exactly as they were the day he died. Death was a very big player in Victorian times in Britain and elaborate rituals were developed around it. Many of the graves and monuments at Highgate are theatrical spectaculars. Among hundreds of graves containing civil servants, lawyers, administrators, local worthies and their families is a roll call of the famous dead. The East Cemetery is the last resting place of, among others: Russian pianist Shura Cherkassky; William Friese-Green, cinematographer; Claudia Jones, Black Freedom campaigner and founder of the Notting Hill Carnival; Karl Marx; Sir Sidney Nolan, Australian artist; Sir Ralph Richardson, actor; Herbert Spencer, philosopher, who coined the terms 'evolution' and 'survival of the fittest'; and Polish artist Feliks Topolski.

In the West Cemetery in 1862 Dante Gabriel Rossetti buried his young wife and model in the family grave plot. So intense was his grief that, against the advice of his friends, he placed a collection of manuscript poems in the coffin. Seven years later he had the grave reopened to retrieve the poems for publication.

Other notables buried in the West Cemetery include Radclyffe Hall, author of *The Well of Loneliness*, and the chemist Michael Faraday. Recently they have been joined by Alexander Litvinenko, ex-KGB, who was poisoned in London with polonium-210. Radioactive, he's buried in a large lead-lined casket.

OLD HAMPSTEAD VILLAGE

DAVID TUCKER

    *Hampstead is London's skybox. It's steeped in privilege. It's fabulously
well appointed. It affords the best views in London. As John Constable put
it nearly two centuries ago, 'this little house* is to my wife's heart's content.
Our little drawing room commands a view unsurpassed in Europe – from
Gravesend to Westminster Abbey.' It was ever thus.*

---

*No. 40 Well Walk (it's marked with a blue plaque)

The best views in London

A few thousand years ago a small band of Mesolithic hunter-gatherers pitched camp on the West Heath (as it's known today). From their camp it was a fifty-yard stroll up to the summit, from where they could see forever.

Indeed, there's an eyrie as soon as you come out of Hampstead tube station: the clock tower. It's part of the old Victorian fire station. They mounted a round-the-clock fire watch from the top of the clock tower because from up there you could see right across the village. And for that matter, you can think of the tube station itself as London's North Face. It's the deepest station in the system. It's no surprise that it was an important bomb shelter during the Second World War.

Steeped and steep (and stepped). Steep is every which way in Hampstead. Out of the tube Hampstead High Street and Fitzjohn's Avenue are practically in free fall. About face, and Holly Hill and Heath Street are almost as vertical as the 'ascenders' in their names.

You hear it said: 'There's something about Hampstead. Something in the air.' Ah, the wisdom of crowds. There *is* something in the air. Hampstead itself. Clouds scudding overhead. Air cleaner and clearer. And thinner? It's, well, exhilarating. But also maybe a little giddy, precarious, vertiginous even – like being out on a yardarm.

WHERE TO READ THIS

Recommended reading venue is the Holly Bush, the wonderful old pub in Holly Mount. Or the park bench on the summit, the one with the view to forever. It's just off Spaniards Road, just a little way along from Heath House. Your eyes will tell you when you're there.

You get that 'read' just about everywhere in Hampstead. Even in Church Row, the finest – it's well-nigh perfect – Georgian ensemble in London. It's right on the edge, clinging to the narrow shelf at the top of the Fitzjohn's Avenue slope. At the far end – down by St John's, the parish church – there's a loophole on your left. It's like looking down the trough of a wave. It's a reminder that the delightful curiosity halfway along on the other side of Church Row – the house with the first floor that juts out over the pavement, a first floor that's made out of white weatherboarding and looks like a fo'c'sle – perhaps isn't so out of place after all.

Shall we inch further out on the 'yardarm'? Surging up from Church Row is Holly Walk. And billowing up right alongside it is the church-yard annex – the overflow (so to speak) graveyard. It's bookended at the top by two handsome old weatherboarded houses. The second one in from Holly Walk was Dame Judi Dench's house. The weatherboarding is the key. It's another touch of old maritime England. The pair of them could be sloops riding out a nor'wester, pitching and yawing up above the whitecaps – the gravestones. And just a few doors further up Holly Walk is that pretty little row of white cottages with their painter's-palette doors. You'd be forgiven for thinking they'd washed up here from Corfu or Santorini.

Or head off in the other direction – up Heath Street. Running off it there are narrow, serpentine footways that are so steep they're hand-railed. Making your way up them you half feel as though you should have a cutlass clenched between your teeth – it's like being in a boarding party using grappling irons and tackle to scramble up the side of a ship. You think I'm kidding? Climb the first one, oh ye of little faith. Following it up you come over the top and you think you're on a ship's poop deck. Complete with a semi-circular railing. And you're looking out over the ocean, the ocean being London. Way in the distance you can see the southeastern rim of the bowl of hills that girdles the Thames basin, the bowl of hills that embraces Greater London. Beyond that rampart is the Weald of Kent. And ten miles beyond that is the sea.

Much nearer of course – well, if five to ten miles or so is *near* – is central London. The Eye. The Post Office Tower. Tower 42. The Gherkin. Manhattan-on-Thames (Docklands, in other words). And then look at your immediate surroundings, the foreground. Hampstead houses. You're standing on the northern rim of that bowl of hills. And if 'ocean' isn't far-fetched, well neither is a touch of vertigo. Because in Hampstead, you're ridge walking.

Another refocusing – and then it hits you: widows' walks. Well, that's what they look like. The balconies and lookouts and roof terraces. Hampstead is bristling with them. Get them into your purview and it all comes together in a rush: widows' walks, windmills and water. That's Hampstead. (Windmill Walk is barely a stone's throw away from 'the poop deck'.)

Especially water. Hampstead's awash with the stuff. Literally, figuratively, historically. All the waters: the Thames, the ponds (there are eighteen of them on Hampstead Heath), the well, the Fleet River, a fountain and, yes, as we've seen, the sea.

Whitestone Pond

Let's navigate some of those waters. And navigate them in style. Let's take a turn by Hampstead's flagship – the Admiral's House, in Admiral's Walk off Hampstead Grove.

The Admiral's House was supposedly the handiwork of an old eighteenth-century seadog, Admiral Matthew Barton. He was what they called a Blackbirder. In other words he bought and sold slaves. He was shipwrecked off the Barbary coast, washed ashore tadpole naked, captured and sold into slavery. Which he richly deserved. His Majesty's government ransomed him home. When they got him home they court-martialled him for having lost his ship. Enough was enough for Admiral Matthew B. After all those trials and tribulations he decided to retire. It might seem a strange place for an old seadog to retire to – up here on the heights of Hampstead, until you remember what he did to the roof of the house. You can see the railings, flagpole, fo'c'sle and satellite dish. And best of all – he put two cannon up there. Four pounders. Which he'd fire off every morning to salute the dawn, and every evening to salute the dusk. And a double charge on the anniversaries of famous British naval victories.

That's the yarn – and it's too good a tale not to tell. But there's not a shred of truth to it. It *was* a naval man who quarterdecked the house but the man in question was Lieutenant Fountain North.

If we set our course by the North Star, just up ahead of us is the Whitestone Pond. Up there you feel a little bit like Noah pitching up on Mount Ararat. And rightly so. Because this is the summit, the roof of London. How high are we? How does 435 feet 7 inches above sea level sound, the soles of your shoes 16 feet 7 inches above the top of the cross on the dome of St Paul's cathedral? It's all rather bracing – and clarifying. Explains why the old Observatory is just here – the air was that bit clearer, the better for stargazing.

The pond is what's called a dew-fed pond (as opposed to spring-fed). In other words, it's a man-made pond. But why put a pond at the top of the highest hill in London? You can understand the reason if you look at either end of the pond. What do you see? Ramps. Now consider Heath Street, which leads up to the pond. It's side-of-a-mountain steep. In the days when the traffic was horse-drawn it was a terrible slog for the horses hauling the wagons and carriages up this tremendously steep hill. So when they finally reached the top they'd drive the team down the ramp and into and through the pond, so the horses could refresh themselves. Then at the far end it would be up the ramp and out of the pond and on their way. (Charmingly, you still see mounted police horses getting that very reward for having summited.)

But it's only part of the answer. There's a far more important reason – a hard-headed, supremely practical reason for putting the pond here. Put yourself up on that wagoner's seat. On a hot summer day as you make the climb up the hill something's going to happen to the wagon wheels that's cause for deep concern. Because of the heat, the wooden part of the wheel will dehydrate a little bit and thus effectively shrink. Because of the heat – and the friction thereby generated – the molecular structure of the iron rims on the wheels will expand. It's an accident waiting to happen. The dehydrated wooden wheel contracts. The iron rim expands. The rim's going to come loose on the wheel. Then when you start down the steep hill at the far end and put the brakes on – the brakes will grip the wheel, but the rim's loose. In short, you don't have any braking. However, drive your wagon through the pond and the water resaturates the wooden wheels. What's more, the water temperature is always a little bit cooler than the air temperature. So when the cold water hits the iron rim it contracts. The iron rim once again fits snugly against the wheel. In short, you've got braking.

Hampstead Heath

Now as long as we're up here, how about if we move along just a little bit. Past the Whitestone Pond and almost to Heath House (where the road forks) there's a footpath (on your right) that takes you on to the Heath – and on to the most sensational 'viewing platform' in London. Trust me. Just go along there, plop down on the bench and, well, feast your eyes on the best panoramic in London. You get there – in body or in spirit – and you'll certainly agree it's the perfect spot to survey Hampstead's history.

Up close – Hampstead

The old cannons in Cannon Lane are fun. They're some of the oldest ones in London. They're 300-year-old Dutch cannons brought back to this country by Sir John Melville, Secretary of the East India Company. The reason for them? There wasn't a Paving Act until the second half of the eighteenth century and before that the wheeled traffic could go wherever it wanted to.

If an iron-rimmed wooden wagon wheel struck the corner of your house – or the corner of your garden wall – it was going to do some fairly serious damage. So householders used the old cannon to protect their properties, flipping them upside down and putting cannon balls one size too large in the mouths of the cannons, then sinking them deep into the road in 'strategic' positions.

As always, we start with the Thames. The Thames, time out of mind, flowing several miles north of here. And then the most important event in London's history: that glacier – that mile-high ice cube – diverting the river more or less to its present location and over the years the river carving out the Thames river valley. The Thames river valley that's spread out before you.

And now we narrow the focus to Hampstead and the last ice age. So we're back thousands of years as opposed to hundreds of thousands. The glacier has pushed down here. It's even bringing its own grit! It's just that it's beneath the ice rather than on top. It's pushing – and laying down – vast deposits of sand. You can see it here – it's underfoot.

Now fast-forward again. Over thousands of years the ice melts. The water from the ice goes down through the sand and hits the subsoil – the seriously old London clay. That clay is largely impermeable. The water from the ice hits the clay and percolates back to the surface in a series of springs. A series of springs giving rise to several of the Thames's tributaries, including the most important of them, the Fleet River.

Forward again, to a mere thousand years ago. If we're standing here then we're standing in the middle of a dense forest. The forest of Middlesex – *the forest of the Middle Saxons*. And it's now that we catch our first glimpse of Hampstead. As the name tells us, 'Hampstead', like many of London's villages, is Anglo-Saxon in origin. Taking the name apart you get *ham* meaning home or farm and *stead* meaning site or place. The late eleventh-century Domesday Book tells us that Hampstead was a pig farm valued at fifty shillings.

Now to Tudor times. Colonies of laundresses wring in this change. They make an important discovery: Hampstead's waters have good bleaching properties. What's more, Hampstead is ideally placed. It's close enough to London and Westminster so they can get some trade from down there. Not only is it close enough, but it's also far enough – far enough away so that the waters are pure.

Pure waters. There's the cue of cues. It rafts us across the centuries to the 'watershed' year: 1698. Hampstead has, well, struck water again. And it's a gusher: a solvent that can turn iron into gold.

Well is certainly the *mot juste*, the well being the Hampstead Well. Its waters proved to be chalybeate, iron-bearing in other words – iron-bearing and thus health-giving. Or so people thought. It was the well that made people well, and Hampstead certainly did well out of it.

Let's explore some more. First to the Vale of Health. It's the village on the Heath – Hampstead's village within a village. It's just a couple of streets, three dozen houses or so, green-remembered lanes, a lake with two white swans – in a phrase, doll's-house delightful, in a word, perfection.

There's more. The Vale of Health is all right in its own right – but what makes it doubly special is the way it counterpoints. Hampstead's all about summits and hilltops and big views – the Vale of Health is hidden, down inside. And all the more delicious for being so.

Back towards Hampstead Village

As is Mansfield Place, off New End Road. It's the smallest street, the most hidden street in London. If you absolutely have to, miss Kenwood House. Whatever you do, don't miss Mansfield Place. Not only is there no other place in Hampstead like Mansfield Place, there's no other place in London like Mansfield Place. It's a cul-de-sac. Two little rows of nineteenth-century cottages tucked in the canyon formed by what's left of the old Victorian New End Hospital. You can see the hospital water tower, the Rotunda, etc. (one of the etceteras being the tall chimney further down the slope – it was for the hospital inciner- ator). Because it's so secluded – so protected – it seems to have a microclimate. The cottage gardens are exquisite. As is the bowered footpath running between the two rows of cottages. Figs, grapes, hops, apples, plums, pears, let alone raptures of flowers – it's a mini Kew Gardens. To find Mansfield Place – to partake of it, however briefly – can be transformative. 'Through the looking glass' was how Lewis Carroll put it. Quantum physicists – and not a few science-fiction buffs – speak of luminous propulsion and wormholes that bend the space–time continuum. Well, whatever the terminology, whatever the theory – Mansfield Place gets my vote. You really do feel as though you've tumbled down a wormhole and come out in the nineteenth century. Way back in the nineteenth century. The sensation is quite extraordinary. It's pronounced – it feels real. So much so that you turn it over in your mind. My theory? Something to do with the utter absence of the automobile in Mansfield Place.

We've done water, so now let's see Hampstead in terms of the other elements, in terms of air, earth and fire.

Its air? Think of the Hampstead Observatory (Lower Terrace). Think of Robert Louis Stevenson coming here – the house he lived in is still there, in Mount Vernon – precisely because of Hampstead's reputation for fine air. Think of the splendid mock-Gothic Victorian sanatorium on Holly Hill. Today it's Celebrityville, a block of luxury flats, home to, word has it, a couple of Arsenal footballers and a Spice Girl or two. Be that as it may, the point here is: it absolutely stands to reason that a hospital for tuberculosis patients would find its way to Hampstead!

And earth? Well, the Heath obviously. There's nearly 900 acres of it, 2 per cent of London's public green. And that's really saying something, because this is the second greenest major city on the planet. But the key to the Heath is the earth: the sand. The soil is so alkaline that it's effectively unable to be cultivated. You can't grow cash crops in a sand pit. The sand – and the alkalinity – is the reason for the gorse and the furze. Wresting a living from sandy soil ain't easy. Most plants can't do it. But that good-for-nothing soil is effectively what's saved Hampstead Heath. You couldn't farm it. So why buy it? And what you haven't bought you can't sell – for 'development'. London – like every city – is a world of dwellings (mostly brick, in London's case) and pavement and roads. And right in the middle – well, near enough to – we've got this vast oasis of green and water and wildlife and playing fields (not to mention a duelling ground, should you need one).

You also get the sand – so to speak – in Golden Yard. It boasts Hampstead's oldest small houses. There's a plaque there that reads: '. . . the area was then largely a disused sand pit, the sand no doubt used in the development of Elizabethan London'. Sand extraction is also what caused the strange landscape at Sandy Heath. Sandscape? Moonscape? Fairyscape? A dunescape in reverse? A touch of a bayou? It's beyond extraordinary. There's no other place in London – perhaps in England – like Sandy Heath. It's pocked with lichen-covered mini-ponds. The secret? It's been quarried. For its sand. The lush, swamp-like mini-ponds mottling this wild and little-known extension of the Heath were sand pits.

And finally, fire. Well, the fire station of course. But also, the *look* of Hampstead. The fiery red brick. Fired in Hampstead kilns. Fired from Hampstead earth, Hampstead clay. And the fire – the reds and oranges and russets – of the gorse and furze on the Heath in the autumn. And the fire at night: the million points of light ablaze down in London when you take survey of the place – 'Gravesend to Westminster Abbey' – from one of Hampstead's eyries (or widows' walks) after night has fallen.

Pull all of the above together – the beauty of the place, its situation, its fine air, its greenery, its interest – and is it any wonder that it's always attracted – that it's *right* for – artists and writers and cinema directors and actors and poets and photographers.* As well as the rest of us.

---

*To name just a few: Constable, of course. But also Ford Madox Brown (The Mount, the scene of his most famous painting, *Work*, looks today very much as it did in 1852 when he painted it), George Romney, Lucien Freud and Michael Ayrton. Cinema directors Ridley Scott and the late Anthony Minghella. Writers John Keats and Leigh Hunt and Rabindranath Tagore and H G Wells and John Fowles and Wilkie Collins and John Masefield and George du Maurier and Katherine Mansfield and D H Lawrence and Robert Louis Stevenson and John le Carré. The list goes on and on.

OLD KENSINGTON VILLAGE

DAVID TUCKER

Kensington takes some getting to know. Not least because time in Kensington is multi-dimensional. A case in point: there's an 'ordinary', nondescript corner of the village where you've got half a millennium of Kensington in the palm of your hand. You can peel the centuries off like the layers of an onion. It's the corner of Thackeray Street and Ansdell Street. And for those who know, Thackeray Street is the true high street of the village. Forget High Street Kensington. Short, sweet little Thackeray Street is the real deal.

Kensington's 'Big Six'

In Thackeray Street you've got three art galleries; you've got Riders & Squires (where you get outfitted for a spot of polo); you've got a very swish French patisserie; you've got the mosaic shop whose other 'branch' is in Paris . . . well, you get the idea.

Three art galleries, Riders & Squires, etc. – and all of them *balanced*, as it were, on a fulcrum of five centuries. To your right, along Thackeray Street (if you're looking down Ansdell Street), there's Kensington Square with its seventeenth- and eighteenth-century houses. To your left, a nineteenth-century mews. Just along Ansdell Street, on the left-hand side, twentieth-century institutional. But that purpose-built American university classroom building isn't the whole story. Take a good look at Ansdell Street itself – notice how it *meanders*. What that arthritic 'layout' reflects is a seventeenth-century lane that led round behind the square to stabling and a bowling green. So: seventeenth century, eighteenth century, nineteenth century, twentieth century. And yes, that's only four. You complete the straight by popping into one of the 'shops' I didn't mention: Ottoemezzo, the little Italian deli. It magics up the best toasted sandwiches this side of Tuscany – ask for the 'Fellini' – *and* they're served up by the prettiest Bulgarian girls in London. And you don't get more twenty-first-century London than that!

And that's just a quick flex of the centuries. What really matters is what's *inside* that arc of time. Which is this: Kensington's all about hidden places and 'enclosures'; about wealth; about greenery and a certain rural character; about the court (this neighbourhood's known as 'the old court suburb'); about *wondrous strange* 'outsiders'; about – yes – horses. Those factors are the Kensington 'Big Six'. They're the keys to its character – and its history. And they're all here, all pivoting round this ordinary nondescript corner.

WHERE TO READ THIS

Either the very swish little French café or the little Italian deli referred to in this chapter. The Montparnasse is at 22 Thackeray Street; Ottoemezzo is at 6A Thackeray Street. Alternatively, pull up a cushion on the low garden wall in front of Hornets, the tiny – and wonderful – little vintage menswear shop in Kensington Church Walk. Be sure to say hello to Bill and Orlando, da man and da capo at Hornets (the cushions are courtesy of B and O).

You've got greenery, of course, in Kensington Square. But also – near the opposite corner of the square and up about a hundred feet (that's up in the air, *straight up in the air*) – the Garden in the Sky. It's the Derry &

Toms Roof Garden, the largest and most astonishing roof garden in the world. Well, three gardens really: a Spanish Garden, a Tudor Garden and an English woodland (complete, like every English woodland, with a stream, a Japanese footbridge and pink Chilean flamingos). It runs to an acre and a half and rejoices in over 1,500 plants and shrubs, including the best roses in Europe (the horticultural secret for that being altitude: at a hundred feet up the Roof Garden's well into the aphid's death zone!).

And as for wealth, well, have a look at Kensington Court Place at the opposite end of Thackeray Street. Its charming little terraced cottages were originally built to house some of the 'domestics' attached to Kensington Palace (the 'court' we mentioned): in recent times one of them – at eight rooms they're not big houses – fetched £1.5 million. Unmodernised.

The mews in the area tell the story of wealth and of horses. Wealth and horses went together like . . . well, like a horse and carriage. And Kensington's awash with mews. Indeed, the prettiest and most unusual mews in London – and London has some 250 of them – are in Kensington. For sheer, rustic, rose-petal-perfect-pretty you want Kynance Mews. For unusual, take a look at Kensington Court Mews, right there at the end of Thackeray Street; and Canning Place Mews, and De Vere Mews. They're that mysterious – it's like peering into a monk's cowl. And then the penny drops: the stabling was on the *first* floor. So where the garages are today, that's where the carriages were kept. There was a curving, gently sloping ramp to get the horses up to the first floor (De Vere Mews is still ramped!). And the stableman and his family lived in the storey and a half at the top. And why do it that way round? After all, it's not easy to get horses up to the first floor. But then it's even harder to get carriages up there. If you look closely at Kensington Court Mews you can see lots of evidence that points to that original use. The depth of the balcony and the width of the doors, for example. The balconies are much deeper than they ever would have been if they had been designed originally for human beings. But they had to be that deep in order to get the horses in and out. Similarly the doors. It's readily apparent that they were originally much bigger – they were stable doors that were 'filled in' to make them people-sized.

And as for *wondrous strange* 'outsiders'? *Voilà!* – just there at the Kensington Square end of Thackeray Street (No. 11), *habitait* the great French statesman and survivor, Talleyrand, pinned and wriggling under Napoleon's verbal dart – *merde dans un bas de soie* ('shit in silk stockings'). Also, in the square itself (at No. 18): John Stuart Mill, forever beating back against the current of the education his father had visited upon him (he could read and write ancient Greek as a three-year-old and Latin followed a year later – the nervous breakdown came seventeen years later). And a young American woman named Isadora Duncan, who pitched up late one night, climbed over the railings of the gardens and danced by moonlight in the verdant green. She was spotted by the very beautiful woman who lived in No. 33, who came out of her house, crossed to the railings and called out, 'Where are you from?' Getting the reply, 'From the moon', the classic beauty responded, 'That's all very well, my dear, but you really must come inside and have something to eat.' That composed, serene beauty was the famous actress Mrs Patrick Campbell (she of mixed Italian and English parentage), for whom George Bernard Shaw wrote the part of Eliza Doolittle in *Pygmalion* (or *My Fair Lady*, as the musical became). And it was that chance encounter – midnight and moonlight-drenched – in Kensington Square that launched Isadora Duncan's fabulous career as a dancer.

Then there was that consummate outsider, William Makepeace Thackeray himself, penning the greatest novel in the English language, *Vanity Fair*, at 16 Young Street, just off the square. Or the Pre-Raphaelite artist Edward Burne-Jones, touching down at No. 41 Kensington Square. Talk about a perfect 'fit' of resident and residence. Medievalist that he was, Burne-Jones eschewed the 'modern age'. And Kensington Square makes its disdain for the goings-on of the last 250 years perfectly clear in the way it resolutely turns its back on – 'cuts dead' – the High Street and 'modern' Kensington.

Much the same goes for the Kensington Church Walk – Holland Street – Carmel Court – Duke's Lane sequence. It's the other must-see Kensington neighbourhood. Must-see, providing you can find it. It's so tucked away you'd think its streets and houses ran up there when they were young, playing at hide-and-seek. Ran up there and got lost – couldn't find their way out. Centuries went by and those 'youngsters' gnarled into the very old streets and houses they are today. At one point in there – it's off Kensington Church Walk – you've got an innermost sanctum of a courtyard tucked away behind a hidden courtyard running off a secret neighbourhood. It's like one of those sets of nesting Russian dolls.

And talk about fabulous 'outsiders' inside deepest Kensington – right there you've got the American poet Ezra Pound and his avant-garde twentieth-century poetic movement, imagism. Pound said, 'Imagism began in Kensington Church Walk.' The house where he had rooms – it's marked with a blue plaque – is surely the most extraordinary small literary house in the world. Counting Pound, it has connections with no fewer than six famous twentieth-century writers. All of them, yes, 'outsiders'. The Americans William Carlos Williams and Robert Frost were put up there by Pound when they were in London. As was D H Lawrence. Laurie Lee courted his future wife there. And T S Eliot, of course, knew it from Pound's time there. For the record, the flat where Eliot lived and died is in Kensington Court Place.

Off Kensington Church Walk is the parish church, St Mary Abbots. Pound married Dorothy Shakespeare there. Was ever a poet's bride better named? Beatrix Potter also tied the knot there, As did W S Gilbert. The church is shot through with high strangeness – and estrangement. There's a plaque that lists all the vicars from 1242 to the present day. The roll call begins with a series of *particuled* Norman French names – Roger de Besthorpe (1260), Thomas de Rysleppe (1328), Gilbert de Raulein (1363). The *particule* is the giveaway – it's like a cockade on a beret! And let's make a 'connection' here – the De Vere of De Vere Mews was Norman French. But then – in 1371 – John Thomas. Followed by John Trigg. Followed by William Baker. Undeniably English names. As is every name that follows that late fourteenth century trio. That sequence is a distillation of the Norman Conquest and its aftermath.

Another plaque commemorates Mrs Jael Boscawen née Godolphin, who was born in 1647 and died in 1730 (what her dates tell us of course is that her formative, teenage years and prime of adulthood coincided with the naughty 1660s and 1670s of the Restoration). It reads, in part: 'She was adorned with rare faculties of the mind; singular acuteness sagacity and judgement, with a generous heart, full of piety and devotion to God, full of modesty candour diffusive charity and universal benevolence to mankind, beloved admired revered by all as well as by her relations, as being confessedly the ornament, and at the same time *the tacit reproach of a wicked age*' [my italics]. What to make of this? What is so revealing is the desperate, lashed-to-the-mast register of the prose. It speaks volumes about the age, and about how Mrs Boscawen née Godolphin of the village of Kensington was at variance with it.

'At variance' could have been the great novelist Thomas Hardy's middle name. Coming as he did from virtually a peasant background in the West Country, Hardy was always impressed by wealth. Attending a service – *and* attending to the wealth – at St Mary Abbot's, Hardy said that when the congregation rose the rustling of the silk dresses was like the beating of the devil's wings in *Paradise Lost*.

Up close – Kensington

Consider the finials of the village. For example, the very pretty little set of them at the western end of Duke's Lane. A finial is the teardrop- or arrowhead-shaped bit of fancywork at the top of many London iron garden railings. Before Prince Albert died, in 1861, London's finials would normally have been painted very bright colours – golds, reds and the like. They were London's bunting! But when the Prince died they were uniformly painted black as a token of respect. And to this day almost all of them are still black.

Kensington Palace Gardens

Now two quick flits. And sips. A stone's throw away from the church, towards the palace, is Kensington Palace Gardens. Or Millionaires' Row, as Londoners call it. It's a gated, private road mightily cliffed with Victorian mansions – Victorian mansions that are some of the most expensive houses in the world. Today many of them are embassies. In its forbiddingness and (restrained) ostentation, its exclusivity and dizzying plurality (Nepalese and Nigerian, Romanian and Russian, Israeli and Egyptian), the street is the diplomatic/architectural equivalent of a masked ball. As for the Palace, like the village it's a part of, it's walled and enclosed and secret-gardened (the Sunken Garden – another must-see) and yet surprisingly accessible. It is quintessentially the Palace of Outsiders. Royal Outsiders, but outsiders nevertheless. Most recently of course, the late Princesses, Diana and Margaret. But also the man who acquired what was a Jacobean country house and turned it into a palace: William III. He was, after all, a Dutchman. The statue of him in front of the palace is beyond compare in its sneering arrogance and prodigious self-satisfaction. Which is by way of saying, what it's *really* all about is the man whose gift it was: Kaiser Wilhelm II, that devil's brew of vanity and insecurity, and paragon of 'outsiders'.

En route to the Round Pond in the Gardens, do spare a thought for

George II and his consort, Queen Caroline (of Brandenburg-Ansbach). Indeed, we have her to thank for Kensington Gardens and the Round Pond. George II died at Kensington Palace. He died in the water closet (on the wrong throne). Caroline was much loved. Intelligent, attractive, cultured, hard-working, she organised everything for her husband. Even unto choosing his mistresses. She made sure they were very beautiful – and very stupid.

And see how the outsiders gather at the Round Pond. There's Virginia Woolf sailing toy boats as a child. And a grown-up Shelley sailing paper boats. Paper boats made out of banknotes – high style and rebellion do often fandango! But that vignette is also forever haunted by what it prefigures: his pregnant wife Harriet's suicide by drowning in the nearby Serpentine and his own death in a sea-storm off Genoa. And there – in another Round Pond spot of time – is J M Barrie meeting the little boy who served as the model for Peter Pan. Barrie was barely five feet tall; he was a Scot in London; he was perhaps a paedophile; he was eternally in the shadow of the shade of his older brother David who drowned, aged thirteen, when Barrie was six: it doesn't come much more alien, more outsiderly than that. Kensington was Never Never Land bacause Barrie was a walking case of Never Never Land and Barrie was in Kensington.*

Now one more hidden Kensington enclave: windsock-shaped, blue-plaque-spangled, Hyde Park Gate West. What a rum lot you find down there. That world-bestriding maverick** Winston Churchill lived and died at Nos 27–28. Above the blue plaque is the window where he made his last 'public' appearance – to wave to the crowd that had gathered outside to pay tribute to him on his ninetieth birthday. Chief Scout of the World Baden-Powell was at No. 9. The sculptor Sir Jacob Epstein – he who could

---

*The statue of Peter Pan – in its dappled glade by the Serpentine – is well worth finding.

**Churchill liked to work in his bed. His small grandson, Nicholas Soames, once burst in upon him and asked, 'Gwandpa, is it twue that you're the gweatest man in the world?' Churchill took out his stogey and growled, 'Yes, now bugger off.'

turn marble into birdsong – lived at No. 18. Across the street, at No. 29, the novelist Enid Bagnold, she who was bedded under a table at the Café Royale by the Victorian roué Frank Harris. At No. 22, the birthplace and childhood home of Virginia Woolf. It's the only house in London with *three* blue plaques – they're like a row of blue buttons. One for Virginia, one for her sister Vanessa Bell and one for their father, Sir Leslie Stephen.

And since the oak is in the acorn let's end at the beginning. The best way to do that is to take your leave – cross the threshold into Westminster and pause on the corner of Kensington Gore and Exhibition Row. London cabbies call it 'the hot and cold corner' because the handsome red brick building there is the Royal Geographical Society with its statue of David Livingstone (of Africa) on the north wall and one of Shackleton (of Antarctica) on the east wall.

And since nothing in London catapults us back further – and faster – than names let's take a ride on Kensington Gore. Gore is from *gara*. Old English, it refers to the triangular patches of ground that were left when irregularly shaped fields were ploughed. As for Kensington – *ton* or *tun* is also Old English (and Old Norse). It means enclosure, farm, estate. And *Kensing*? Nobody knows for sure, but the best guess is that it comes from the name of an Anglo-Saxon chieftain or smallholder. Fit those two ancient linguistic shards together and you get – scholars say – *Cynesige's farm*.

And there – in those ancient names – is Kensington's DNA: enclosures, irregular nooks and crannies, rural character and Englishness. And, yes, obduracy.

Without being too schematic about these matters, maybe those are the qualities a place has to have – the shell it has to secrete about itself – if it is to survive, remain true to itself, indeed thrive anent the mighty ocean of London. Certainly – as we've seen – that ancient village is still there. But – as we've also seen – to find it you have to do some exploring. Like Shackleton, you have to find your way back.

OLD CHELSEA VILLAGE

BRIAN HICKS

When you are spewed out of the underground station at Sloane Square you emerge into a genteel world. Sweaty bodies give way to scented silk scarves wantonly sprayed by wealthy ladies who 'shop'. Gentlemen here do not push and shove, but give way with polite gestures of their delicately manicured hands. That breed dressed in a uniform of Burberry and Barbour, known as 'Sloane Rangers', may be all but extinct but their good manners and courtesy still survive in petite, well-tailored pockets of Chelsea. Chelsea has not always been so tasteful. Its fortunes have ebbed and flowed with the tides of the nearby Thames.

Sloane Square and the Royal Court

The Chelsea story begins with those ruffians who established so many English towns and settlements – the Anglo-Saxons. No perfumes for them. No shopping. They took what they wanted and they took this land from the Celts. Their settlement was a landing place, a *hithe* or *hethe*, built on chalk, *chele* in Anglo-Saxon. So this becomes *Chele-hethe*, synthesised over the centuries to 'Chelsea'.

The subsequent village founded by them became known, in the sixteenth century, as the 'village of palaces'. Its location, so close to the medieval motorway of the Thames, made it a convenient stopping-off place for the wealthy when they ventured up- or downstream with the assistance of a benign tide. King Henry VII had a house here, so did the Earl of Shrewsbury and his wife Bess of Hardwick. The Bishop of Winchester resided here and so did the saintly Lord Chancellor, Sir Thomas More.

In the early seventeenth century Chelsea was dominated by one man. His legacy permeates the very air of this district. The station, the square, the streets bear his name. He was Hans Sloane. He was born into the Restoration in 1660. His family were wealthy. Hans studied in London and Paris and became an accomplished physician. He attended Queen Anne and her successors and he was appointed president of the Royal Society, remaining so for twenty-six years. In Chelsea he was responsible for ensuring the survival of the Society of Apothecaries' Physic Garden. His collection formed the foundation of the British Museum. To his daughter Elizabeth he left his Chelsea property of over a hundred acres. She in turn married Lord Charles Cadogan and, as you will gather if you stroll around here, the Cadogans are still around. The current Lord Cadogan is one of the country's wealthiest people, primarily because of his land holdings here. So Hans's family still have a firm grasp of his estate.

WHERE TO READ THIS

The Fox and Hounds pub, at the corner of Graham Terrace and Passmore Street: to say this is an intimate pub is a bit of an understatement. The pub is now twice the size it was and it is still remarkably small. It was created to cater for servants from the local big houses. It dates from 1830 and has a select clientele, including the odd monk, but it is peaceful and friendly. So get yourself a pint of Young's 'Dirty Dick' and have a read. An alternative is to enter the Chelsea Physic Garden and find yourself a shaded bench. The garden has a delightful tea room, so if the time is right perhaps you should also treat yourself to one of their wonderful cakes and a pot of Darjeeling.

The boundary for Chelsea was almost completely aquatic, to the south the Thames, to the east the River Westbourne and to the west the Counters Creek. The northern boundary was the Fulham Road. These boundaries have been tampered with most prominently here under your very feet. Arriving by train you may have glanced up and seen a large structure scaling the platforms, studded, boxed and contained. Contained because within this structure is the rather sad remains of one of London's lost rivers, the Westbourne. One-time boundary and trout stream but now reduced to the function of a sewer. In more refined days Sloane Square station was one of only two complete with a bar. This bar was called 'Drink Under the River' because that's exactly what you would do.

Outside the station your eye may well be caught by the Royal Court Theatre, founded in 1888. Chelsea has always been popular with 'theatricals'. Actors and writers abound and the 'court' has been associated with experimental and avant-garde theatre. Shaw premiered plays here. George Bernard Shaw was an influential 'Fabian', a socialist, who mixed with such people as H G Wells and Sidney and Beatrice Webb. His socialist beliefs underpinned most of his writing. He could be an old rogue. He said of himself he was an 'immoralist and heretic'. Sometimes grumpy but always witty, once at a party he was asked, 'Are you enjoying yourself, George?' His reply was the rather cutting, 'Well, there is nobody else here to enjoy.'

Shaw's plays have had many performances here at the Royal Court. *St Joan*, *Heartbreak House* and *Back to Methuselah* all premiered here in the 1920s. The theatre became a cinema in 1935 and remained so until it was bombed in 1940. When the building was restored in the 1950s it became once again a theatre and it was here that the angry young man John Osborne premiered his plays such as *Look Back in Anger* and *The Entertainer*.

If you leave the square and make your way down one of the side streets such as Holbein Place or Lower Sloane Street you will eventually bump into the Royal Hospital in Royal Hospital Road, the home of the Chelsea Pensioners. You don't have to be sick to come to this hospital, but you do have to have served in the army. 'Hospital' in this instance relates to 'hospitality'. The hospital has a proud history that stretches back to its famous founder, King Charles II.

Charles was a tall man, over six feet in height with a dark complexion. He was physically fit, a good swimmer and rower. By all accounts he could be charming and lovable. He was a born pragmatist and would always work to his own strengths. He had learned a hard lesson from his father Charles I, who had been executed in 1649 for his autocratic style and his abuse of Parliament. After a civil war fought by the Parliamentarians against the Royalists, the King was beheaded and England became a Puritan Republic termed the 'Commonwealth'. The eventual head of state was one Oliver Cromwell, a man who lacked vanity, and who saw the world for what it was, 'warts and all'.

The young Charles II was forced to live abroad, most notably at the court of his cousin Louis XIV of France. While at the 'Sun King's' dazzling court in Paris he promised he would convert to Catholicism if he should become King of England, and he also noticed that Louis had provided a retirement home for old soldiers called Les Invalides.

When Charles was restored to the British crown in 1660, it was with the help of the British army and a man called General Monk. Charles decided it might be politic to show his appreciation to the army, and what better way to do this than to set up a grand retirement home for old soldiers, based upon the French model. It was founded in 1682. Charles apparently donated some £7,000 to help towards its establishment and was able to get the finest architect in the land to construct the dining hall and chapel wings – none other than the designer of St Paul's Cathedral, Sir Christopher Wren.

Charles is quite rightly celebrated here. In the quadrangle there is a fine statue by Grinling Gibbons, more renowned for his woodcarving than his sculpture. This bronze was gilded to commemorate the present Queen's Golden Jubilee in 2002. Apparently some, even among the ranks of the Pensioners, think it now looks rather gaudy.

The statue is the focus of Oak-apple Day, 29 May, Charles II's birthday. On this day each of the 350 or so 'Boys of the Old Brigade' march up to the statue armed with a piece of oak branch. They place these around the statue until the King lies hidden in the oak leaves. The ceremony commemorates the escape of Charles II from the Parliamentarians in 1651 after the Battle of Worcester. Charles II had been defeated by Oliver Cromwell and had to escape. He made his way to Boscobel House in Shropshire. The Penderel family were loyal to the King but felt it was unsafe for him to reside in the house so he slept in an oak tree in their grounds, attended by Colonel Carlis and a cushion. While Charles hid in the tree, Cromwell's men came and searched the house and, according to legend, when they went outside and stood under the very oak tree which shrouded the King, the soldiers began talking about what they would do if they laid their hands upon his person. Charles escaped and enjoyed recounting that story again and again. It is recorded in the diary of none other than Samuel Pepys. Oak-apple Day became a public holiday celebrated throughout the land right up until the nineteenth century, and is still remembered in some other places in Britain even today. Numerous public houses remember that 'Royal Oak' in their names and the Pensioners get double rations on Oak-apple Day.

Oh, and about that promise to Louis XIV about converting to Catholicism if he was restored to the English crown . . . well, Charles, ever the pragmatist, realised that this would be a very unpopular move with the British people, but he wanted to keep a promise made in good faith – so he converted to the Catholic faith on his deathbed in 1685.

Up close – Chelsea

The building of the Albert Bridge in 1873 coincided with the construction of the Chelsea embankment. Designed by Rowland Mason Ordish, the bridge's delicate design is similar to a bridge – the Franz Josef bridge – Ordish designed to cross the Danube and which was demolished in 1949. The Albert Bridge was decked out in lights for the Festival of Britain in 1951 and they have stayed ever since, making it a glittering spectacle on the Thames. One local who loved the bridge was John Betjeman, poet laureate and architectural writer. When the bridge was under threat in the 1950s he formed a protest group to save it – one of the earliest architectural 'conservation campaigns'. The bridge has a sign on it dating from the Second World War which advises soldiers to break step when marching across the bridge.

Just around the corner from Royal Hospital Road lies Tite Street, whose most famous resident was Oscar Wilde. He lived at No. 34.

Oscar was the son of a baronet and eye surgeon in Dublin. His mother Jane Wilde was a nationalist and poet published under the name of 'Speranza'. Oscar went to Trinity College Dublin and then subsequently to Magdalene College, Oxford. Students at Trinity like to say that he was 'sent down to Oxford'. Wilde graduated from Oxford with a double first and soon after met Constance Lloyd, whom he married. They moved into this house where he wrote in the ground-floor studio on a desk that had belonged to Thomas Carlyle. In 1884 he met Lord Alfred Douglas, or 'Bosie' as he was known, and almost immediately there was a spark of attraction between the two men. This became common knowledge in London and one person who found out about this was Bosie's father, the Marquess of Queensbury (the man who drew up the rules of boxing). The Marquess believed there was something 'going on' between his son and Oscar, so he came down to Tite Street, barged in through the front door and threatened Oscar in his own family home. Oscar apparently said to his servant, 'This is the Marquess of Queensbury, the most infamous brute in London; never allow him into my house again.' The Marquess did not stop there; he made his way up to Wilde's club, the Albermarle just off Piccadilly, and there he left his famous calling card with the words inscribed upon it, 'To Oscar Wilde posing as a somdomite'. Apparently he couldn't spell. When Oscar saw what was written upon the card he was quite calm, but Bosie was mortified. After much encouragement from Bosie, Oscar went along to his lawyers to begin an action for defamation against the Marquess. He lost the trial and was later charged with gross indecency. After what many regard as a show trial he was imprisoned in 1895. He was released in 1897, left England and never returned. Wilde died on 30 November 1900 in Paris, his last words supposedly, 'Either that wallpaper goes or I do!' The blue plaque on his house was put up in 1954, the centenary of his birth. One local magistrate was apparently against this 'honour', stating that Oscar was nothing but 'a common filthy criminal'.

Back into Royal Hospital Road and to the Chelsea Physic Garden. Established in 1673 by the Society of Apothecaries, its purpose was to grow plants to be used as medicines for 'physicians', thus the name. It is not the oldest physic garden in Britain – the Oxford Botanical Garden dates back to 1621 – and it is certainly not the oldest physic garden in Europe, the first physic garden being formed in the university city of Pisa in about 1543. Nevertheless this is a very significant garden and more than a hundred years older than the Royal Botanic Gardens at Kew.

During the later part of the seventeenth century one visitor was the diarist John Evelyn. He was fascinated by the 'subterranean' heaters used to keep the plants alive during the very cold winters of this period. Carolus Linnaeus came here to study plants. A seed exchange was estab-

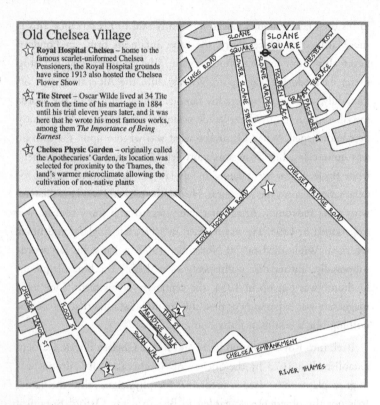

Old Chelsea Village

☆ **Royal Hospital Chelsea** – home to the famous scarlet-uniformed Chelsea Pensioners, the Royal Hospital grounds have since 1913 also hosted the Chelsea Flower Show

☆ **Tite Street** – Oscar Wilde lived at 34 Tite St from the time of his marriage in 1884 until his trial eleven years later, and it was here that he wrote his most famous works, among them *The Importance of Being Earnest*

☆ **Chelsea Physic Garden** – originally called the Apothecaries' Garden, its location was selected for proximity to the Thames, the land's warmer microclimate allowing the cultivation of non-native plants

lished here in the seventeenth century. The first Cedar of Lebanon trees in England were grown here. John Wesley, the founder of the Methodist Church, visited in 1748 while, later, Wilfred Owen and Siegfried Sassoon visited the garden to escape the hell of the First World War. The garden still has links with Imperial College, part of the University of London, and studies have been done here on the Madagascar periwinkle, from which is derived an alkaloid used in the treatment of leukaemia, and the woolly foxglove, with reference to digitalis used in the treatment of heart conditions.

When Hans Sloane became the Lord of the Manor here in 1712,

this land became part of his estate. The Society of Apothecaries had wanted to purchase the land to secure it but Sloane instead agreed that he would rent it to them at £5 per annum. Another condition was that they should send to the Royal Society five specimens of dried plant per year until this august body had received two thousand specimens. Hans was president of the Royal Society himself for twenty-six years and this collection of plants not only ensured the continuing study of plants here but also forms part of the collection of the Natural History Museum today.

The garden became a registered charity in 1983. Annual rent still has to be paid to the successors of the man who gave the station where we began our visit its name, Hans Sloane. A cheque has to be written out to the Cadogan Holding Company, still for the sum of £5. The cost of entry today is £7, so with one visitor they have paid their rent for the year and have a £2 surplus. Now that has to be the way to run a business.

Chelsea has a lot to thank Hans Sloane for.

OLD SOHO AND ITS PUBS

ED GLINERT

Soho has long had London's best pubs. But then it has long had the best of everything. Here the shops are fancier, the food in the restaurants tastier, the streets livelier, the nightclubs louder, the nights out longer, the people happier, even the prostitutes – of either sex, sometimes both – better-looking. People come here from afar to marvel at the capital of chic, the centre point of style. When they arrive they find glamour, glitz and glitter, as well as great pubs.

Thomas Burke, writing his *Nights in Town: A London Autobiography*, knew it in 1915. 'Soho – magic syllables!' he waxed. 'When the respectable Londoner wants to feel devilish he goes to Soho, where every street is a song. He walks through Old Compton Street, and, instinctively, he swaggers; he is abroad; he is a dog.'

No one ever drank in Soho for the quality of the beer, rather it was to sup in the presence of glamorous ghosts hovering over the bar stool – Dylan Thomas, Nina Hamnett, George Orwell, Charles de Gaulle, Arthur Rimbaud, Karl Marx – the thought that some of that mystique that made those names so celebrated might rub off, and for the quality of the pub as a saloon of sophistication.

In Soho the inspired imbiber has an insatiable choice. Within a few streets of Soho Square there is the mouth-watering prospect of De

Hems on Macclesfield Street; the Crown and Two Chairmen at 32 Dean Street; the John Snow, 39 Broadwick Street; the Dog and Duck, 18 Bateman Street; the French House, 49 Dean Street; the Golden Lion, two doors along at No. 51; the Carlisle Arms of Bateman Street; and the Coach and Horses at 29 Greek Street – most of which Burke would have known a hundred years ago.

Turn every corner and there is another glittering glass gin palace with a shattering story to tell: the Red Lion on Great Windmill Street where Karl Marx devised the *Communist Manifesto*; the Argyll Arms at 18 Argyll Street, with its well-preserved Victorian fittings, where the novelist George Orwell chastised BBC colleagues for failing to show sufficient proletarian credentials; the Sun & 13 Cantons on Great Pulteney Street, named after the Swiss woollen merchants that used to be based locally.

Of these some have so enticing a reputation it is barely possible to walk past without being sucked in. A pub has stood on the site of De Hems, to the south of Shaftesbury Avenue, since 1688 when it opened as the Horse and Dolphin. De Hem, a retired Dutch seaman, took over the premises early in the twentieth century. He had a passion for molluscs and decorated the walls with some 300,000 oyster shells, the last of which were removed in the 1950s. Fittingly, it was here during the Second World War that Dutch resistance fighters gathered.

In the 1960s De Hems was popular with music-business types, particularly Pete Meaden, the Who's first manager, who once described himself as 'neat, sharp and cool, an all-white Soho Negro of the night', and who would come here every lunchtime to buy rounds of Scotch and Coke. Both the Soho newcomer and the seasoned Sohoite looking to re-indulge might try to take in the lot . . . perhaps over the course of a few weeks.

WHERE TO READ THIS

An ideal place to read this chapter would be Bar Italia on Frith Street. It's the best coffee house in London and one of a dwindling number of stylish independent outlets that hark back to Soho's great pre-Frappuccino days and the arrival of the Gaggia machine locally in the 1950s. Bar Italia has retained the correct period detail – neon signs, chrome pedestal bar stools, mirrors, two-tone Formica striped with steel – has a shrine to the boxer Rocky Marciano, and even a scooter club whose members preen and parade outside in good weather, revving their machines as if auditioning for *Quadrophenia*. It remains effortlessly chic – and the coffee's great. Line your stomach with a panino or two before an assault on the Soho pubs, and come back here the next day to wipe out that hangover with some of the black stuff.

A drink from the rudest landlord in London

Come out of Tottenham Court Road tube, head towards sedate Soho Square with its Tudor-styled folly and prestigious company headquarters (Paul McCartney Ltd, the Football Association), and then start on nearby Greek Street, south of the Square, at the Pillars of Hercules. The pub is aptly named, for the two ends hold up the bridge that runs over Manette Street. The Pillars of Hercules has stood here since 1733 and a century and a half later was a favourite of Francis Thompson, the cricketer-poet who in 1888 was rescued from the doorway, where he was lying in a drunken stupor, by Wilfred Meynell, editor of *Merry England*, who subsequently gave Thompson his first chance of being published. In the 1970s up-coming authors Martin Amis, Julian Barnes and Ian McEwan frequented the Pillars, as did those who worked for the literary magazine the *New Review*, then based at 11 Greek Street.

A few hundred yards south on Greek Street is Soho's best-known and most crowded pub, the Coach and Horses. Until recently it had long been presided over by Norman Balon, the self-styled 'rudest landlord in London' – there are even coffee mugs in local offices bearing that legend – and it is where *Private Eye* magazine holds its fortnightly lunches. To get on that guest list is an honour barely with parallel. Those so honoured include Melvyn Bragg, Germaine Greer, Salman Rushdie – even Margaret Thatcher – but not all on the same day. Rushdie scoffed away while Special Branch officers downstairs, on the lookout for suspicious fatwa-supporting characters, posed as ordinary drinkers. Usually the most dangerous encounter was with Balon himself, who was known to terrorise lunch guests with a playful 'Oi, where the x#&%#x! do you think you're going?' as they furtively made their way upstairs to the dining room.

In the last half of the twentieth century the Coach and Horses was a home from home for the *Spectator* columnist Jeffrey Bernard: four-times-married gambler, journalist and fervent alcoholic who could regularly be found perched on a favourite stool regaling customers. According to Soho chronicler Daniel Farson '[Jeffrey Bernard] paid for his formidable intake of drinks by writing very funnily about the disastrous effect the drinks have on him'. Keith Waterhouse turned Bernard's life into a West End show, *Jeffrey Bernard Is Unwell*, the excuse often found on the page where his *Spectator* column should have been.

The Golden Lion and the French House

Further west a couple of streets over along Dean Street are two neighbouring but highly contrasting hostelries: the Golden Lion, intense and irreverent, and the French House, louche and loud. The Golden Lion at No. 51 has been a gay pub since the 1920s. It was frequented in the 1970s by Dennis Nilsen, the mass murderer who killed at least fifteen men in the London suburbs. Here in November 1981 he picked up Paul Nobbs, one of the few targets he failed to murder.

The French House at No. 49 couldn't be more different. It opened as the Wine House in 1910 and was run by a German, Schmidt, who was deported when the First World War broke out. He was replaced by the Frenchman Victor Berlemont, then the only foreign landlord in Britain. Berlemont would eject troublesome customers by announcing, 'I'm afraid one of us will have to leave, and it's not going to be me.' During the Second World War the pub became a meeting place for the French Resistance, where Charles de Gaulle allegedly drew up his Free French call-to-arms during lunch upstairs. After the war painters such as Lucian Freud and Francis Bacon became regulars. By then Berlemont had been succeeded by his son, Gaston, who despite being born in Soho and serving in the RAF during the war played up his Gallic background to the full by sporting a flamboyant moustache and engaging in much hand-kissing.

It was in the French House in 1953 that Brendan Behan ate his boeuf bourguignon with both hands. It was also here that year that Dylan Thomas left the only copy of the hand-written manuscript for *Under Milk Wood* a few weeks before he went to America – for good – in 1953. Thomas told a BBC producer, Douglas Cleverdon, that if he found the original he could sell it. All Thomas knew was that he had dropped it somewhere in Soho, probably in a pub, but had no idea where. Eventually Cleverdon realised that the French House was a likely choice. He found the script and sold it for £2,000 (£40,000 in today's money). The French House retains its raffish Gallic Bohemian atmosphere. Beer is only served in halves, but alas the blue wisp of a Gitane curling to the ceiling is no more.

The centre of Soho – Old Compton Street

In Soho all roads lead to Old Compton Street. Only a few hundred yards long, it consists almost entirely of shops, cafés, bars and restaurants, and is packed day and night with tourists, shoppers, restaurant-goers, theatre-lovers and late-night revellers. By midnight Old Compton Street is the liveliest spot in the capital and its pubs are still going strong. At the eastern Charing Cross Road end is the awkwardly named Molly Mogg's. It was the Coach and Horses from 1731 to 1981 and features in the 1961 Colin Wilson novel *Adrift in Soho*, which perfectly captures the transient world of the Boho Soho drifter. The hero, Harry Preston, ends up here after leaving the Midlands, lonely and ignored. 'After a few minutes a bearded youth came in with an arty-looking girl; she wore thick red stockings and a duffle coat. I tried smiling at her when she glanced in my direction, but she looked away as if I were invisible.'

Bar Soho at Nos 23–25 was the King's Arms in 1839 when the German composer Richard Wagner stayed here. Inspired by a rough voyage he had recently endured on the Baltic Sea, he began work on his opera, *The Flying Dutchman*, in Old Compton Street. In 1871 the French symbolist poets Paul Verlaine and Arthur Rimbaud fled Paris following the fall of the Commune and briefly lodged here. By then the pub was the Hibernia Stores, which put on radical lectures upstairs that the two poets attended along with, possibly, Karl Marx. Rimbaud, who once confessed to embracing degradation and trying to 'derange all his senses' so he could write a new kind of verse, met the 28-year-old Verlaine when he was 17 after writing him a fan letter. They scandalised literary Paris by eloping to Soho, where Rimbaud complained that the gin tasted like 'concentrated sewage water', that London was muddy with a constant fog, and described the city as being 'as black as a crow and noisy as a duck'.

The Admiral Duncan at 54 Old Compton Street is Soho's leading gay pub, and it was here, on 30 April 1999, that David Copeland, a Nazi sympathiser waging a one-man war against minority groups, nervously asked the barman directions to the nearest bank, and deposited a holdall containing a bomb packed with 500 nails in the bar before leaving. Fifteen minutes later the bomb exploded, killing three people and injuring scores of bystanders. Copeland had detonated similar bombs in Brixton and Brick Lane over the previous few weeks, resulting by chance in much less damage, and it was later revealed that the police, suspecting that Old Compton Street could be a target, had alerted some gay businesses and organisations but sent the gay rights group Stonewall a warning letter with a second-class stamp, which failed to arrive until the day of the bombing.

Opposite the Admiral Duncan is Compton's. It was built in 1890 with a facade that featured swags, elaborate heads and a figure of Pan and was topped by a steep mansard roof that was later removed. Here in 1958 Harry Webb became Cliff Richard after deciding that 'Harry Webb' wasn't rock'n'roll enough. A decade earlier it was where the cultish dilettantish writer Julian Maclaren-Ross discovered from the poet Tambimuttu that the glamour of the area created its own problems for writers, as he described in his autobiographical *Memoirs of the Forties*:

'It's a dangerous place, you must be careful,' Tambi said.

'Fights with knives?'

'No, a worse danger. You might get Sohoitis, you know.'

'No, I don't. What is it?'

'If you get Sohoitis,' Tambi said very seriously, 'you will stay there always day and night and get no work done ever. You have been warned.'

Maclaren-Ross evidently caught Sohoitis, for his masterpiece, *Memoirs of the Forties*, for which he was paid chapter by chapter, was still unfinished when he died of a heart attack in 1964, just after finishing an entire bottle of brandy to celebrate a new commission.

Up close – Soho

To most people walking along Broadwick Street in the heart of Soho it's just a pillar box. It's been there so long it probably says 'J R' (Johh Rex, as in the old king John, not a dog). OK, it couldn't be John as the pillar box wasn't introduced to British streets until 1852 (by the great Victorian novelist Anthony Trollope, no less). But they are stamped with the Latinate name of the monarch of the time, although there aren't many for Edward VIII. The red mail monster on Broadwick is no ordinary pillar box. For it was here that one of London's funniest comic troupes, the Crazy Gang, staged their great 'lost postman' gag. The two perpetrators were 'Monsewer' Eddie Gray and Tommy Trinder. The pair were calmly walking by one day when they stopped at the pillar box. Gray peered into the hole and shouted down: 'Well, how did you get in there? Don't panic. I'm sure we can get you out.' As a crowd gathered, he turned to Trinder and explained, 'It's a postman. He's fallen in. I'm going to get help. Can you lot wait here?' He and Trinder then made off, never to return. The crowd slinked away embarrassed once they realised they had been duped.

The most exciting Soho pubs can be found in the oddest places. The King's Arms at 23 Poland Street is dwarfed by Marks & Spencer's Pantheon building. The Ancient Order of Druids first met here on 28 November 1781, their activities precipitating a revival of interest in the Ancient Britons. Literary historians like to believe that William Blake, who celebrated his twenty-fourth birthday that day and lived locally, was present. The John Snow at 39 Broadwick Street is always packed, probably because the beer, Sam Smith's, is about a pound cheaper than its rivals. Don't wander in without a thought for Snow, an inspired local nineteenth-century physician whose surgery stood on this site. It was there he single-handedly solved Soho's 1850s cholera epidemic. The Endurance at 90 Berwick Street was the King of Corsica for decades. It was one of the oddest pub names in the country, chosen in honour of the French mercenary Theodore Neuhoff, who was once invited to become king of the island of Corsica and died in Soho in 1756. He is buried in the disused churchyard of St Anne on Wardour Street and took to his grave the knowledge of where he buried his vast hoard of treasure. Experts believe it may be under West Ham United's Upton Park football ground, but no one has tried digging up the pitch yet. Kingly Street, right over at the West End of the neighbourhood, is easy to miss. It is a tiny street, almost an alley, tucked away behind Carnaby Street. Until recently it sported one of London's greatest greasy-spoon cafés, Voltaro, but still has the Caledonian-themed Clachan pub, which has some of its original Victorian woodcarvings.

Back to Old Soho

Running north–south through the centre of Soho is Wardour Street. Long ago it was known as Old Soho, an evocative and romantic name remembered by Ray Davies in the opening of the Kinks 1970 hit 'Lola'. It should be *the* great Soho pub street, but it is more of a working place; advertising agencies and film production companies are rife on Wardour. For decades its best-known pub was the Intrepid Fox, home of bikers and hair freaks. The Intrepid Fox was named after Charles James Fox, the Whig politician whose support for the French Revolution convinced many of his colleagues to join the Tories. Fox frequented the pub and the landlord was so impressed he offered free drinks to anyone who promised to vote for him. The pub is currently closed but will probably reopen soon under a different name.

That is what has happened nearby at the corner of Great Windmill Street and Archer Street, where what was the Red Lion is now the B@1. Karl Marx attended the Communist debating club that met here in the 1850s. He was watched by the Prussian government agent Wilhelm Stieber, who was monitoring Marx under instructions from the Prussian Minister of the Interior, Ferdinand von Westphalen – Marx's brother-in-law. Stieber reported back to von Westphalen that the Communists were plotting in code to kill Queen Victoria, and though von Westphalen reported this to Lord Palmerston, the foreign secretary, the latter sat on the information. When the Prussians complained that the British authorities were not showing sufficient concern the home secretary explained that 'under our laws, mere discussion of regicide . . . does not constitute sufficient grounds for the arrest of the conspirators'. The cell was wound up in September 1850 and moved to Cologne, where it was rounded up by the Prussian police.

It was also to the Red Lion that Marx and Friedrich Engels brought the outline of their new *Communist Manifesto* to the Communist League congress. It must have seemed strange at the time. No such body as the Communist Party then existed nor was the work really a manifesto. As a piece of literature *The Manifesto of the Communist Party* is clumsy and pedestrian. Its famous early line – 'The history of all hitherto existing society is the history of class struggles' – pales alongside its precursor Rousseau's great epithet from the *Social Contract*: 'Man is born free; and everywhere he is in chains'. But as a piece of political propaganda its resonance has been phenomenal.

Only one other book – the Bible (and that is of unsure translation) – has had such an impact on humanity. *The Manifesto of the Communist Party* was the cornerstone of a philosophy that powered the Soviet Union, China, Mongolia, North Korea and much of east Europe for the latter half of the twentieth century, and that still propels much political thought worldwide. It is certainly the most influential book that ever arose from a meeting in a pub in Soho.

Mystery and Secrets: Hidden London

SECRETS OF THE CITY

HILARY RATCLIFFE

The best way to find the secrets of the City is, of course, to walk. And as you go, to look up, around and even down, and there they are, secrets waiting to be discovered. The first and perhaps most surprising secret is that in a city where 300,000 people go to work and that encompasses only a square mile, there are over one hundred gardens.

Gardens to discover

One of the people responsible for such a verdant centre was Fred Cleary, President of the Metropolitan Parks and Gardens Committee in the 1970s. He was determined that there should be open spaces in what is a very overcrowded area where land is at a premium. So, as a salute to Fred, start your walk in Cleary Garden off Huggin Hill near St Paul's. The garden is built up the hill and in the ancient past this was where there were Roman baths. The Romans used the water from a spring on the hill. At one time the baths were communal and mixed, but in the time of Hadrian (was he a prude?) separate baths had to be provided for men and women. The name of the Hill relates however to a later period when pigs were kept here, hence pigs – hogs – Huggin Hill.

Another very pleasant garden to discover is at St Dunstan's-in-the-East in the remains of the church: dating originally from around

1100, a tower was added later by Sir Christopher Wren, it was rebuilt by David Laing in the 1820s only to be destroyed by Adolf Hitler in the Blitz of 1940. Rather than rebuild a church that the city didn't need, the site was turned into a beautiful garden with a gentle fountain in the middle. Just the place to rest as you pound the city streets on your walk.

A real gem is the churchyard garden of St Vedast on Foster Lane (north of St Paul's across Cheapside). It is hidden behind a blue door that looks like somebody's front door and you seem to have to dare to enter. Go in and you will find a bust by Jacob Epstein, a tablet set in the wall written in ancient Sumerian script and part of a Roman pavement. Plus a memorial to Petro, a soldier, who is described on the memorial by his friends, 'This was a man'. What a wonderful tribute. It makes you want to know him.

WHERE TO READ THIS

Sitting in the churchyard of St Dunstan's-in-the-East, one of the special places in the City. There, surrounded by flowers, shrubs and the singing of birds, the noise and bustle recedes and you can listen to the gently trickling water of the fountain that spills over the yellow-coloured stone in the middle of the garden, perhaps in the shade cast by the Christopher Wren church tower.

About street names

Walking around, another thing to look for is street names. They always give a clue as to what was there in the past and so uncover secrets. Take for example Hanging Sword Alley. As people in the past couldn't read, outside your shop or place of work you would put up a picture of what you did. A hanging sword was a fencing master's house.

What about Cloak Lane? That gets its name from Cloaca, a Roman sewer, but this is now a salubrious street near Guildhall. While on the subject of sewers, the first public toilet in London was established by Richard Whittington, better known as Dick Whittington. As the character in the story Dick Whittington is viewed as simply a young man who came to London to seek his fortune. Through his faithful cat, according to the tale, he gained fame and fortune and became Lord Mayor of London three times. So is this true? Well yes, he was Mayor three and a half times in fact, taking over on the death of the previous mayor. He was wealthy and he did marry the merchant's daughter. We know this because there is a beautiful Christopher Wren church on the site of where he was buried in 1423 called St Michael Paternoster Royale in College Hill. In the church you will find some wonderful stained-glass windows by John Haywood that show Dick Whittington with his faithful cat. So did he have a cat? After the church was bombed in 1940 and they were clearing the mess ready to rebuild, a mummified cat was unearthed from the rubble. But perhaps the truth lies somewhere else. Richard Whittington made his money from bringing sea coal from the northeast into London and this was transported in boats called cattes, so perhaps this is the 'cat' of the story.

But back to Whittington's toilet. He didn't have any children and so used much of his money to benefit the City. Among his endowments was the first public longhouse or toilet, a 64-seater – 32 for women, 32 for men – that overhung the river where the effluent ended up.

Another street name to conjure with is Hatton Garden to the northwest of St Paul's. The land used to belong to Sir Christopher Hatton, a courtier at the time of Queen Elizabeth I. He became her favourite apparently because he was good at dancing and he danced his way into Elizabeth's heart. She gave him land in the area and he built a house. It was pulled down in the eighteenth century and a garden put in its place, hence the name. Now the area is the centre of the London diamond trade.

Pubs

Pubs are great at providing clues to the past. Take for example the Crutched Friars on Hart Street. The name comes from the Augustinian monks who lived in this area in the Middle Ages. They all wore a large cross and so were known as the crossed friars, which corrupted became crutched friars. The Blackfriars near Blackfriars Bridge also relates to the monks that used to be here, named after the black habit they wore. This was one of the most important religious communities and it was to this monastery, inside the great hall, that Henry VIII came for his divorce case to be heard, by Cardinal Wolsey and Cardinal Campeggio from Rome. It was here that the case was revoked to Rome, which led to the monarchy's break with the Pope, Henry's divorce and subsequent marriage to Anne Boleyn. If you look at the outside of the pub you will see a large, jolly, black-habited monk and inside it is a riot of monks: bronze monks, painted monks, mosaic monks.

Another pub, one of the oldest in the City, is Ye Olde Cheshire Cheese. It is on Fleet Street and dates back to 1667, just after the Great Fire of London. We managed to burn down four-fifths of the city then, including the great St Paul's, 87 city churches, and left scores of thousands of people homeless . . . so what do we rebuild first? The pubs. Obvious really, because a workman likes his drink! Why is it called the Cheshire Cheese? In Tudor times London's standard cheese came to the city from Suffolk. But when the market for butter grew, more fat was skimmed from the milk, making the resulting cheese harder than it was before. Samuel Pepys, the seventeenth-century diarist, complained that 'my wife vexed at her people for grumbling to eat Suffolk cheese'. In 1650 the first cheese from Cheshire was brought into London and was immediately preferred to Suffolk cheese, and became popular, hence the name of the pub.

Along the streets

As you walk along the streets there are many other things to look for, such as pavement bollards. These are used to stop traffic going down a street and to prevent parking. In the City they are painted red, white and black, and on them they have the coat of arms of the City. If you look carefully you should be able to find some that are fixed to a block that goes into the pavement. This means you are looking at an original cannon and cannonball that has been upended and turned into a bollard. Walk along St Bride's Lane and you can find three that date from the Napoleonic wars at the beginning of the nineteenth century. There is also a gun that has been turned into a lamppost in the front courtyard of Staple Inn on Holborn (near Chancery Lane underground station). This one dates from the Crimean War of 1854–56.

Adorning the streets are many of the original red telephone boxes, designed by Giles Gilbert Scott. These are now protected and so will survive, despite mobile phones. There are many of them but some good examples are on The Strand near the main law courts. You'll also notice postboxes, sometimes called pillar boxes because the earliest ones were in the shape of a pillar. All postboxes have on them the royal cipher from the time that the box was installed, for example 'E II R' for Queen Elizabeth II. There are two side by side on St Andrew's Hill near St Paul's Cathedral. If you look at them you will see that one has the cipher of Edward VII and the other George V.

Up close – Secrets of the City

Look beneath your feet and you'll discover coal holes with metal lids. Up until about the 1960s, heating in most houses was coal-fired and houses had deliveries from the coal man. The cart would come around the street with sacks of coal, which would be tipped down through the coal hole into the cellar. It was always important to count the empty sacks so that you knew you had been given the right amount. These coal holes have metal covers that are different depending on which company made them. Some people even do coal hole rubbings (like brass rubbing) as a hobby.

The City's churches

Another of the gems you can enjoy in the City are the area's City churches. There are 39 of them in the City area and, because the number of people living in the City is only about 9,000, there are too many to act as normal parish churches. So the City churches have a unique mission to the office workers around the churches. Many are open only during the week but closed at the weekends.

Inside the church of St Helen's Bishopsgate on Bishopsgate look for the tomb of Sir Thomas Gresham (1519–79). On top of it you will find a grasshopper. Why? Well, he was a wealthy merchant and financier in the time of Queen Elizabeth I. He visited Antwerp and was very impressed with the Bourse that he saw there. He came back to London determined to create a similar place and so founded the Royal Exchange. But why the grasshopper? According to an ancient legend of the Greshams, the founder of the family, Roger de Gresham, was a foundling abandoned as a baby in the long grass in Norfolk in the thirteenth century. He was found there by a woman whose attention was drawn to the child by the noise made by grasshoppers. A beautiful story; it is more likely that the grasshopper is simply an heraldic rebus (pun) on the name Gresham. Even so, you'll find the grasshopper on his tomb, on a bank sign on Lombard Street that used to be Gresham's bank, and on top of the Royal Exchange.

Thinking of foundlings, in St Andrew's Holborn on St Andrew Street you will find a memorial to a very special man, Thomas Coram. He was a sea captain who made a great deal of money. When he retired back to London in 1720 he was horrified by the number of abandoned children in the streets and determined to do something about it. He persuaded, with great difficulty, some eminent people such as William Hogarth, the artist, and G F Handel, the composer, to support the establishment of the Coram Foundation, which was the first foundling hospital in England, set up to take in children from their mothers, an option to mothers abandoning their children on the streets. On his memorial you will see an image of a child crying. There were, however, too many children for the places available and they used coloured balls in a basket to allocate places. When the mother was interviewed she had to pick a ball from the basket. If it was white the child got a place, if black not, and if it was a red ball, the child was put on a waiting list.

Another church with a fascinating story connected to it is St Katherine Creechurch. Each 16 October in this church the Lion sermon is preached. John Gayer, a Lord Mayor, was travelling around the coast of Africa in 1646 for the Levant Company and at one point in his travels found himself face to face with a lion. Falling on his knees he begged the Lord to spare him. Miraculously, the lion lost its appetite and failed to eat him! On his return home, Gayer endowed an annual sermon to be given, in perpetuity, in gratitude for his escape.

The church of St Andrew's Undershaft on St Mary's Avenue is so named because it used to have outside a maypole (or shaft). This custom was described by Chaucer in the fourteenth century:

Right well aloft, and high ye bear your heade
The weather cocke ,with flying, as ye would kill
When ye be stuffed, bet of wine then brede
Then looke ye, when your wombe doth fill
As ye would beare the great shaft of Cornhill
Lord, so merrily crowdeth then your croke
That all the streete may heare your body cloke.

On May Day the maypole would be decorated with garlands and ribbons and the apprentices would dance around it and make merry. In 1549 this led to the maypole being condemned as an idol, put on trial for corruption and sentenced to be burned. Luckily times changed, and if you look carefully above head-height in Shaft Alley just near the church you should be able to see a maypole.

As you walk you will see statues on buildings and on the street. The City has a policy of putting new statues in open spaces. So you can meet Hodge, 'a very fine cat indeed', owned by Dr Samuel Johnson. He sits in Gough Square on the first English dictionary and next to two oyster shells. The shells refer to the fact that cats in the eighteenth century were given and liked eating oysters, far too expensive now of course. Near Cannon Street you can find the statue of a LIFFE trader (London International Financial Futures). He is in the striped blazer that traders used to wear and is, of course, depicted glued to his mobile phone. On the church of St Andrew's Holborn on Holborn you will see statues of a boy and girl. They are charity-school children and the statues were originally on a charity school run by the church that was in Hatton Garden. The children are in the uniform of the school and are both carrying a book. They are delightful statues, made from a special stone called Coade stone. This was manufactured in a factory in Lambeth from 1720 to 1840. When in 1840 the owner of the factory, Eleanor Coade, died, the secret of Coade stone died with her, although not for ever as later the stone

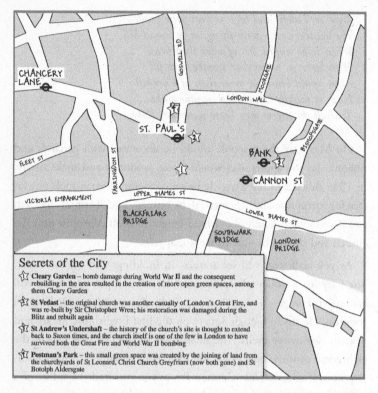

Secrets of the City

☆ **Cleary Garden** – bomb damage during World War II and the consequent rebuilding in the area resulted in the creation of more open green spaces, among them Cleary Garden

☆ **St Vedast** – the original church was another casualty of London's Great Fire, and was re-built by Sir Christopher Wren; his restoration was damaged during the Blitz and rebuilt again

☆ **St Andrew's Undershaft** – the history of the church's site is thought to extend back to Saxon times, and the church itself is one of the few in London to have survived both the Great Fire and World War II bombing

☆ **Postman's Park** – this small green space was created by the joining of land from the churchyards of St Leonard, Christ Church Greyfriars (now both gone) and St Botolph Aldersgate

was analysed and its formulation discovered. It is manufactured now for specialist restoration projects.

A final gem that brings together so much of the idea behind walking to discover the secrets of the City is Postman's Park, located between King Edward Street, Little Britain, and Angel Street. This is one of the pretty gardens talked about at the beginning of the chapter. It was the churchyard of St Botolph's Aldersgate, a church that has been extensively and lovingly restored recently and is now an active City church. The garden got its name because of its popularity as a lunchtime garden with workers from the nearby old General Post Office. Beneath the park runs the post railway, now no longer used by the post office for moving letters around the central London area. In the garden is a wooden gallery that houses a range of tiled plaques. These were the inspiration of G F Watts, a Victorian painter. He was saddened that great men and women are remembered with statues but that ordinary people who had committed acts of bravery were generally ignored. So he established this hall of fame for ordinary people who had lost their lives saving the lives of others. It is a poignant memorial to people like Alice Ayres, a nursemaid, who saved children in a fire that took her life.

Secret Westminster

DAVID TUCKER

Prisons and palaces and towers and moats and secret redoubts on a lost island . . . It sounds like something out of Edgar Allan Poe. It isn't. It's Westminster. But not that Westminster. Not the 30-million-tourists-a-year Westminster. We'll give that – and them – a miss, thank you very much. So how do you find Secret Westminster? Sometimes it's a case of knowing where to go. Sometimes it's a case of knowing where to look. Sometimes it's a case of just knowing.

Heraldry is one 'way in'. A crowned portcullis is the symbol of Parliament. A portcullis is the symbol of the City of Westminster. The portcullis is everywhere in Westminster. The exterior of the Henry VII chapel is waffle-ironed with them. The new parliamentary office building is called Portcullis House. Its atrium features great wooden struts converging towards the middle of the ceiling. They're engineered to open in the event of a fire, creating a chimney so the building won't fill with smoke. Not to put too fine a point on it, the roof of Portcullis House is essentially a portcullis. You can't get away from it here. The grille on the front of the Division Bell up on the wall behind the bar in St Stephen's Tavern – the MPs' 'local' – resembles a portcullis. You're even carrying it around with you. Pull a few coins out of your pocket. Got a penny? Take a close look at its reverse side. It's a portcullis.

A portcullis. Just what you'd expect on a lost island creaking with prisons and palaces and towers and moats and secret redoubts.

The island comes first. It supplies the genetic code. The sequence runs like this: Westminster was an island. Its secret places are islands. They're the islands on the island in the island within the Isles. And since, as they say in Ireland, we don't own the land, the land owns us, the mentality – the *genius loci* of Westminster – is insular.

We get the island from two rivers: the Thames and the Tyburn (*Ty – burn*: the two burns or two streams). The Tyburn came down through what is today St James's Park and swabbled along about where Abbey Orchard Street turns Thamesward. (An orchard by a stream – merrily, verily, the names carry us far back.) And then it branched, the two forking arms of that stream creating our island, Thorney Isle. *Thorney*: covered with bramble bushes. Anticipating another element of the Westminster heraldic symbol: the rose.

Now, according to the *mythos* of Westminster, once upon a time (some 1,400 years ago) the Anglo-Saxons built a little church on the island. The night before the consecration a miracle occurred. There was a fisherman living on the island. He was awakened by voices calling to him from the far shore, the Lambeth shore. They wanted him to row over there because there was a ferry passenger. So he did. And so there was. Some ferry passenger: *St Peter himself.* So the fisherman rowed St Peter across the Thames and when St Peter set foot across the threshold of the little church it exploded into a supernova of light – as if with the light of a thousand candles!

WHERE TO READ THIS

St Stephen's Tavern, across from the Houses of Parliament (it's the MP's 'local' – perfect for overhearing some political gossip). Or St Margaret's, Westminster – the House of Commons 'parish church'. Winston Churchill was married in this ancient church. Sir Walter Raleigh – well, most of Sir Walter Raleigh (from the neck down) – is buried here.

Westminster Abbey

And that's essentially the creation myth for Westminster and the Abbey. The Abbey is where it is – and it's called what it is (the formal name is the Collegiate Church of St Peter at Westminster) – because Edward the Confessor, who built the first Westminster Abbey in the mid-eleventh century, wanted to be buried where St Peter was supposed to have walked.

And the layers just kept being added. Much of the nave in today's Abbey is mid-thirteenth century and the work of Henry III. He spent one tenth of the entire wealth of the kingdom on the Abbey. He stumped up £40,000 of his own money – this at a time when a labourer's annual wage was £1. And the call he was answering? A burial place for himself. Similarly, the early-sixteenth-century Henry VII chapel – boasting the finest stone roof in the world – was to be a burial place for Henry VI. And, yes, why not push the envelope: *Westminster Abbey is essentially an English pyramid.*

Its tombs are inner sanctums. Or, if you prefer, last redoubts. Or even hatches. And the same goes for secret doors and hidden gardens. The oldest door in England, for example. It's off the passageway leading to the Chapter House. Or the oldest garden in England, the Abbey Garden. It's through a secret door and along a passage off the hidden of hiddens: the Little Cloister with its tiniest-of-tiny garden. Finding the Little Cloister is like following a treasure map to X marks the spot (though that's true of much of Westminster). The sequence is: Great Cloister, Dark Cloister (the windowless bay along its south side is believed to have been a strongroom or prison), Little Cloister. You zig and you zag – the Dark Cloister especially is like walking through a tomb – and then there it is, just ahead of you . . . *an emerald in a casket.* The Little Cloister is, quite simply, a masterpiece. It's a tiny chalice of light and green. An English oasis.

The Little Cloister is deep within the integuments of the Abbey complex. But Westminster's most hidden 'garden' was the one on the roof of the Citadel. The 'redoubt on the Mall', it resembles a huge, vine-covered pillbox. A bomb-proof bunker, it was where the last stand would be made if the Nazis clanked into London. Its green crew cut – the lawn on its roof – was put there to fool the Luftwaffe.

And the most important garden? No question about it. The walled garden of 10 Downing Street. Much of the Balfour Declaration, which green-lighted the creation of modern Israel was hammered out in the War Cabinet meetings held in that garden in the summer of 1917. Historical pivots don't come any more momentous – or far-reaching.*

And now the scene switches to the forecourt in front of the great

---

*The three most important 'turning points' in the twentieth century took place in London, two of them here in Westminster. You'll read about the second Westminster 'historical pivot' later in this chapter. The third one was in Bloomsbury on 12 September 1933 when Hungarian physicist Leo Szilard conceived the idea of the nuclear chain reaction that made possible the atomic bomb.

twin-towered west front of the Abbey. Secret places aplenty here. Westminster Gatehouse, for example. The monument to 'those of Westminster School fallen in the Crimean War' marks the spot today. It was the seventeenth-century chokey of 'stone walls do not a prison make' fame. The lines were penned by Richard Lovelace, the Cavalier poet, when he was locked up here in 1642.

And glance over at the Clock Tower (the 'Big Ben Tower') of the Palace of Westminster. Sure enough, it's got a lock-up as well – for refractory politicians. And for another one of the Clock Tower's 'secrets' look at the slate-grey 'dunce cap' at its apex. Directly beneath it you can see five or six elliptically shaped, gilded windows. Inside the room they give on to is an extremely powerful lantern. When Parliament's sitting at night the lantern is lit. You can see it from all over central London. That's when those who know go to the Strangers' Gallery in the Palace of Westminster to watch Parliament in action. The point being that there's never a queue at night – you can always sail right in. Just look for that 'on if by night' light.

Closer to hand – it's just over the way in Parliament Square – is Middlesex Guildhall. It always gets missed. It shouldn't do. Pustulating with gargoyles and gaitered with a riot of relief sculptures, it's both a visual peal of bells and a history lesson – some warm-up act for the new Supreme Court proceedings inside. And round behind it – and set into it – is the 1665 gateway from the old Bridewell Prison in Greencoat Row. The croaking old inscription reads like a death rattle: 'for such as will beg and live idle'. The past doesn't come much more austere and drear and cold. Rather that, though, than the fiery hell shadowing the present. It's there to see as well, In the shape of what could pass for a round, stone picnic-table top in front of the Queen Elizabeth II Conference Centre. It isn't. It's a vent to a bomb shelter. But not a Second World War bomb shelter. A hydrogen-bomb shelter. (Not that it would have protected the scoundrels – the scurvy politicians – it was designed for.)

Any more? Sure. Right next to Portcullis House is the Norman Shaw Building (as it's known today). It was New Scotland Yard – that is, Metropolitan Police Headquarters. A mordant touch: its 'Dartmoor granite' was quarried by convicts. And as for quarries – well let's not forget what's underfoot there. Which is by way of saying, even the new Underground station partakes of the Westminster mind's walls! In Simon Bradley's, er, lapidary phrase, 'anyone who has ever pored over Piranesi's prison engravings will shiver with recognition in this vast space, which reads as a kind of dark unconscious to the tightly controlled architecture above'.

And if you want to know what the torque of six centuries has done to Westminster's underlying idiom of surly bonds, just saunter from Westminster station's twenty-first-century Piranesian vision to the moated, fourteenth-century Jewel Tower. Noting, in passing, the line of stone sentries – the little towers – that *fence* in Parliament. The one on the corner – the 'officer' – is much taller. Beside it, like an aide-de-camp standing at attention, there's a lamp standard. Atop it, like a golden diamond on a sceptre, is a four-sided lamp with the word 'Taxi' in sober black lettering across each of its amber panes of glass. It's the House of Commons 'taxi lamp'. When an MP wants a taxi the light comes on and flashes on and off. The firefly of Parliament Square, it's very eye-catching, especially at night. Passing cabbies spot it and they know an MP wants a taxi. A delightful touch to the country's political life.

Then there are Westminster's hidden streets. One of these is Queen Anne's Gate, arguably the finest Georgian street in London. And around the corner from it, Cockpit Steps – London's most hidden 'street'. Ninety years ago Queen Anne's Gate was the home, in London, of men who bestrode the world like a colossus – the Great War titans First Sea Lord Jacky Fisher ('Organizer of the Navy that won the Great War' as the inscription on the footstone of his grave reads) and Sir Edward Grey, the Foreign Secretary and *primus inter pares* of the great and the good. Seeing their houses – they're both blue-plaqued – domesticates them. And to domesticate them is to bring them – and their milieu – to life in a way that no cold, historical record on the printed page could possibly do. Because so little has changed, to come here is to walk into their world and their time.

Take 3 August 1914, for example. The cliff edge of the Great War. Standing there in his room at the Foreign Office, looking out the window at the gathering dusk in St James's Park, Sir Edward famously remarked, 'The lamps are going out all over Europe: we shall not see them lit again in our lifetime.' To stand in front of the Foreign Office today and look over at St James's Park – yes, at dusk – and then stroll over to Queen Anne's Gate, exactly where Grey will have walked that evening nearly a century ago, is to feel you have a very good chance of seeing him, just ahead of you. *Up there, in the gloaming . . .*

Gathering dusk. And gathering ghosts. In 1931 the War Graves Commission, in a bid to give people an idea of the scale of the losses in the Great War, reported that were the dead of the Empire to form up in Trafalgar Square and march down Whitehall, four abreast, it would take that ghostly column – that parade of death – three and a half days to pass the Cenotaph. There may be something else about that tableau. Something that in its own unwitting way is as stark – even perhaps as iconic – as Goya's *Disasters of War*. It's this. Looking out over St James's Park, Sir Edward had already turned his back upon that will-it-ever-end? 'death march'.

There's more here. There's always more. Just past the sandbagged entrance to the Cabinet War Rooms is the entrance to the Treasury. The first-floor window setts that run along there – from the Treasury entrance to the corner of the building – are necklaced with square patches of discoloration. The reason for them? They mark the holes that were drilled for the pegs for the steel anti-shrapnel shutters that were fitted to those windows. Steel anti-shrapnel shutters that protected the man who got this country – and indeed Western civilisation – through its darkest hour. In short, Winston Churchill spent most of the Second World War on the other side of those windows. No plaque there to tell you this; it's another item in that catalogue that is Secret Westminster. That set of rooms was called the Annex. It was a first-floor flat in the Treasury that was specially created for Churchill. They didn't want him in 10 Downing Street because it was a 250-year-old brick building, which wouldn't have survived a direct hit from a bomb. The thick stone walls of the Treasury could take it.

Up close – Secret Westminster

Here's a party trick for you. Put the following question to any Londoner: 'You're standing in Victoria Tower Gardens (just along from Parliament) – which side of the river, by the compass, are you on?' The answer invariably will be, 'Don't be a fool, mate, you're on the north side.' Wrong. You're on the *west* side. Every Londoner orients by the Thames, which basically flows west to east, bisecting London, but at this point the Thames has gone round a sharp bend and is flowing due north. Which means Victoria Tower Gardens is on the west side of the river. Ask that same Londoner where Docklands and One Canada Square (the tallest building in the UK) are and they'll point in the direction in which the river is flowing. Whereupon you smile knowingly and say, 'No, the next time you're driving across Lambeth Bridge at night from this side of the river keep your eyes peeled; you'll see it way in the distance, straight ahead of you.' The *disorientation* is compliments of the bend in the river.

Smith Square, Lord North Street, Cowley Street, Barton Street

This is a congeries of magical 'hidden streets'. The sensation you get when you find your way back into this little nest of perfectly preserved early-eighteenth-century streets is quite extraordinary. They're a salient into the past. This is a London *Field of Dreams* – a build-it-they'll-come neighbourhood. Except it's already built. It's very real. And they're here already.

Lawrence of Arabia at No. 14 Barton Street, for example. He rewrote his masterpiece, *Seven Pillars of Wisdom*, in the attic room – 'a haven of peace' – under the eaves. And Lord Reith, the first Director-General of the BBC, at 6 Cowley Street. And just over the way – at No. 16 – the greatest English actor of the twentieth century, Sir John Gielgud. Round the corner, at No. 2 Lord North Street, the Tory PM, Anthony Eden. At No. 4, Sir John Anderson – who came up with the idea and gave his name to the eponymous Anderson Shelter. (If you look closely you can see faded old 'Public Bomb Shelter' signs on several Lord North Street houses.) At No. 5, Sir Harold Wilson, the Labour PM. At the far end, No. 12, William Stead, the great campaigning journalist who went down with the *Titanic*. (His is the only house in the street that has a plaque.) Next door – No. 14 – Marilyn Monroe spent the night. It was the house of Binkie Beaumont, who ruled the West End of London for a generation. In other words, he was the most important theatrical impresario of his day. And that meant that anybody who was anybody in that world – Noël Coward, Laurence Olivier, Vivien Leigh, Richard Burton, Arthur Miller, etc. – sooner or later crossed that threshold.

And since this is a surprise-round-every-corner neighbourhood, by all means pop round to No. 8 Smith Square. It was the house of Sir Oswald Mosley – he who on precious little evidence believed he had one of the most powerful minds of the twentieth century. It was there that Mosley – great admirer that he was of Mussolini and Hitler – masterminded his cadres of Black Shirts, this country's home-grown fascist movement.

Point counterpoint, because back round the corner – at No. 8 Lord North Street (the most important political salon on this country) – was

The statue of Winston Churchill in Parliament Square, looking to Big Ben. It was in the nearby prime minister's House of Commons office in May 1940 that Churchill addressed a full cabinet meeting on Dunkirk. 'If,' said Churchill, 'our long island story must finally end, let it end only when the last one of us is lying on the ground, choking on his own blood ... whatever happens at Dunkirk, we shall fight on.' (David Tucker)

This plaque at St Paul's Cathedral commemorates St Paul's Cross, which once stood in the cathedral's churchyard. A wooden pulpit surmounted by a cross, St Paul's Cross served as a place where proclamations were made and where felons were punished.
(Man Vyi)

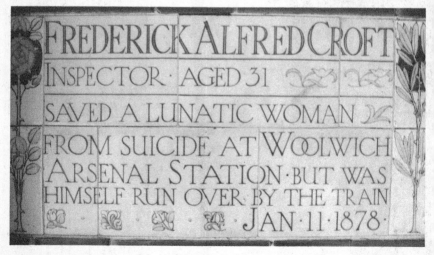

FREDERICK ALFRED CROFT
INSPECTOR · AGED 31
SAVED A LUNATIC WOMAN
FROM SUICIDE AT WOOLWICH
ARSENAL STATION · BUT WAS
HIMSELF RUN OVER BY THE TRAIN
JAN · 11 · 1878 ·

One of the tiled plaques to be seen in Postman's Park. The collection of plaques was created by G F Watts to recognise the heroism of ordinary people.
(Joan B Ingram)

Above Looking along Roupell
Street in Lambeth, a street
frontage that could be straight
out of the mid-1800s.
(John Willoughby)

Left A detail of a fountain in the
beautiful Kensington Gardens.
(Harold Slatore)

Above A detail from Rocque's map of London published in 1746. The map is formed of 24 sheets; this sheet shows the river and London docks at the time. Almost everything came to London via the docks and quays of the Thames.

Right This print by Charles Soar is a 1750 view from the south-east of old St Mary Abbots in Kensington. Although the site is now occupied by the 'new' (1872) church, the form of the church wall and arched entryway are still recognisable today. (Museum of London)

Left The Argyll
Arms in Soho is a
well-preserved late
Victorian pub.
(Peter Moore)

Below The Museum
Tavern opposite the
British Museum in
Great Russell Street.
(John Willoughby)

Above Bar Italia is for many one of the best coffee houses in London. One of a dwindling number of stylish independent outlets, it harks back to Soho's great pre-frappuccino days and the arrival of the Gaggia machine. (Michael Hewson)

Below The impressively illuminated Royal Exchange, one of the must-sees when walking in London at night. (Matthew Starling)

Above St James's, together with Green Park, is, for many Londoners, a favourite of the city's parks.
(John Willoughby)

Left After the destruction of St Dunstan in the East during the Blitz, the site was turned into a beautiful garden oasis rather than re-built. It is one of London's special places.
(Mark Paulda)

where the anti-appeasement movement got started. It was the home of Brendan Bracken, the owner of the *Financial Times*, but more importantly, the ally, confidant, friend and lieutenant of Winston Churchill. Churchill and others of a like mind – such as Duff Cooper and Harold Macmillan – regularly met there, schemed there, trying to figure out how they could muster the support in the House of Commons to get Chamberlain out and Churchill in, so he could draw a line in the sand and say to the little Austrian guttersnipe in the Reichschancellory, 'You cross that line, Herr Hitler, you're at war with the British Empire.'

The 8 Lord North Street story doesn't end there. Thirty years ago a group called the Conservative Philosophy Group regularly met in this house. They were addressed by luminaries from that end of the political spectrum, notably Richard Nixon and Henry Kissinger, but also the conservative economists Frederic Hayek and Milton Friedman. These weren't idle chats. Those confabs laid down the intellectual foundations of Thatcherism.

Up until a few years ago 8 Lord North Street was the home of Jonathan Aitken, the prominent Conservative MP who was at the centre of one of the two biggest scandals to engulf the Tory party at the end of the twentieth century.

Parliament Square

Let's end by heading back out to the 'public face' of Westminster. If you stand by the statue of Winston Churchill in Parliament Square and look in the general direction in which he's looking, you're looking at the spot where the second of the two most important moments in the twentieth century occurred. You're looking across at the Prime Minister's House of Commons office. It was there late on the afternoon of 28 May 1940 that Churchill addressed a full cabinet meeting – a cabinet meeting of frightened, demoralised British politicians.

Some context. The British army – 340,000 men – was trapped at Dunkirk. The panzers were just ten miles away. The evacuation had just started the day before. They'd only got 10,000 off that first day. They thought *if they were lucky* they'd get 100,000 off. In the event, the miracle occurred. Well, two miracles. For some reason Hitler didn't pull the trigger and send the panzers those last few miles to those beaches. And the cloud cover came in, so the Luftwaffe couldn't deliver the *coup de grâce*. The flotilla of little vessels – one of them to this day is sometimes anchored right there in the Thames – got almost all of that army off – 334,000 of them. But on 28 May that happy outcome was in the future, undreamed of, unhoped for. Nor did Churchill pull his punches. He told his colleagues exactly how things stood. He said, 'We could all be dead in a few months.' And then this: 'If our long island story must finally end, let it end only when the last one of us is lying on the ground, choking on his own blood – rather than surrender to that man.' And closed it thus: 'Whatever happens at Dunkirk, we shall fight on.' And that was the turning point. As one, those frightened, demoralised politicians leaped to their feet, cheering. The war was not Churchill's to win – that would require the entrance of the Americans – but it was his not to lose. He did that then. Did it just over there – where you're looking.

The next time you look at a newspaper hoarding in London, perhaps spare a thought for the hoardings that went up all over London just a couple of weeks later, on the day the French surrendered. The hoarding read: 'French Surrender – We're in the Finals'. The insouciance of that is very British – but that flame couldn't have been lit had it not been for Churchill's 'mobilising the English language and sending it into battle' (in the words of the great American reporter, Edward R Murrow) the way he did in that modest little room off the Commons on that fateful day in May 1940.

The Royal
City

The Old Palace Quarter

ANGELA DOWN

London is full of wormholes, the sort that if you know where they are and can wriggle through them you can go back in time. One such place is the old quarter of St James. This area was, along with the square mile of the medieval City of London, really all there was to the capital for hundreds of years. Between these districts and around them was rolling countryside and copious wildlife, and although the more dangerous sort had politely withdrawn some time ago, there were still plenty of deer for the hunting.

The Old Palace Quarter was really the old backyard of the Palace of St James and that story starts with the tale of a king's lust. The king was Henry VIII, who has been described by an eminent British historian as one of our most repellent monarchs. Maybe. Certainly it is said that the build-up of noxious gases in his somewhat corpulent corpse caused it to explode in his coffin, which is a fairly repulsive picture.

Henry's appetites were prodigious, and one of them was for pretty girls. Anne Boleyn debuted at Court in the 1520s. Her education was French, and French in the English Court meant style, fashion, sophistication. So here was this new girl at Court, exotic with French glamour, with a sharp mind and strong will to go with it, and much before anyone could blink she had most of the men enslaved and most of the women spitting feathers. Of course she was going to come to the attention of the King, and when she did she said no. Imagine! Nobody ever said no to the King. But Anne was playing what might be described as the Long Game, determined to occupy a position rather more elevated than that of king's mistress. After all, her own sister had been one of those. But there was the irritating fact that the King already had a Queen, having been married for twenty years or so to Catherine of Aragon. They had a surviving daughter but Henry had no legitimate son.

It being human nature to want what we can't have, Henry's ardour increased at a ferocious pace. When the Pope refused to annul his marriage to Catherine, Henry dumped the Catholic Church and brought in the Reformation. By the time Henry and Anne married in 1533 she was pregnant, and although the marriage actually took place in his Palace of Whitehall, it was to the little Palace of St James that Henry immediately took his bride. He had had it developed from an old leper hospital and used it mainly as a hunting lodge, or, in this instance, a honeymoon lodge.

It was one of a dozen or so residences Henry had within a day's travel of London. It was set in fields, orchards and parkland, and in the early, halcyon days of their marriage, Henry would ride out at dawn to collect fragrant boughs of blossom for his bride. Apart from the agreeable setting of the hunting lodge it had the major advantage, unlike the Palace of Whitehall, of being well away from the river. Advantage, because the Thames stank. It was the main sewer. There was no underground sanitation and everything, gutters, streams and tributaries, emptied straight into it. Although for centuries it was a very beautiful river frontage, the smell was appalling; it was said that you could smell London from twenty miles away. And stench, delicate reader, would be the first thing you would notice in the city any time before the twentieth century. It wasn't just from raw sewage in the streams and rivers, the streets full of animals, both domestic and farm, but also smoke from a multitude of open fires, rancid oil in oil lamps, tallow (rendered animal fat) in candles, and butchers and fishmongers whose wares would have been strangers to Health and Safety. Woven through this rich, olfactory tapestry would have been the stink of unwashed bodies. If you were wealthy when you went out, especially if you had to go anywhere near the Thames, you went with your nose wedged in a strongly scented nosegay, or, in the case of Henry VIII's Cardinal, Wolsey, a hollowed-out orange in which was a sponge soaked in sweet vinegar.

When later in 1533 Anne gave birth, it wasn't the son that Henry was so desperate for, and it was partly his devastation that allowed the treacherous factions of the Tudor Court to start spreading their poison against the new Queen. By 1536 Anne Boleyn was in the Tower of London awaiting execution. Had she had a son perhaps her fate would have been different.

WHERE TO READ THIS

The prettiest place to read this would be Green Park when the thousands of daffodils are out, but as these days they come out in February this might be a bit chilly. By the time the weather's warmer the daffs are over, so I would suggest St James's Park by the lake, so that when you glance up you'll be endlessly entertained by the many different sorts of sweet little ducks. Or you could sit outside the café next to St James's Church on Piccadilly, under the trees in the churchyard, the advantage then being if it's cold you can simply move inside.

St James's Palace

All that remains of Henry and Anne's little hunting-lodge palace is the gatehouse – today the clock tower – and inside a poignant H and A entwined above the fireplace in the tapestry-room. St James's Palace, however, rebuilt and extended, is still very much there at the south end of St James's Street, a street which certainly existed in some form by the middle of the seventeenth century, although described at the time by the diarist John Evelyn as 'a quagmire'! Any monarch between Henry VIII and Queen Victoria spent time in St James's Palace, especially after the Palace of Whitehall burned down in 1698 and the Court became centred at St James's.

Charles I spent his last night there in 1649 after the Civil War of the 1640s between the Crown and the Parliamentarians under Oliver Cromwell, before crossing a frozen St James's Park on a bitter January morning to his public execution in Whitehall. His dog, Rogue, followed at his heels.

With the return of the Court from exile and the restoration of Charles II, the Merry Monarch, in 1660, the English cheered up. They'd found the Puritan ethic of Oliver Cromwell's Commonwealth a little stringent for their generally and generously convivial tastes. Now with the opening up of the theatres again, and music and dancing back on the agenda, the citizen was as merry as his monarch.

Charles had a soft spot for St James's Palace and the nearby St James's Park, so perhaps it was inevitable that someone should notice the ripe potential for development of the area north of the Palace. And the someone who stepped up with a dazzling plan to create a new, fashionable 'West End' was Henry Jermyn, the Earl of St Albans. He was a very close friend of the widowed Queen Mother, Henrietta Maria. In fact there was a rumour that they had married in exile. But if that sounds quite dashing, he was also described by a contemporary, the poet Andrew Marvell, as having 'a drayman's shoulders and a butcher's mien'. Not a big fan, then. Nevertheless, there is an elegant, gracious shopping street that still bears his name.

The first part of the new district to be completed was St James's Square, one of the oldest squares in London, in which by 1700 there were said to live seven dukes and seven earls. At the end of the little Duke of York Street, named after the King's brother, on the north side of the Square, in 1684 a newly built church had been consecrated: St James's, Piccadilly. It was designed by the genius Christopher Wren, was acoustically brilliant and typically full of light and air. Since the main entrance to the Church was originally on the south side, it was a very short step for the seven dukes and seven earls on a Sunday morning to rock out of fourteen residences and into their pews. In Sheridan's 1777 play *A Trip to Scarborough* (his version of Vanbrugh's *The Relapse*), Amanda asks Lord Foppington which church 'does he most oblige with his presence?' To which he replies, 'Oh, St James's, there's much the best company.' Then when asked if 'there is good preaching too?' he replies, 'Why faith, madam, I cannot tell, a man must have very little to do that can give an account of the sermon.'

Maybe it was Charles II's famously libidinous nature that began to give the area its notoriously licentious reputation. After all, two of his more high-profile mistresses, Barbara Castlemaine and later Nell Gwyn, had residences in the vicinity. Certainly by the middle of the eighteenth century the area had taken over from Covent Garden, known for fruit, flowers, vegetables and the girls who charged, as the centre of excellence, you might say, for the girls. It was to St James's you went for the most elite establishments. This was the heart of the demimonde, with its classy bordellos, and the more sensational women set up in their own little town houses, conveniently placed not only for the Court but Parliament at Westminster as well.

It was a world that ran on a parallel track to that of polite, respectable London society, and one in which these women had considerable standing and some power. They were the style icons of their day. These were the ladies with the Jimmy Choo shoes and Prada handbags, conspicuous expenditure. They were entirely socially acceptable in public, and when at the opera and theatre usually enjoyed much the same attention as the spectacle on the stage. Indeed, many of them had started their careers on that side of the curtain. Men and women were equally engrossed, although usually for different reasons, the women making mental notes as to what they might, discreetly and tastefully, be able to copy in the way of fashion and coiffeur, and (vital in any age) accessories, especially the sort that catch the light. They were to be seen in the public parks and gardens, and if out riding every detail from the rider's costume to the equipage of her horse was noted, if not out loud. It was not unknown for people to form an orderly queue to watch one of their own celebrities, Kitty Fisher, eat her dinner in her box in Vauxhall Gardens.

While it is perhaps not possible to describe these women as the first feminists, nevertheless they enjoyed a great deal more autonomy and control over their own lives, especially financially, than their respectable married sisters, who had none whatsoever. Some, but only some, went on to form loving, enduring relationships with their clients, even marriage, although that was no guarantee of an upgrade to polite society. On the contrary, the wrath of the conventionally married sisterhood descended and ensured that the 'fallen' woman, even though now upright, remained beyond the pale and never became socially acceptable.

Alongside the development of St James's racier reputation came the establishment of its peculiarly masculine character and the area's evolution as the domain of the male. By the early eighteenth century there were coffee houses all over London, at least three on Jermyn Street alone, and they were exclusively male. Tea still being expensive, coffee and chocolate were the popular choices, the chocolate often enriched with egg, sack (a sort of dry, white wine) and spices, so pudding really. The air was also thickly enriched with tobacco smoke. Many of the coffee houses later became gentlemen's clubs, where not only was hospitality extended to the gentlemen, but fathomless opportunities for gambling, which had become a ferocious addiction of epidemic proportions by the end of the eighteenth century.

The gentlemen's clubs still stand along Pall Mall and St James's Street and the area even today has a unique personality: gentlemanly, gracious, moneyed. It's a bit like being in the presence of an elderly but still elegant relative, who, though now sedate enough and beautifully mannered, you know has this rollicking, roaring past. St James's has charm, and that lies partly in the beguiling nature of the shops. Although only a stone's throw or two away from the brash chaos of Oxford Street's high-street fashion chain stores, here the shops are independent, individual and old-fashioned but in a really good way. There's the dowager-duchess of department stores, Fortnum and Mason, on

Piccadilly, 300 years old but still glamorous, whose fabulous, dreamlike window displays have long been an attraction in themselves. Fortnum's was built on candle-wax. William Fortnum, a footman in service to Queen Anne, made the most of the Queen's desire to have fresh candles every night in the palace by replacing the previous night's supply with new candles, and selling on the more serviceable candle-ends to the ladies of the bedchamber. Eventually he'd made enough to be able to open a modest establishment on Piccadilly with his landlord, Mr Mason.

Fortnum's is known for its tea. Queen Victoria in the 1850s especially requested that the store send crates of its famously recuperative beef tea to Miss Florence Nightingale in Scutari. And so some of the soldiers who survived the ghastly battlefields of the Crimean War were helped to claw their way out of the jaws of death by the Lady with the Lamp and Fortnum and Mason's beef tea. It's about the only type of tea you can't get there these days.

Up close – Old Palace Quarter

The oldest gentlemen's club in this area, Whites, stands at the top of St James's Street near Piccadilly. It was started by an Italian, Francesco Bianco. One of its most famous members was George Brummell, better known as Beau. He used to sit in Whites' renowned bow window so that passers-by in the street could benefit from his fashion choices, it being well known at the time that his taste in all things sartorial was unequalled and unchallengeable, sort of the Kate Moss of his day. One of his fashion tips was to have one's boots polished in champagne, the soles as highly as the uppers, and it was so he didn't have to put glassy sole to street that he required the sedan-chair bearers to take him right into the club.

Behind Fortnum's in Jermyn Street is Floris, the gorgeous perfumier, started in 1730 by a Minorcan, Juan Famenias Floris, attempting to re-create the scents of his Mediterranean island and still run today by his direct descendants. A couple of doors along is Paxton and Whitfield, cheesemongers for over two hundred years, and scattered all along the street are the shirt and suit makers. On St James's Street is John Lobb, crafter of beautiful hand-made boots and shoes since the middle of the nineteenth century; Lock and Co., hat makers since the end of the seventeenth century; and at the bottom of the street Truefitt and Hill, suppliers of gentlemen's shaving and grooming requisites and toiletries since 1805. Some of their products were found in the wreck of the *Titanic* at the bottom of the Atlantic Ocean.

Turn around from Truefitt and Hill and there is the place where it all started – St James's Palace. Ambassadors are still accredited to the Court of St James, but Queen Victoria removed the Court from there to Buckingham Palace. It had been her uncle, George IV, who seems to have been determined to introduce a note of vulgarity into royal residences by commissioning the grandiose enlargement of Buckingham House, but he died before his vision of grandeur was completed and it was his niece who first occupied it as a monarch. It was he who, as Prince of Wales, in 1795 was married in the Chapel Royal of St James's Palace. He and his bride, Caroline of Brunswick, disliked each other intensely. In fact so dismayed was he by her appearance at their first meeting he said to an aide: 'Harris, I am not well. Pray get me a glass of brandy.' It may have been a personal hygiene problem. At some point someone was dispatched to suggest tactfully that she might change her stockings more often. Anyway, her reluctant bridegroom on their wedding night drank himself senseless and spent the night with his head in the bedroom fireplace. Presumably it was a warm night. At some point he rallied, because nine months later Caroline gave birth. It was her only child.

St James's Palace is still used from time to time as a royal residence. Prince Charles moved in after his separation from Princess Diana, although after his grandmother's death he moved next door to her old place, Clarence House. It was in the Chapel Royal that Diana's body lay between her being brought back from Paris and the night before the funeral. But it's a more muted place today, being mostly grace-and-favour apartments for members of the royal household and administration.

Looking now at the old palace, with its Tudor gatehouse and the changes of brick on either side, set as it is between the pretty serenity of St James's Park on one side and Green Park on the other, one can only wonder at the quiet and unquiet lives lived within its walls.

A RIGHT ROYAL ROUTE

RICHARD ROQUES

> *Between the two cities, London and Westminster, stood the mansions of the wealthiest of the aristocracy, rising from the river, accessible by land and water, ideally situated for commerce and court. Today there are still signs of these lost palaces hidden among the shops, railway stations and crowded streets of the twenty-first-century West End, but for most of the city's history the space between the two cities was open land where people would come to hunt or for a breath of fresh air outside the foul, overcrowded walls of the medieval city.*

Charing Cross and Trafalgar Square

Standing outside Charing Cross railway station is the cross that gave this station its name. But things are not quite as they seem . . .

In 1290 Eleanor of Castille, the wife of Edward I, died in Harby in Lincoln and her body was brought to be buried in Westminster Abbey. At each of the twelve places that the funeral cortege rested on its way to London, a cross was erected in her memory. Two of these 'Eleanor crosses' were set up within the city, at Cornhill and at the village of Charing, the name of which means 'to turn', where the road turned away from the River Thames to head west.

The cortege had passed out of the old city of London through the gates at Temple Bar, past the heads on spikes (the heads boiled in salt to prevent birds pecking away at the features). Eleanor would have been glad to leave London: when she had been imprisoned in the Tower and had tried to escape she had been pelted with rubbish by Londoners. Now, Eleanor's coffin moved down the Strand, with fields to the right and the river to the left, past the Savoy Palace, ever closer to her resting place. Durham House shielded the river from her sightless eyes and now the procession paused at the village of Charing.

A cluster of cottages stood here where the cross is today outside Charing Cross station. An ancient medieval cross outside a railway station . . . except the cross that stands here is the wrong cross in the wrong place. To find the site of the original Eleanor cross we need to walk a little further along the Strand to Trafalgar Square. Here is the original place the cross was located in the 1290s. The Square has vital significance for Londoners, in fact, as this is the dead centre of London. From here are all measurements calculated.

Here you'll find a statue of Charles I, beheaded just a few minutes' walk away in Whitehall on 30 January 1649. After Cromwell had abolished the monarchy he gave the statue, built in the 1630s by the Frenchman Hubert le Sueur, to John Rivett, a brazier. Rivett subsequently made a killing from the regicide by selling commemoration knives and forks he claimed were manufactured from the melted-down statue of the dead king. When Charles II was restored to the throne, however, he asked Rivett if he knew anything of the whereabouts of the statue of his father and it turned out that the brazier had hidden it in his garden. He returned it to Charles II, who was never so hypocritical as to admonish another conman. The fish shop that stood there was pulled down and the statue put on the spot of the original twelfth Eleanor cross. When the railway came to be built the Victorians named the station Charing Cross and asked Thomas Earp to build a replica of the cross, which they placed outside their terminus. So what you have today is a copy, and in the wrong place.

WHERE TO READ THIS

It has to be Gordon's Wine Bar down the steps from Villiers Street. The river was not embanked until the 1850s and now this spot is a little park on land reclaimed from the Thames. Gordon's Wine Bar has tables with large umbrellas where you can eat and drink, even in the rain. Also the balcony of Somerset House, with fabulous views of the South Bank and the dome of St Paul's Cathedral. There is a café with tables.

Villiers Street and Embankment

Down a narrow flight of steps off Villiers Street, by the side of the station, is Gordon's Wine Bar, a fantastic old cellar. At the end of the tables is the water gate from the 1670s, now stranded a hundred yards away from the river. Built in elegant Portland stone, this was the entrance by water to the Duke of Buckingham's mansion. Servants in rich livery would help you out of a gilded barge, through the stone archway into Buckingham House. The building is no longer here but the entrance by water remains.

Walking down the side of the water gate into Embankment Gardens you will see a large area with deckchairs, free to sit in, arranged facing a large open-air stage. You might even get to see a concert there in the summer. If you walk out on to the Embankment itself there's a wonderful view of the river. Further down is Cleopatra's Needle. This, however, has nothing to do with Cleopatra as it predates her by a thousand years. If it looks familiar it's because it's one of a pair – the other is in Central Park, New York. The sphinxes, by the way, are the wrong way round; they look *at* the obelisk, whereas they should be looking out, guarding it.

Back up at the water gate, if you walk over the archway and up the steps, this will take you in to Buckingham Street. Here you will find a plaque to Samuel Pepys, the diarist of the 1660s. If you were going to write a diary this was a good time to be doing it. The year 1660 was the restoration of the monarchy. Pepys himself, only a young man, went out on a ship to the Low Countries to bring Charles II back to be restored to the throne. Later, in 1665, Pepys's diary records red crosses on the doors of houses in nearby Drury Lane and the words 'Lord have mercy on their souls'. Pepys survived the Great Plague and the next year, 1666, the Great Fire. He describes digging a hole with Sir William Penn (whose son was to found a state in the US) and burying his Parmesan cheese in it, then digging it up again when the fire was over.

Pepys was not living in the house that bears the plaque when writing the diary; he came here after he'd been imprisoned in the Tower of London. For a wonderful account of the life of Pepys, read Claire Tomalin's *The Unequalled Self*.

Opposite the plaque to Pepys is a house with the original fanlight window above the door and link snuffers. Until Sir Rowland Hill invented the penny post in 1840, houses did not have numbers. Instead, on letter-headed notepaper or on an invitation to visit would be the name of the street and a copy of the pattern on the fanlight window above your front door.

The link snuffers, the upturned cones attached to the railings, were to snuff out a 'cressit' or 'link', a naked-flame torch made from hemp rope dipped in pitch. It was so dark along London's streets in the days before street lighting that those travelling by carriage would frequently pay someone to light them through the streets, the person running in front of the carriage holding a rope torch aloft. John Gay (best known for *The Beggar's Opera*) wrote in his work *Trivia* that:

> *Though thou art tempted by the Linkman's call*
> *Yet follow him not along the lonely wall*
> *In the mid way he'll quench the flaming brand*
> *And share the booty with the pilfering band.*

A warning of those linkmen who had mates hiding down a dark alley and who might lead your carriage driver down there, drop his 'link', and in the dark he and his friends then leap out and rob the people in your coach. Those who did manage to get home in one piece would extinguish their rope links in the up-turned link snuffers.

Buckingham Street still has some lovely eighteenth-century houses in it, now all business premises. Further up you'll find a house with masks, some like gargoyles with a fearsome aspect, protecting the occupants from evil spirits. Charles Dickens as a twelve-year-old worked here in Warren's blacking factory while his father and the rest of the family were in the Marshalsea debtors' prison. He came back to live in this street as a young man and used the area, before it was embanked and reclaimed from the river, as Murdstone and Grinby in *David Copperfield*, drawing directly from his own time working in the factory.

Further along the Strand is the Zimbabwean High Commission, built in 1907 as the HQ of the British Medical Association. Jacob Epstein was commissioned to decorate the facade and he did so with full-length representations of the human body, some clothed, some not. The nude statues caused an outcry; 1907 was, after all, the year in which the tango was banned for being too sensual. The company that owned the building on the other side of the Strand fitted opaque frosted windows so their employees could not see the scandalous naked figures. The BMA themselves eventually got a man with a hammer and chisel to remove the heads of the sculptures in the hope that this would make them seem less naturalistic. This was an act of terrible cultural vandalism, as Epstein was one of the greatest sculptors of the twentieth century. Time, the weather and the frost played its part, and other bits gradually dropped off as well, rendering them less of an offence to public decency.

The building that installed the frosted windows was in Durham

House Street, the name 'Durham House' all that remains of the mansion that had been there since medieval times. Simon de Montford lived there, the baron who convened the first parliament without the permission of the King and then convened representatives of the burgesses of the shires to sit as commoners. When later Henry III was proceeding down the Strand and there was a terrible storm, de Montford came out of Durham House and offered him shelter. The King replied that 'thunder and lightning fear I much, but by the head of God I fear thee more'. He kept going and got wet.

It was during the reign of Henry III that the next palace was built. Henry gave the land here – east along the Strand from Durham House Street – to his wife Eleanor of Provence's Uncle Peter, the Count of Savoy. Today the hotel on the site – the Savoy – is one of the most famous hotels in the world. Look carefully at this road. It is different from any other road in the British Isles because drivers must drive on the right-hand side.

In the Peasants' Revolt of 1381, Londoners destroyed the Savoy Palace because the hated Duke of Lancaster, John of Gaunt, lived there. Disdaining to steal from the burning palace, the rioters threw a box that was thought to contain jewels on to the fire. It contained gunpowder and destroyed the great hall.

Up close – the Strand

If you go down a tiny, steep alley just past the Savoy Hotel, you will find all that is left of the old Savoy Palace, the Queen's Chapel. Geoffrey Chaucer was married here and in the eighteenth century John Wilkinson conducted illegal weddings advertising 'five private ways by land to this chapel and two by water', presumably so you could get away quickly if anyone turned up to put a stop to the nuptials.

Next to the Savoy is the Coal Hole, a great pub where Edmund Kean the actor formed the Wolf Club for repressed husbands whose wives wouldn't let them sing in the bath. Richard D'Oyly Carte built a theatre here, also called the Savoy, for Gilbert and Sullivan. It was rebuilt in the late 1920s and is a lovely example of Art Deco.

The Savoy Hotel had the first suites of rooms in England and the first electric ascending rooms. The dance floor rises as well. It's a great place to have tea, but a riverside suite will cost you several hundred pounds a night. Auguste Escoffier was chef here and he invented peach melba in honour of Dame Nelly Melba, the Australian soprano who stayed regularly. I used to see Richard Harris there a lot, particularly in the Coal Hole, where he always appeared to be talking, not to friends, but to people he'd just met. He had a permanent suite in the hotel. Nice, if you don't like washing up or housework.

Further east along the Strand is Aldwych with one of my favourite parish churches in London, St Mary-le-Strand. Pop your nose in. The interior is like a jewel box, a riot of Italianate baroque.

One palace that does remain is Somerset House on the Strand. Somerset House was rebuilt in the eighteenth century as offices for civil servants in impressive Portland stone. This elegant baroque courtyard looks more like a palace than nearly anything else in London. The original renaissance palace that stood there was built for Edward Seymour who was made executor of Henry VIII's will. The new King, Edward VI, was only nine, so a council of regency was formed to help the little guy out. Edward Seymour was his uncle (the new king was Jane Seymour's son, the only male heir to Henry). Now in a powerful position, he had himself made the Duke of Somerset and set about building himself a great palace befitting his new status. However, he did not enjoy his dukedom or his palace, because he got his head chopped off a few years later. But the name stuck and this is Somerset House, home to three fantastic art collections, the best of which is the Courtauld.

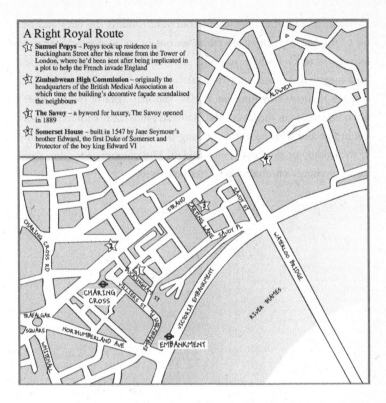

A Right Royal Route

☆ **Samuel Pepys** – Pepys took up residence in Buckingham Street after his release from the Tower of London, where he'd been sent after being implicated in a plot to help the French invade England

☆ **Zimbabwean High Commission** – originally the headquarters of the British Medical Association at which time the building's decorative façade scandalised the neighbours

☆ **The Savoy** – a byword for luxury, The Savoy opened in 1889

☆ **Somerset House** – built in 1547 by Jane Seymour's brother Edward, the first Duke of Somerset and Protector of the boy king Edward VI

It was George III who ordered these buildings constructed. Look for the statue of him here. It's hilarious. It looks nothing like him, the sculptor was so eager to flatter that George's wife Queen Charlotte had no idea who it was. There are now fifty-five fountains here, which dance on the hour and half-hour and are lit up at night. There are tables and chairs strewn around which don't belong to any café and a few clever people have realised you can take a picnic and a bottle of wine and just sit. If you have children on a warm day they will just run in and out of the fountains for hours, quite safely as there is no traffic and it's very difficult for them to escape out of sight. If it is winter there may be an ice-skating rink.

Walk through the magnificent courtyard towards the river and out on to the balcony. There are tables set out in an outdoor café that no one seems to find where you will get a fantastic view over the river. This huge balcony leads on to Waterloo Bridge. You could walk over and see if there's anything on at the National Theatre (where there's often free music in the foyer), the National Film Theatre (literally under the bridge and with a great happening bar), the IMAX cinema (on top of the bridge) or the Royal Festival Hall. Music, drama and film, then, for an evening's entertainment after your walk.

South of
the River

Historic Greenwich

NICK DAY

Greenwich is a strong candidate for having the most famous place name on Earth. The story of how it came to be so is a remarkable chain of chance that continues even to this day. To visit Greenwich, it's best to approach it by river, either at speed on an exhilarating commuter catamaran, or more slowly by tourist cruiser – where the occasional distinctively accented commentary from a crewman, whose Thames waterman family lineage might well stretch back to Shakespeare's time, will entertain us with homespun wit and enlighten us with fascinating non-facts like the derivation of the word 'wharf': 'WareHouse At River Front'!

As you come downriver you might like to imagine the brightly decorated flotilla, filled with optimism, pomp and fawning favourites, that brought the dashing King Henry VIII with his second and sexy young wife, Anne Boleyn, to the favourite of his many palaces. It was a journey Anne was to make in sombre reverse a mere three years later. There is nothing we can see, above ground, of that magnificent Tudor palace that stood in Greenwich. Greenwich Palace, in which Henry had been born, had everything the fun-loving king could want. In front of him was fast transit to some of his other magnificent homes upriver. Deptford and Woolwich dockyards, founded by his father, lay to port and starboard of his palace and gave him ample opportunity to play ships. He had his tiltyard and, near to them, the huge towered armouries where magnificently decorated suits of armour were continually and expertly tailored to his expanding girth. There was a deer park for hunting and hawking, and a huge banqueting house where riotous enactments of daring feats were played out over multi-course feasts. And there were the orchards and gardens in which he could flirt with his enticing young bride, confident that when he lay beside her that night she would arouse him sufficiently to produce the one thing he craved – an heir.

But this great Tudor palace came about almost by accident. To trace its history we must go back to the sudden end of a previous Henry's reign – that of the hallowed victor of Agincourt, Henry V.

Henry V's famous reign was in fact one of England's shortest. He died, quickly and unexpectedly, after contracting dysentery in France at the age of thirty-four. His son, the new King Henry VI, was merely nine months old – the only king, incidentally, to be crowned King of England in London and King of France in Paris – and obviously unable to rule. In fact, the apparently weak and reputedly feeble-minded king was never to be an effective ruler at all and was ever heavily influenced by the powerful and ambitious people who schemed to gain his ear.

WHERE TO READ THIS

The finest and most famous view of Greenwich is to be had from Island Gardens. You can get there by crossing the river on foot. There's no need to get your feet wet, you go via the foot tunnel built early last century to enable workers to get to the Millwall and West India docks in the Isle of Dogs. Think of the firm who got the tiling contract – 200,000 tiles! As you reach the northern end you will pass through an especially narrow section that was a temporary repair to Second World War bomb damage. If you're going to Greenwich by Docklands Light Railway you could get off at the stop before Cutty Sark and make your way into the gardens for a short but satisfying detour.

The other vantage point from which you can view Greenwich advantageously is from up by General Wolfe's statue at the top of the hill on the south side of the Queen's House. You look down the precipitous hill that provided popular sport in the nineteenth century. Young men and women would join hands and run down the hill. Inevitably the girls, unable to keep up with their longer-legged beaus, would tumble down the slopes, providing hopeful spectators a peep of petticoat and other forbidden delights. The park café is not far away down André Le Nôtre's grand avenue, so you can fetch a coffee and a bun to chew on as you gaze across Greenwich to its capital. What did Louis XIV's landscape gardener intend, do you think? It's probable that he never visited the site to see that his avenue would not take a visitor direct to the Queen's House. Perhaps he knew about this hill and planned this great excitement for approaching visitors, who would come along the avenue seeing nothing but sky ahead of them, and then suddenly and unexpectedly, as they stopped at the brink of the hill, have their vision launched across a simply vast expanse of court and countryside.

The seeds of a terrible dissent were sown by Henry V's will in which the baby king's uncle, Humphrey, Duke of Gloucester, was appointed Protector of England. A fateful rivalry was assured by the appointment of the young king's great-uncle, Henry, Cardinal Beaufort, to the boy's personal care. The one had charge of the king, and the other of the realm. It wasn't going to work. The two men were each rich and powerful, with strong retinues of devoted followers. Shakespeare chronicled their disputatious careers in his *Henry VI* trilogy where we hear Humphrey rail against the 'presumptuous priest' who plots against him:

> *No, prelate; such is thy audacious wickedness,*
> *Thy lewd, pestiferous, and dissentious pranks,*
> *As very infants prattle of thy pride.*

Humphrey had inherited the manor of Greenwich in 1427. With its commanding view of the river, his great house, 'Bella Court', was to be an ideal home for a man embroiled in a threatening power struggle. A licence was granted 'to empark 200 acres of land, pasture, wood, heath and furze, to enclose the manor house and mansion with walls, to crenellate the same, and to build a tower of stone and mortar in the park'. This tower was, as we shall see, the foundation of a significant legacy. We can assume that Humphrey built it because from its crenellated battlements he and his security staff would have a commanding view of that other great highway to Europe, the Dover road. From there, and from his bedroom window looking out on the river, he could keep a watchful eye on significant comings and goings.

Humphrey set himself to arrange a strategic marriage for the young king with one of the three available Armagnac heiresses. Meanwhile Beaufort, determined to further consolidate his influence over the young king, cunningly and deviously manoeuvred the bright and vivacious Margaret of Anjou into the boy's affections. Humphrey's cause was lost and, perhaps to rescue his future and favour, he rashly offered his splendid Greenwich home for the young couple's honeymoon. We can imagine Margaret sitting at the great dining table, admiring the view over the enwalled private park. She instantly fell in love with Bella Court and, it seems, determined that it should one day soon be hers.

Humphrey was to lose the power struggle. His wife was sentenced to life imprisonment for practising witchcraft on the young king, and he himself was to die in most mysterious circumstances while awaiting trial in Bury St Edmunds on a concocted charge of high treason. Margaret lost no time in occupying the handsome Greenwich house. Now it was cleared of Humphrey's fusty books, she redecorated and refurbished, celebrating her occupation with ornamental sprays of marguerites all over the place. During the next five years she was to upgrade the house with the latest in interior design, extending it with pavilions, arbours and a jewel house. So now, with a *royal* resident, the house was no longer simply a house, but a *palace*: the Palace of Pleasaunce.

Now we should race ahead across a hundred years of history to the great Tudor Palace of Placentia that had accrued on the site, the palace to which Anne Boleyn came downriver in 1533. The wilful and seductive Anne Boleyn, Henry's second wife, had been enlisted at great political cost. Henry's expectation was that she would help correct a humiliating and persistent failure to create a male heir. But Anne's magic failed to produce the desired male heir in Henry's image. A (probably female) child was stillborn in the summer of 1534, and Anne was to suffer a second stillbirth the following year. Henry's affection for her lasted barely twelve months. He regularly and openly sought his pleasures elsewhere. Anne's only surviving child was the flame-haired Princess Elizabeth – the future virgin queen – whom we can picture in the early months of 1536 trailing around the palace with her forlorn and threatened mother watching the whispering in corners, and secretive comings and goings that were signs of a simmering plot to free the king for yet another marriage.

On 24 January 1536 an unwise opponent had unseated the king in the Greenwich lists. Henry was unconscious for several hours and undoubtedly concussed. A wound was re-opened on his leg that would remain unhealed for the rest of his life. The painful abscess would severely limit the degree to which he could joust and dance in future. Now the once sporting and competitive athlete comforted himself by consuming colossal calories which he was unable to burn off. Anne would find her increasingly obese, bad-tempered husband, with his permanently suppurating leg ulcer, distinctly unattractive, and Henry was impatient to be rid of her. On 29 January, an already difficult day when Catherine of Aragon was being interred at Peterborough Cathedral, Anne discovered her husband with a young lady-in-waiting named Jane Seymour sitting on his knee. Tragically, that night Anne miscarried of a fifteen-week-old foetus – the prince that might have saved her.

So we can picture the scene at the great May Day tournament. The frustrated and stony-faced king sitting with his queen in the royal box overlooking the tiltyard. We can imagine their total lack of rapport. Sir Henry Norris and the Earl of Rochford were listed to joust against each other. The former was a favoured courtier and trusted intimate of the King, the latter another favoured courtier and brother to the Queen. The story goes that they rode up together to the great tower overlooking the tiltyard in order to salute their master and monarch. Anne took out a handkerchief and let it fall to the combatants. Henry Norris caught it and, thrilled with the intimate gesture, tucked it into his armour as a token of good luck.

Henry was furious and stormed straight out of the tiltyard. Norris was arrested and sent to the Tower. The next day Rochford was dispatched after him. They were to be joined by two further gentlemen of the privy chamber, Sir William Brereton and Sir Francis Weston. Anne herself was taken upriver to be accommodated in the same chamber in which, a mere three years before, she had tremulously anticipated her royal progress down to Greenwich as Henry's new queen.

The king had badly needed a fresh marital start. There was a strategic imperative to make peace with Emperor Charles V, and disposing of the queen who had controversially displaced Spanish Catherine would be politically most expedient. The small committee of advisers especially assembled by the King advised him that his wife must be proved to have been plotting against his life. The charge could be seasoned with accusations concerning the kind of carnal behaviour of which people would judge her capable. The perfect solution. It needed only appropriate evidence and ready confessions. Gossip of licentious behaviour was fomented and collected.

Norris, Brereton and Weston were tried in Westminster Hall. In spite of their spirited denials, none of their judges could dare to find them innocent. Anne and her brother had special hearings in the great hall of the Tower, where seating was built for some two thousand spectators. Rochford's trial was a sensation. His behaviour with the queen, it was claimed, had not merely been flirtatious but adulterous and also, of course, incestuous. The court heard lurid accounts of how brother and sister kissed with their tongues in each other's mouths. A further charge against him was so explosive that it could not be read out in court. It was passed to him in a written document. Rochford, utterly careless now of his fate, made it clear to all what the charge was: he had apparently put it about that the King was unable to perform. The humiliation for the proudest of kings was unbearable. Rochford would be lined up with his companions beside the execution block on Tower Hill, and suffer the torment of being the last to go. They were executed one by one on 17 May as Anne was forced to watch the succession of executions from a window in the Tower. Henry ordered that Anne herself was to be executed within the Tower walls, with a swift and sharp sword wielded by an executioner specially brought over from France. So she was dispatched on 19 May after a careful speech telling the thousands of spectators that her husband had been 'one of the best princes on the face of the earth, who has always treated me so well that better could not be'.

Was Anne guilty of 'daily carnal lust' and 'vile provocations'? Who can know? Certainly she invited the attention of young men of the court. Certainly she was sexually coquettish, and certainly there was a tradition in her time, that she indulgently promoted, of courtly love. And her intimates would often visit her quarters to pay court. The degree of her guilt is anybody's guess, but her forwardness with men and her insouciant outspokenness allowed people at the time to be unsurprised at the judgement against her. The fact that Henry, notwith-standing his pride and sensitivity over matters sexual, commuted her sentence from the traditional ghastly hanging, drawing and quartering for treason, to simple decapitation, seems the best evidence for the innocence of all concerned.

Henry impatiently paced up and down at Whitehall Palace until he heard the cannon fire from Tower wharf confirming Anne's execution, then immediately set off to see the young Jane Seymour. A mere two weeks later, on 1 June, they sat together as King and Queen in the magnificent banqueting house adjacent to the Greenwich tiltyard.

So much of our journey through Greenwich's past has been with the help of our imagination. It must be time to consider what we can actually still see. At the very centre of the extraordinary assembly of architecture, which has been designated a World Heritage Site, sits Inigo Jones' impudent and bijou conceit, the Queen's House. We should consider it without the colonnades that extend from either side – they were added in the early nineteenth century to shelter pupils at the

Up close – Greenwich

There is a fascinating detail, unnoticed by almost everyone, in James Thornhill's hagiographic celebration of the Hanoverians on the west wall of the Painted Hall.

George, Elector of Hanover, was the son of the childless Queen Anne's cousin, Sophia, who by the Act of Settlement had been declared heir to the throne. There were some fifty-six people ahead of her in the line of succession but they were all Catholics. Sophia was a convenient Protestant. You'll see Sophia of Hanover standing proudly just up and to the right of her son. That little house on her head was all set to be replaced by the English crown, but after running to take shelter from a rain shower one day, the eighty-three-year-old Electress expired. So her son inherited the crown.

Over thirty years before, George had wed his cousin, Sophia Dorothea, in a marriage that brought bling but not bliss. He sought regular satisfaction from his wife's maid of honour, Ehrengard Melusine. This affair was public and permissible. His wife, on the other hand, was having a rip-roaring affair with the dashing Count von Königsmark, whom she had loved since she was a young girl. George was so incensed by the continuing affair that during one furious row he threw his wife to the floor, tearing out great hanks of her hair, and was only prevented from strangling her when attendants pulled him off.

The affair could not be suffered to last. One morning in 1695, the sated count was waylaid as he was about to let himself out the back door. Enormous sums of money had been paid to secure his demise. He was never seen again. Sophia Dorothea was sent far away to Ahlden Castle and forbidden to see her children again. The wife who should have ridden in the coronation coach to Westminster Abbey was hidden away from the world for more than thirty years.

So what fascinating detail did the mischievous Thornhill provide for us? Look at the carpet fringes below George's feet. You'll see a small pale patch in the painted marble step where it looks as if someone has started to clean the painting. Look carefully just to the left of that patch and you will see the ghostly form of a lady's hand reaching out from where she has been swept under the carpet!

Royal Naval Hospital School from inclement weather. We should also exclude the former school buildings at either end of those colonnades and which now house the stirring galleries of the National Maritime Museum.

Now we must advance our story by leapfrogging two queens. The Stuart King James I and his wife, Queen Anne of Denmark, were not the best of friends. Their already difficult relationship had been severely strained when Anne had accidentally killed her husband's favourite hunting dog. In an attempt at reconciliation James granted Greenwich to his wife for her personal resort. Inigo Jones was an admired designer of court masques who had travelled to Italy and was enthralled by the exactly proportioned Renaissance architecture he had seen there. His commission to build for the Queen a small house of her own, behind the old palace, was to have a profound influence on the further development of architecture in this country. The novelty of Jones's 'curious devise' can be appreciated if we imagine its clean, pale stucco exterior set against the small-windowed and crenellated red-brick gateways of Hampton Court or St James's palaces; for so Greenwich Palace looked when Inigo applied his genius to the Queen's commission in 1616. There is a fine model on the ground floor of the Queen's House that helps us to imagine how things looked at that time.

Greenwich Palace had been bedevilled by an unfortunate geographical coincidence. It so happened that the dockyards of Woolwich and Deptford had developed into sites of enormous importance for this island nation. Most inconveniently, the traffic generated between them was channelled along a right of way that passed between Greenwich Palace and its backyard. It was on to a puddle in this very thoroughfare that Sir Walter Raleigh courteously threw his cloak lest his beloved queen should muddy her beautifully embroidered shoes.

We can stand on the very spot under the Queen's House and imagine the road stretching away in each direction. Inigo Jones had the splendid idea of building the queen's new house in two equal halves, one on each side of the road. He would join those two rectangular buildings with a single bridge so that the Queen could enter her front door and go out of her back door without ever having to step in puddles. Sadly, Queen Anne never lived to take advantage of this pretty conceit.

Not long after, Henrietta Maria, the Catholic wife of Charles I, inherited it for her own pleasure and delight. The scorching political temperature of the 1640s, however, drove her and her son into the arms and succour of Louis of France. At the magnificent and extravagant French court, the young Prince Charles learned how a monarch might live. So, once the British monarchy was restored by popular request in 1660, the ambitious king engaged John Webb, Inigo Jones's pupil and nephew, to build him a fabulous new palace at Greenwich overlooking the Thames. Webb was also to expand the now Dowager Queen Mother's House of Delights at the back of the palace by building a bridge at each end, turning Jones's innovative little H-shaped villa into a rectangular house.

Part of the reason for the demise of Charles I had been his insistence on the right to raise and spend money without reference to Parliament. After the Restoration the monarch's expenditure was to be far more constrained and the new King Charles II was continually strapped for cash. The sum granted by Parliament for constructing his grand new palace ran out when only one of the three planned ranges had been built (and before even that had been completed).

Charles II was succeeded by James II, whose Catholic tendencies could not be tolerated and whose reign did not last long. In 1689 William of Orange landed with his army at Torbay and marched unopposed on Whitehall. James's daughter Mary had married the Protestant Dutchman as a tactical alliance, but had grown to love him tenderly and, estranged from her father, was complicit in the plan for her husband's accession.

It is this caring woman that we have to thank for the sublime array of buildings on the Greenwich riverfront. In 1692 the British Navy had achieved an extraordinary victory over the French at La Hogue and thwarted an invasion of England. Mary had been distressed to learn that the heroic seamen, many of them now with significant parts missing, had no provision for their future. She determined that something must be done in the way that Wren's hospital for retired soldiers had been founded in Chelsea. William, who so adored her, indulged this wish and determined that her Uncle Charles's unfinished palace in Greenwich would be an ideal location 'where the great number of ships continually passing and re-passing would afford constant entertainment'.

Christopher Wren was thoroughly exercised by the project and offered his services for free. First he would build a matching block facing King Charles's unfinished building. His own architectural style had progressed somewhat from John Webb's and he would add to the south a magnificent and separate building in his distinctive and eccentric baroque style. Now that he was an ingenious dome expert, he would place a huge dome over a chapel at the centre of his richly flowing design that would knock France's Les Invalides into touch.

The old Tudor palace, seriously decayed since the Civil War, was demolished and used to embank the river. When Mary saw the broad view of the Thames that was then opened up from the Queen's House she was horrified that Wren proposed to block it. She demanded he go back to the drawing board and devise a plan that would preserve her view. The result is an odd, but strangely satisfying, assembly of buildings, which Samuel Johnson described as 'too much detached to make one great whole'. Certainly the Queen's House is not quite up to the task of being the focal point of such a substantial perspective. When Canaletto painted the view from across the river he couldn't resist adding a few details to the house to better balance the composition. The Observatory, set off the axis on top of the hill, is a further oddity that reminds us that so much of this visual feast was arrived at by chance rather than design.

Charles II recognised himself as a monarch of a new age and he took great interest in matters scientific, sponsoring the foundation of the Royal Society to promote innovation and research. He was ruler of a nation whose powerful naval and merchant fleets were to make this tiny island master of the largest empire the world has ever seen. Dominance of world trade and security of the high seas were paramount. Safety at sea had historically been severely compromised by the simple fact that one of the two vital dimensions of space remained accurately incalculable. A ship's position north to south could be determined by observations of the sun and the stars. The other horizontal dimension, however, could only be roughly calculated by a system known as 'dead reckoning'. A ship's direction of travel could be determined by its compass. A log would be tossed over the side attached to a knotted rope; the number of knots running overboard over a set time measured by sand-glass would give a figure for speed. Some speedy chartwork could then plot an estimated position. But it's evident how maritime navigation was prone to significant and catastrophic error. Ships were forced to keep to familiar, well-travelled routes that were consequently insecure.

To this intractable problem there was a tantalisingly simple theoretical solution in that the Earth turns through its 360-degree axis every 24 hours. Knowing the difference between the time at your present position from the known time at a standard point further back round the globe (perhaps where you started) would tell you exactly how far round that 360 degrees you might have ventured. It was a simple method that was simply impossible; the necessary accuracy of timekeeping was unachievable. Clocks were driven by a pendulum mechanism that would not stand the rolling of a ship. Metal expands and contracts, oil thickens and thins. An inaccuracy of just one minute a day would render calculations a hundred miles out in just a week.

Louis XIV of France was in the vanguard of the search for an answer. He had established an observatory in Paris that sought a solution in the skies – and that might one day give France ownership of the world prime meridian. It was a great stroke of fortune for Charles II, therefore, that his French mistress – 'the Catholic whore' – Louise de Kérouaille, should have a friend, Le Sieur de St Pierre, who knew what to do and how to do it. He was invited to London and outlined the theory to the king and the Royal Society.

It had long been known that the moon and the stars move in a repeating and predictable pattern. The position of the moon against the backdrop of the stars, because it is so much closer, varies according to one's position on the Earth. As a system for navigation, however, using the moon's transit had seemed beset with unpredictable and inaccurate variables, because the moon has an irregular and complex orbit. But Le Sieur de St Pierre convinced Charles that it would be a worthwhile project for some committed R&D. With minimal financial resources, Wren was persuaded to build an observatory from architectural scrap using the foundations of Duke Humphrey's tower. The resulting building was, Wren said, 'for the Observer's habitation and a little for pomp'. John Flamsteed was appointed the first Astronomer Royal, and in an exhausting forty years made some thirty thousand separate observations. The task was complicated by the fact that the moon has an eighteen-year cycle. It was only after the diligent efforts of a succession of Astronomers Royal, over one hundred years, that the first tables were published enabling navigation by the so-called lunar distance method. Meanwhile, catastrophic maritime loss due to inaccurate reckoning continued. In one shocking shipwreck that was a direct result of his faulty navigation, Admiral Sir Clowdisley Shovell lost four of his five ships and two thousand men. To stem this tide of loss the Longitude Act of 1714 offered a huge prize for the manufacture of a reliable and accurate timepiece. Such a clock, in fact a series of such clocks, was submitted by a Yorkshire carpenter named John Harrison. The story of this remarkable man and his friction-free timepieces is told up there in Flamsteed's Observatory. Harrison's final offering to the nation was a chronometer, five inches in diameter but weighing several pounds, that lost only four seconds in eighty-one days.

Navigation using time alone was simple, elegant and accurate, but the lunar distance method, while necessitating some arcane mathematics, was much cheaper to implement. The accurate chronometer was fearfully expensive, whereas a carefully machined and optically perfect sextant and the necessary tables could be purchased for a mere twenty pounds. Anything could happen to a clock in the hostile oceans, but the heavens were ever there. So we have much for which to thank Le Sieur de St Pierre. And the French have much to resent.

It was Sir Neville Maskelyne, the fifth Astronomer Royal, who first drew the prime meridian through Flamsteed House so that it passed diagonally across the Royal Park and on over the Thames. His meridian was to be only one of many under consideration at the Washington conference convened in 1884 to settle the matter once and for all. A decision in favour of Greenwich was by no means secure, but it was a lucky chance for us that the Canadian delegate had calculated that three-quarters of the world's shipping already used Greenwich as their standard. He persuaded the conference that the most practical and least bothersome solution was to finally approve the line through Greenwich as the worldwide standard meridian. We needn't be surprised that the French clung obstinately to their own meridian, measured two degrees east of Greenwich, until 1911 when they insisted they would fall in with the rest of the world only if Britain fell in with the metric system. In fact their formal adoption of Universal Time calculated from the Greenwich Meridian came as late as 1978, four years after the metric system began to be taught in British schools. It's ironic that in Greenwich Market today, right under the old sign bearing the legend, 'A false balance is an abomination to the Lord but a just weight is his delight', you can still buy coffee measured out before your eyes to an exact 227 grams – that's half a pound to you and me.

LAMBETH – SOMEWHERE ELSE LONDON

ADAM SCOTT

Having harboured a number of villains in her time, one would have thought that sly old Lady London would have picked up a few tips when it comes to concealing the city's history and modus operandi. There have been tutors enough, surely. From John Christie to the Krays to Professor Moriarty, the Napoleon of crime, the metropolis has played home, backdrop, hideout and perhaps even muse to the world's most notorious criminals. But the clues to London's whereabouts over the centuries gone by lie strewn throughout the city. Nowhere is the half-forgotten, line-drawn and sepia city more poorly concealed than in the part of town where angels – and intransigent taxi drivers – fear to tread: south of the river, down Lambeth way. Lambeth, the southeastern quadrant of central London, remains for many an undiscovered country – 'Somewhere Else London'.

If you commute south and east, you may have caught a glimpse of the jewel in the crown of Lambeth as you travel out of Charing Cross on the main line through London Bridge via Waterloo. A flash-frame view of London of 1818, glimpsed at Waterloo East Station in a gap between the red-brick railway wall and the structure of Platform A. It is a view so brief that, if the train has built up any head of speed to speak of, it leaves you wondering if it wasn't just some trick of the light. It is a view so thrilling, with such a true feeling of having seen back through time, that when one calls it up in the mind's eye to cherish it again, one inadvertently fills in the blanks: the chimneys, smokeless now some fifty years since the Clean Air Act of 1956, seem to once more be belching forth their sooty breath, casting that famous grey pall over the city. Present-day, watercolour London is once again, if only in the imagination, the charcoal smudge of yore.

WHERE TO READ THIS

The bar of the Olivier Theatre at the National, particularly in summer on the terrace, affords a marvellous view of the north bank of the river. And while the show is up and running it is deserted, giving it a delicious, clandestine, secret London feel. A little further upstream at the Royal Festival Hall, the public viewing gallery, while having no immediate liquid refreshment outlet, is, to all intents and purposes, a public space. Drag a chair out there and enjoy the commotion of architectural styles over on the Embankment. Traditionalists should head for the King's Arms on Roupell Street. Deep in the heart of Somewhere Else country, this scrubbed and cosy corner boozer was once an undertakers. With an open fire, sofas for lounging and a serious respect for real ale, this is a bright star in the ever-dwindling firmament of London corner pubs.

From ground level, down in the streets themselves, the railway above lends its rumbling soundtrack. Half-closing the eyes, the picture is completed by adding the gaseous, lung-clogging emissions from the long-gone ghost trains of the 'Golden Age of Steam'. Along Roupell and Brad Streets and along Windmill Walk, those pretty details that many a preservationist Londoner cherishes along with their Routemasters and red phone boxes, have their underbelly exposed in this original context. Those oh-so-collectible fire plaques hint here at tales of private fire brigades leaving numberless souls to perish because the residents hadn't paid the insurance premium. The ornate tiles of a corner pub – made so often right here in Lambeth, the birthplace of Royal Doulton– so shiny, such a stamp of authenticity, were placed there not merely for dressing, but to allow the piss of the punters to cascade down the wall and into the open sewer that was the street.

On nearby Cornwall Road, that picturesque little Franciscan chapel of St Patrick marks not only the Catholic Emancipation Act of the late 1700s, but also the ever-present Irish diaspora, fleeing poverty and starvation in Ireland only to wash up in the far from fecund pastures of Lambeth. In 1800 the Catholic population of London was around 40,000. By 1840 it was nearer 300,000, many of those the Irish navigators – 'navvies' – who carved out the roads and railways out of this transient London enclave so associated with travel. While those highways and railroads afforded those Londoners with sufficient disposable cash access to the coast and the countryside, the navvies and their families were left behind in the smog of their tawdry Promised Land.

Lambeth is also where London chose to hide the body of post-war Utopian architecture. And in true cack-handed London style, the corpse was not weighted and dropped into our 'dirty old river', as the The Kinks sang in 'Waterloo Sunset' (only songwriter Ray Davies could have called it a dirty old river and meant it as a loving compliment). Nope, the cadaver was dumped on the riverbank, in plain sight of the well-heeled denizens of the north bank. And it is in this brutalist relic, within the walkways and wide-open concrete spaces of the National Theatre, that we find the link between the dingy riverside Lambeth of the early nineteenth century and the shiny Londoner's playground of the twenty-first.

The Old Vic

Cesspits. Smoke. Murk. Smog. It is perhaps a strange place to find another of the world's most renowned theatres. But that is exactly what can be found nearby. Built in 1818 as the Coburg Theatre, renamed the Royal Victoria in 1833, it has been known officially this past century and a half by what was once its affectionate nickname – the Old Vic, to be found on The Cut.

The clamour for a British national theatre had rung out from the early 1700s. The cast list of movers and shakers central to the plan through the ages reads like a who's who of British theatre: Garrick, Irving and Granville-Barker among them, merely the more garlanded of the players. Sites were mooted in Bloomsbury and Kensington, but as the plan limped through the centuries, our nearest neighbouring republics of Ireland and France beat us to the punch, establishing fine theatres in Dublin and Paris. It wasn't until 1963 that the National Theatre of Great Britain and Northern Ireland was established at the Old Vic, under the auspices of Sir Laurence Olivier, and took up residence – where else? – in unlovely Lambeth. Olivier's legendary National Theatre company . . . with Kenneth Tynan as literary manager and a cast of legends: O'Toole, Redgrave, Jacobi, Plowright and, of course, 'Sir' himself. (For a portrait, slightly veiled, of Olivier in his pomp, rummage the bookstalls beneath Waterloo Bridge for Michael Blakemore's shamefully out-of-print *Next Season*.)

It was an outing to this very theatre that inspired Kevin Spacey as a boy to become an actor, and he is on record as counting it a privilege to be its Artistic Director. Amid the slings and arrows of critical misfortune, Spacey has also returned the traditional pantomime to the old house. This populist move echoes the spirit of Lilian Baylis, the mighty A.D. of the O.V. from 1912 to 1937, whose first act as boss of the theatre was to stage a barnstorming programme of affordable Shakespeare – 'Shakespeare for the People'.

Up close – Lambeth

Slowing down for long enough to safely look up is just one of the great advantages of walking. Look up in Cornwall Road, and you will see that the bell tower at St Patrick's Franciscan church has space for only one bell. Following the Catholic Emancipation Act (which began its protracted journey into law in 1780 – see Charles Dickens's *Barnaby Rudge*), Roman Catholics were allowed to worship openly in their own churches. Hitherto, their masses had taken place literally underground, in such covert locations as the basements of the embassies of the great Catholic powers. Due to financial constraints, many of the churches were small and the bell towers unable to bear the weight of more than one bell. Glance up here, or in Hampstead at St Mary's, or listen out for Corpus Christi on Maiden Lane chiming the Angelus at 6.00 p.m. daily (eighteen single tolls) or standing up gamely to the bells of St Martin's every Sunday morning.

The National Theatre

Prince Charles said of the National Theatre that it was a clever way of building a nuclear power station in the middle of London without anyone objecting. The other side of the coin was presented passionately and poetically by Sir Richard Eyre in his BBC television series and book *Changing Stages*. Focusing on Lasdun's concrete walkways, with their angular split levels, Eyre likened them to the prow of a ship pointing down the River Thames. In this take, the National becomes not a landlocked and parochial institution, but a mighty vessel firing down the river and out into the wider world, there to retrieve theatrical gems and return them to London for our delectation. Eyre cites particularly the great Irish plays of which this building has seen many a landmark production. Appropriate, this, given the strong Irish flavour of the local population and that Ireland played home to the first subsidised theatre in the English-speaking world. The circle is completed by the benefaction of a noted Southeast Londoner,

Forest Hill's Annie Horniman, daughter of the tea merchant and a major influence in the founding of Dublin's Abbey Theatre.

In the interests of impartiality, however, I am compelled to look from the Prince Charles side of things. To do so, I will draw a quote from the manifold London wags who have turned their wit southward to Upper Ground, Lambeth over the last thirty years: the great thing about being inside the National Theatre, is that you don't have to look at the *outside* of the National Theatre. A rather cheap and harsh assessment for my money, but it does reveal a hidden London truth. Of a summer's evening, one of the finest secret pleasures of the capital is to sip at something long, cold and inspiring on the NT's terrace while the show is up and running. A peaceful central London bar is a rarity indeed. And the view – that of the most readable section of the River Thames, from Parliament to Somerset House – is certainly worthy of a toast. Or two.

The OXO Tower

Another London 'secret' is but a few steps downstream. At the top of the OXO Tower – the O-X-O-shaped windows of which form an ingenious circumvention of a riverbank advertising ban – is the Harvey Nichols-owned restaurant. Head for the cocktail bar at the rear. There you will find not only a bar staff as knowledgeable as any in the metropolis, but a view to rekindle your passion for London all over again. Being on the south-facing side of the building, the vista is both seldom seen and epic. Eschewing the spires and domes of postcard London, what unfolds before you is best described as backstage London – where all the London players prepare for their turn on the main stage of the West End and the City. It is the view that also brings us full circle in Somewhere Else London, as we gaze down on the ranks of chimney pots of the workers' houses of 1818, now so desirable as central city homes complete, as they are, with indoor toilets, the Lavender Men long gone. Named for the bunches of lavender tied around their necks, these public servants emptied the cesspits of human waste once a week.

But for all its current movie-star glamour and upward mobility, Lambeth by dusk can still be dark and dank – and deliciously so. Indeed when Beat Generation writer and erstwhile Londoner William Burroughs described London on a wet, smoggy day as resembling 'an attic full of mildewed old trunks', he could still be describing this very place. This Lambeth of the mind's eye, still evoked in these secret streets at the fag-end of a winter's day, dark, tough, straight-talking, what-are-you-looking-at-guv London, can be found in the pages of arguably George Orwell's best novel, *Keep the Aspidistra Flying*. In that paean to the pains of nonconformity and poverty, when respectable, aspiring poet Gordon Comstock falls from middle-class grace, it is in the murky streets of Lambeth where Orwell has him land. And, just as when Dickens wrote of poverty on the south bank, Orwell too is writing from painful experience, the bleak colours of that novel drawn from a palette assembled during the writing of his *Down and Out in Paris and London*, set both in Lambeth and in her sister manor of Whitechapel.

The final cameo, unlikely as it may seem, goes to William Burroughs's compadre, Jack Kerouac. As detailed in the all-too-brief London pages of his *Lonesome Traveller* anthology, Kerouac made a pilgrimage to the Old Vic at Easter 1957, leaving the brouhaha of his *On the Road* to rage through the US in his absence. Inspired to travel – as was Orwell – by the works of Jack London, Kerouac had taken in the *St Matthew Passion* at St Paul's, eaten Welsh rarebit at the King Lud Pub (now a branch of Abbey bank) and headed to 'see Shakespeare as it should be performed' at the grand old theatre on The Cut. There, he saw a production of *Antony and Cleopatra* which would have featured a future luminary of British stage and screen at the dawn of her career in a play-as-cast role: the young Judi Dench.

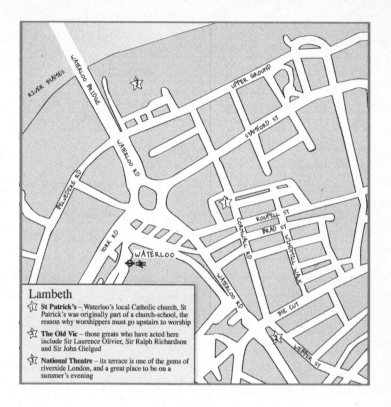

Lambeth

☆ **St Patrick's** – Waterloo's local Catholic church, St Patrick's was originally part of a church-school, the reason why worshippers must go upstairs to worship

☆ **The Old Vic** – those greats who have acted here include Sir Laurence Olivier, Sir Ralph Richardson and Sir John Gielgud

☆ **National Theatre** – its terrace is one of the gems of riverside London, and a great place to be on a summer's evening

Early and Medieval London

THE ORIGINS
OF LONDON

KEVIN FLUDE

Once upon a time someone knew who founded London. In the twelfth century Geoffrey of Monmouth* said that that someone was the Trojan King Brutus – descendent of Aeneas, slayer of the indigenous race of Giants, who built London as Trinovantum (New Troy) in what we would now call the Bronze Age. Geoffrey peopled the city with a glorious host of kings, descendants of Brutus such as King Cole, King Leir, King Belinus. King Lud, for example, was said to have renamed Trinovantum 'Lud's Dun' or London.

Doubts as to the trustworthiness of Geoffrey began to creep in as early as the sixteenth century, but even archaeologists in the twentieth century were fantasising about a London that was old when the Romans came.

Merchants from Gaul sailed up the Thames in small ships, and made fast at these harbours to trade in the mineral products of the island long before Caesar planned to gain new glory and acquire the wealth he had heard of.**

---

*Geoffrey of Monmouth (trans. Lewis Thorpe), *The History of The Kings of Britain*, Penguin Books, 1966
**S R James, *London Triumphant*, The Studio Publications, London 1944

The heroic archaeologist Sir Mortimer Wheeler* put the evidence together to deny the existence of a pre-Roman London as early as 1928, and excavations in post-Blitz and post-big-bang London confirmed the lack of any credible evidence for a pre-Roman city. Closer reading of Julius Caesar's** account of his crossing of the Thames in 54 BC show no reference to an existing city. So the founder of Londinium is more likely to have been a Roman.

When I discovered what the enemy's plans were, I led the army to the River Thames and the Territory of Cassivellaunus. There is only one place where the river can be forded, and even there with difficulty. When we reached it, I noticed large enemy forces drawn up on the opposite bank. The bank had also been fortified with sharp stakes fixed along it, and, as I discovered from prisoners and deserters, similar stakes had been driven into the river bed and were concealed beneath the water.

I immediately gave orders for the cavalry to go ahead and the legions to follow them. As the infantry crossed, only their heads were above the water, but they pressed on with such speed and determination that both infantry and cavalry were able to attack together. The enemy, unable to stand up to this combined force, abandoned the river bank and took to flight.

. . . In the meantime the Trinovantes sent a deputation to me. They are perhaps the strongest tribe (civitas) in the southeast of Britain, and it was from them that young Mandubracius had come to me in Gaul to put himself under my protection, having

*R Merrifield, *London City of the Romans*, Batsford, 1983
**Julius Caesar (ed. Anne & Peter Wiseman), *The Battle for Gaul*, Chatto and Windus Ltd, London 1989

had to flee for his life after his father, the king of the tribe, was killed by Cassivellaunus.

There is, however, one lingering piece of evidence in favour of a pre-Roman London – linguists insist that the name Londinium is pre-Roman in origin. Previous suggestions of the meaning of the name such as Lake Side Town, Lud's Castle, Londinos's settlement, have not survived scrutiny. More recently, Richard Coates* has suggested the original name was Plowonida – or 'settlement by the wide-flowing river'. Plowonida must have been a small settlement (insofar as nothing significant archaeologically has yet been found) and whoever was the founder of that settlement will, barring a miracle, never be known.

WHERE TO READ THIS

City Wall St Alphage High Walk. If you turn left when you leave the Museum of London and walk along the High Walk, past the Pizza Express, after about 200 yards, on your right you will find St Alphage Church – ruined since the Blitz, and once part of a monastery. Turn left again, and by some steps you will see a huge section of Roman wall complete with battlements. The battlements are brick and date to the 1470s. Here you can get a true idea of why London was such a formidable place crucial to all military disputes in England.

Deprived of their prehistoric city, twentieth-century archaeologists placed the foundation of the city in the context of the Roman conquest of AD 43. Aulus Plautius, general in charge of the invasion of Britain, had successfully established the bridgehead, and was forced to await

---

*Richard Coates, 'A New Explanation of the Name of London', *Transactions of the Philological Society* Volume 96:2 (1998), pp. 203–29

the arrival of the Emperor Claudius to partake in the military glory. Archaeologists assumed he occupied his troops by building a bridge across the River Thames at its lowest bridging point and establishing an advanced military supply base on the north bank. London was thus a military foundation, and Aulus Plautius a credible founder of Londinium.

A new generation of archaeologists, following the Second World War, was prepared to reconsider the evidence and found that the likely foundation date was not AD 43 but some few years later, and so London, they believed, was more likely to be a civilian foundation. During the excavation of No. 1 Poultry* in the 1990s a wooden drain beside the main road was found and dated accurately by tree-ring dating to AD 47 – the likely date of the layout of the new Roman city. The founder then was an unknown official or trader in the governorship of Publius Ostorius Scapula (AD 47–52).

The nature of the Roman city was not spelled out by Geoffrey of Monmouth in the thirteen century, but he believed the line of British kings continued unabated, interrupted only by occasional Roman re-invasions. Later historians, steeped in the British Empire, thought differently; they saw the Romans as kindred spirits to the British Imperialists, and the Ancient Britons they saw as barbarians. Londinium was cloaked in the spirit of Roman civilisation and recast as a provincial example of the 'Glory that was Rome'. At its centre was the Roman town hall and market – the Forum, surrounded by Roman palaces and villas, temples and bath houses, theatres and amphitheatres, its citizens as educated Romans, proud to be Roman. The native Britons were absent from this picture – either Romanised, enslaved or ignored, as illustrated by this Roman writing tablet found

---

*Peter Rowsome, *Heart of the City*, Museum of London, 2000

in London in which the Latin named Rufus is referred to as the son of the Briton Callisunus*:

> Rufus, son of Callisunus, sends greeting to Epillicus, and all his fellows. I believe you know that I am well. If you have made the list please send it. Do look after everything carefully so that you turn the girl into cash.

Archaeologists duly found most of the missing Roman buildings: the Forum by the Lloyds building; bathhouses at Cheapside and Huggin Hill; temples and religious arches dotted around the town; an amphitheatre underneath the Guildhall; and a pattern of development that fitted into the Roman paradigm – no London before the Romans, an increase of Roman stone-built buildings as the Roman province developed, and an abrupt halt to the city when the Romans left. Maintaining town life in London seemed to need the civilising influence of the Romans, the narrative suggested, the Britons were incapable of it themselves.

As the baby-boomer archaeological generation matured, attitudes and discoveries changed the picture. In the 1970s developer madness led to a boom of archaeologists rescuing history from the jaws of the JCB. A surprising series of discoveries were made that revealed a wholly unexpected phase of early Roman timber-built construction, which reversed the perceived flow of development. The analysis of stone buildings was shown to give a false picture of Roman London. The early timber buildings demonstrated that Roman London had grown almost explosively in the first hundred years, despite the destruction of the city in the Boudiccan revolt of AD 60–61. By AD 140 it was at its height, and it then began

---

*P. Marsden, *Roman London*, Thames and Hudson, 1980

a long decline, punctuated by short-term recoveries, into oblivion.* The evidence could be interpreted to suggest that town life did not sit comfortably with the native economy – it only boomed in the initial period when the Romans 'gave private encouragement and official assistance to the building of temples, public squares, and good houses'**.

Up close – Roman Origins of London

In the crypt of Wren's St Bride's Church in Fleet Street is a small museum and some archaeological remains. Here you will see fragments of a Roman structure with tessellated floor, cut by early church foundations. Archaeologically there is nothing to link the Roman remains with the later church, although fifth-century pottery has been found here. But sit here and enjoy the unscientific speculation that nearby St Bride's Well was a holy well dedicated to the Celtic goddess of fertility Brigantia, that this became an late Roman Church and was dedicated to St Brigid of Kildare, the patron saint of brides, in the Saxon period. Wouldn't it be nice?

Archaeologist Neil Faulkner*** sees the Romans as robber barons failing to impose their ways on the British, and he sees the building of massive town halls and Roman city centres as being huge white elephants. In London, for example, the symbol of Roman Imperium the Forum**** appears to have been in a sorry state before being pulled down shortly after AD 300. By AD 400 no new Roman coinage was being circulated, the town centres were in terminal decay, Roman industries destroyed and Londinium, renamed Augusta, empty of

---

*Kevin Flude and Paul Herbert, *Citisights Guide to London*, Author's Choice Press, 2000
**Tacitus (trans H. Mattingly), *The Agricola & The Germania*, Penguin Books, 1948
***Neil Faulkner, *The Decline And Fall of Roman Britain*, Tempus, 2000
****G. Milne (ed.), *From Roman Basilica to Medieval Market*, Museum of London, 1992

citizens. London disappears from the historic record for nearly 200 years; archaeologically it disappeared for 400 years.

For historians since Geoffrey of Monmouth, this was an Armageddon – a descent into anarchy, barbarity, illiteracy, paganism, plague and genocide – the Dark Ages, when the Ancient Britons were all but exterminated by the Anglo-Saxons.

For some post-modern archaeologists it was nothing of the sort. They believe that the Roman civilisation was a thin veneer on a robust British society (Frances Pryor* for one sees a continuity of society from prehistory well into the medieval period), and see the Anglo-Saxon invasion hypothesis as much exaggerated. Some believe the decline of London has been exaggerated as cemeteries around London do not confirm the decline in population, and the shrinking urban area depends on a particular interpretation of a horizon called the 'Dark Earth' as a result of decline. The final abandonment of Londinium in AD 410 meant little more than that the robber barons had gone and the Britons would now pay tax to someone who lived more locally. The Saxons did not wipe out the natives, they integrated with them. But the lack of coins, formal pottery industries and the decline of towns means that dating evidence is so difficult to come by that an agreed narrative on what actually happened in the post-Roman period has not yet fully emerged. Reputable scholars advance diametrically opposed opinions – ranging from the full-blown disaster scenario to a complacently patriotic view that nothing much changed behind the comings and goings of Romans, Anglos, Saxons and Jutes.**

But within the walled city of Londinium, archaeologists found that

---

*Francis Pryor, *Britain A.D.*, Harper Perennial, 2004
**Bryan Ward Perkins, *The Fall of Rome and the End of Civilisation*, Oxford University Press, 2005

nothing much happened until the ninth century, when town life revived. However, history tells us that St Paul's was founded in AD 604 and that London was the chief town of the Saxon Kingdom of Essex. These two facts could not be reconciled until the 1980s when archaeologists suddenly realised that a series of excavations in the Aldwych and Covent Garden area which revealed Saxon period 'farms' had in fact discovered a previously unsuspected urban centre – Saxon London* – or Lundenwic as it was known. For unknown reasons, Londinium had died and a new city with a similar name revived 200 years later a mile or two to the west of the old city. This new unwalled city was attacked by Vikings in the ninth century and the people moved back behind the safety of the old Londinium defences – possibly when King Alfred instituted his policy of defence in depth behind walled Boroughs.

So archaeologists, through dint of repeated excavations on hundreds of sites, have revealed completely unknown 'facts' about London, creating a revolution in our understanding of the city. Londinium was founded first as a city by the Romans in AD 47, and probably named after a small pre-Roman settlement called Plowonida. Lundenwic was then refounded in the sixth century around the Aldwych, and moved back into the city in the ninth century as Lundenburgh, where it has remained ever since, and is still known as the City of London.

The remaining mystery is what happened in those 200 years from AD 400 to AD 600? In 2006, archaeologists working at St Martin's-in-the-Fields, Trafalgar Square found a burial site of a man – radio carbon dating suggested he was buried in 410 AD making him a contemporary of the real St Martin. Nearby was a brick kiln. Also found was a piece of pottery of a type used by early Saxons dating to about AD 500, and nearby in St Martin's Lane are further early Saxon

---

*A. Vince, *Saxon London*, Batsford, 1990

remains. Was the man the last Roman Londoner and did the pot belong to the first Saxon? Was this a cemetery that served both Roman Londinium and Saxon Lundenwic – was there a Roman settlement around St Martins, which survived the end of Roman London and which formed the heart of the new Saxon settlement? Putting aside romantic speculation, the 200-year gap is beginning to be closed.

LIFE IN THE MEDIEVAL CITY

SUE JACKSON

On Christmas Day 1066, William the Conqueror was crowned King
of England in Westminster Abbey, and the Middle Ages began. Or at least
this is as good a starting point as any. William would largely control his
new kingdom by force but, faced with the 'restlessness of its large and fierce
population', he was wise to approach the citizens cautiously.

In a gesture of conciliation, William confirmed all their existing rights and privileges in a document known as William's Writ. For his part, he inherited a city that was already well organised, and to a degree self-governing, a city that was wealthy, proud and conscious of its power. By the early Middle Ages, the boundaries of the city had expanded beyond the old walls to encompass an area of about a square mile, the Square Mile that is virtually unchanged to this day. The great Old St Paul's Cathedral dominated Ludgate Hill and throughout the area a forest of spires rose above the skyline. Beyond the walls to the north was the 'smooth field' – corrupted to 'Smithfield' – an open space used for entertainment, sport, executions and where a weekly horse fair and meat market was held.

Outside the wall to the west flowed the River Fleet, a natural defence and the means by which goods could be brought deep into the city. At the end of the eleventh century, a prison was built on its banks. On the south side of the city, the remains of the old riverside wall were at this time crumbling into the Thames, to be replaced by stone warehouses. London was now a thriving international port and the river, the main highway of London, 'teeming with craft'.

By 1209, a stone London Bridge over the Thames had been completed that was to last more than six centuries. At its centre was a chapel dedicated to St Thomas Becket, a Londoner who had risen to become Archbishop of Canterbury. The bridge was crowded with houses and shops. Its gatehouse displayed the gruesome sight of severed traitors' heads.

Huddled together along the narrow streets and alleys of the city were overhanging thatched houses and shops. Down the centre of the stinking and filthy lanes ran gutters, overrun with rats, into which everything, including human slops, was thrown. Cats, dogs, hogs and chickens wandered freely. Rubbish piled up and some streets served as open sewers, most obviously Cloak Street, which was originally Cloaca (sewage) Street.

WHERE TO READ THIS

You might sit and read this story in the old churchyard of St Bartholomew's Church, Smithfield. Here you will be sitting in what was once the covered nave of St Bartholomew's priory church of 1123, later the graveyard – which is why you are four feet above the level of the remaining south aisle! The lower part of the gatehouse dates from the late thirteenth century and one side of the cloisters still remains.

William balanced the benevolence of his Charter by building formidable strongholds. The wooden stockade he had built on the east side of the city would, by the end of the eleventh century, be replaced by the great stone keep later known as the White Tower, with walls up to fifteen feet thick. Commanding the eastern approach to the city, it served as a threatening presence not only to possible invaders but to the Londoners themselves, and it was echoed on the western side by Baynard's Castle and Montfichet Tower.

Little remains physically of the medieval city, except the Tower, parts of the walls, the odd crypt and sections of churches, but it is still possible to conjure up a vivid picture of what it must have been like from the street names which haven't changed, the multiplicity of blue plaques recording the location of many 'lost' churches and livery company halls.

The Normans were nothing if not organised and efficient. All over the city, churches were built or rebuilt. By the end of the twelfth century, there were an estimated 126 parish churches, one on virtually every corner. Many were dedicated to the same saint – there were sixteen St Mary's for example – often with a distinguishing suffix. Sometimes this was the name of the church's benefactor, for example, St Martin Orgar or St Lawrence Pountney. St Margaret Patten refers to the raised iron shoes or pattens made in the adjacent lane to protect clothes from the mud, and St Mary-le-Bow in Cheapside is named after the arched vaulting in the crypt. And it was the great tenor bell of that church that signalled the nine o'clock evening curfew when all citizens had to be back within the walls. True citizens of the city were those who lived within the sound of Bow Bells.

The churches, part and parcel of everyone's life, were tiny and dark, lit by candle and perfumed with incense. The walls were painted with biblical stories – most people were illiterate. The mass was murmured through the sanctuary screen, confessions were made (though probably only once a year, in Lent), marriages performed in the porch, and the dead buried in the churchyard, which over the centuries rose to several feet above ground level. The seatless naves of churches were often used as public meeting places or, as time went on, for commerce.

Sermons would be attended elsewhere – and the citizens loved a good sermon, particularly at St Paul's Cross in the cathedral's churchyard. A wooden pulpit surmounted by a cross, it also served as a place where proclamations were made – to announce royal deaths and births, victories or defeats – and where felons were punished. In 1087, the Saxon cathedral burned down, to be replaced by a vast stone building, the spire rising to 450 feet above the ground. The rose window on the east wall became so famous it was replicated in embroidery, as on Absalom's slippers in Geoffrey Chaucer's *Canterbury Tales*.

In the churchyard was the Jesus Bell Tower, which summoned the citizens to the great assembly or folkmoot on Christmas Day, Midsummer's Day and Michaelmas Day. Booksellers, usually itinerant, set up their stalls permanently here, and became known as 'stationers' as they were no longer on the move.

From the thirteenth century, monasteries, priories and abbeys found space on the edges of the city – Augustinians, Franciscans, Carmelites, Benedictines, Carthusians, Dominicans and others – all came to preach to and help the poor. Chaucer, living above Aldgate as a collector of dues on goods entering the city from the east, was able to observe them, and have them find a way into his *Canterbury Tales*. Of the nine religious characters on pilgrimage to Canterbury Cathedral, virtually all of them are corrupt. Right under Chaucer's nose in Aldgate was the vast Holy Trinity Priory (some of the remains of which are preserved in an office building in Mitre Street). Founded by Queen Matilda in 1108, the priory spent so lavishly on fixtures and fittings that the brothers hadn't enough money for food. Further, its prior forced the brothers to swear that a Mrs Joan Hodgiss was the official embroideress, rather than his mistress. When Henry VIII closed the priory down in 1532, no one was sorry to see them go.

It wasn't unusual for unmarried women to enter a nunnery, where life might be pretty comfortable. St Helen the Great's Priory became notorious for its frivolity, the nuns having to be ticked off for rushing through their services, wearing ostentatious veils and kissing secular persons. The prioress was ordered to keep to her own room.

Up close – Life in Medieval London

Still surviving on Smithfield are the remains of St Bartholomew's Priory Church. Built in 1123, and with vast Norman columns and arches, it is the oldest parish church in the City. Although the nave has been pulled down, two stumps of pillars that supported the south aisle roof remain.

So the Church was part of the daily fabric of life in the Middle Ages and its teachings and strictures influenced almost every aspect of life. Diet, for example. At certain times during the year meat was forbidden by religious observation and fish was substituted instead – its importance evident in street names such as Fish Street Hill, near Billingsgate, where most fish was landed, Old Fish Street and Friday Street, near St Paul's, where fish was also sold. The local church was St Nicholas Cole Abbey in Queen Victoria Street, St Nicholas being the patron saint of sailors and fishmongers. Many of them are buried here.

But meat was the staple, and Smithfield was the meat market. Beasts and poultry were brought to market along the nearby lanes, which gained predictable names such as Chick Lane and Cowcross Street. Sold and slaughtered, the offal from the animals was thrown into the River Fleet. Smithfield apart, the main market streets were Cheapside and Eastcheap – 'cheap' from the Anglo-Saxon for 'market'. The names of their side streets tell us where the various traders had their houses and shops, each gathered together in one area, for example Bread Street, Milk Street, Honey Lane, Ironmonger Lane, Poultry.

To practise a trade meant joining the relevant guild that protected and promoted that trade. A young boy of about fourteen years would serve a seven-year apprenticeship and it was the Master's responsibility to house, clothe and feed him. If his work 'passed Master' he could set up on his own and gain the freedom of the City. And being a Freeman was the passport to possible position and fortune. But apprentices had a reputation for getting involved in fights at the drop of a hat, drinking too much and being only too easily distracted by the lure of sport and entertainment. Chaucer sums it up in 'The Cook's Tale':

There was a prentice living in our town,
Worked in the victualing trade and he was brown.
At every wedding would he sing and hop

And he preferred the tavern to the shop
Whenever any pageant, goodbye to his profession
He'd leap out of the shop to see the sight
And join the dance and not come back that night.

And, indeed, in the first written description of London of 1177 by William FitzStephen, though waxing lyrical about virtually every aspect of the city, he condemns the 'immoderate drinking of fools'.

By the Middle Ages, there were over one hundred guilds. By the late fifteenth century, in an attempt to settle the many disputes that had arisen over precedence, the companies were put in order and the top twelve were, and are, known as the Great Twelve. Unsurprisingly, it was the merchant element that held sway over the craft guilds. Number one were the Mercers, controlling the fine cloth trade – but the Fishmongers and the Salters were there too, salt being so important in preserving meat and fish. Numbers six and seven were the Skinners (furs) and the Merchant Tailors. So persistent were the latter in arguing that they should be number six, that in the end the Skinners and Tailors were ordered to swap places each year, a custom that, it is said, gave rise to the expression 'to be at sixes and sevens'.

Every August, in the precincts of St Bartholomew's, a cloth fair was held, with merchants coming from all over Europe. Temporary courts were set up to deal with any complaint that arose and these were known as 'courts of pie powder', a corruption of '*pieds poudrés*' – or dusty foot, the notion of justice on the hoof along the dusty roads before the fair moved on. Here, a local tavern called the Hand and Shears was used as a court and its successor still stands today on Cloth Fair.

Most of these livery companies and their rebuilt halls still exist, though many are no longer actively involved in the original trade. Exceptions are the Fishmongers, whose Fishmonger's Hall still stands alongside London Bridge and whose members still examine the quality of fish at Billingsgate market. The market is now located in Docklands, where the rent is one fish a year. Meanwhile the Goldsmiths still weigh new coinage in the Assay Office at the Trial of the Pyx and are still involved in the jewellery trade. Down near the river was and is Vintners Hall in Upper Thames Street, where the wine merchants dealt, and the name of the nearby church, St Michael Paternoster Royal, College Hill, is a reminder of La Reole, a district of Bordeaux where the wine came from.

There was time for recreation in daily life. There was always the chance of a game of football on Smithfield, miracle plays to watch, dog fights, archery and ice-skating on the frozen watery meadows of Moorfields in winter, where skates could be fashioned from animal bones. The youth were nothing if not reckless and games were often dangerous, if not fatal. Best of all, there might be an execution – perhaps a beheading on Tower Hill or a hanging, drawing and quartering on Smithfield. Citizens were expected to attend executions, which were intended as a deterrent. You got a day off and plenty to drink and eat and you could cheer it all on. In 1305, William Wallace suffered a horrific traitor's death at Smithfield, his head later ground on to a spike and placed on the gatehouse of London Bridge as a terrible warning. The Tower itself was of course an object of fear associated with dark tales of imprisonments (often of the high and mighty), torture and escapes. The Bishop of Durham famously swung to freedom from the top of the White Tower on a rope which had been hidden at the bottom of a barrel of wine he'd spirited into his cell.

And the Tower continued to grow, to include two concentric walls and further towers circling the central keep. A menagerie was set up during Henry I's reign and he received as a gift three leopards and lions, alluding to the royal coat of arms, a polar bear and even an elephant, which no one had ever seen before.

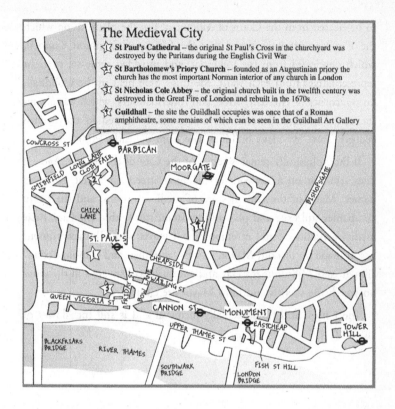

The Medieval City

⭐ **St Paul's Cathedral** – the original St Paul's Cross in the churchyard was destroyed by the Puritans during the English Civil War

⭐ **St Bartholomew's Priory Church** – founded as an Augustinian priory the church has the most important Norman interior of any church in London

⭐ **St Nicholas Cole Abbey** – the original church built in the twelfth century was destroyed in the Great Fire of London and rebuilt in the 1670s

⭐ **Guildhall** – the site the Guildhall occupies was once that of a Roman amphitheatre, some remains of which can be seen in the Guildhall Art Gallery

As the Middle Ages progressed, wealthy individuals built fine houses all over the City. These were usually merchants or aldermen who made most of the vital decisions regarding the affairs of the City. Power resided with them, and the City gradually but inexorably consolidated its independence. In 1215, King John confirmed its right to elect a Mayor on condition that an oath of allegiance be sworn to the monarch at Westminster. Thus was born the Lord Mayor's Show, which continues to this day. Then, as now, within the City the Lord Mayor took precedence over everyone except the monarch.

The Mayor, who would already have held the post of sheriff, came to be elected from the Court of Aldermen. But the platform on which the City's government rested was the Court of Common Council, which developed from the folkmoot, and provided some six to eight representatives from each ward. Meetings were held in the Guildhall, on the corner of Gresham Street and Aldermanbury, which was always the centre of civic government and certainly existed in the twelfth century. Parts of today's building date from the early 1400s.

If little physically remains today of the City of the Middle Ages, it does still rest on a network of medieval streets and their evocative names. Many of the churches are of medieval origin, and the livery companies still exist and play an important role within the City, their medieval traditions and ceremonies still played out. The government is still made up of Lord Mayor, sheriffs, aldermen and common councilmen, and Midsummer's Day and Michaelmas Day are still the dates on which the sheriffs and Lord Mayor are elected.

The City is still fundamentally medieval and is still the 'flower of cities all'.

Of Law and
Newspapers

LONDON LEGAL

TOM HOOPER

Established on private land once owned by the Knights Templar, the Honourable Societies of Inner Temple and Middle Temple are two of the formidable four surviving legal areas referred to as Inns of Court. For centuries barristers, who held the monopoly of audience in courts, lived and practised in the Inns and from here went to the Courts – often taking a ferryboat upstream to the key courts at Westminster from the Inns' own pier known as Temple Stairs.

Cases were conducted in French or Latin. Not surprisingly, all this has changed. The ferryboats have vanished, Temple Stairs were swallowed by the development of the 1860s Embankment, cases are conducted in plain English and even Latin has been expunged. The monopoly of audience has disappeared too, the accommodation has dwindled and barristers can practise from outside the Inns. These and other seismic changes have had little impact, though, on the visitors' impression of these unexpectedly quiet and beautiful places. Many leave with an indelible overarching sense of history stretching back through the 400 years the Inns have owned the land and beyond to the mighty influence of the Templars.

WHERE TO READ THIS

On a sunny, warm day sit on a bench in Temple itself to immediately immerse yourself in the atmosphere of this extraordinary place and to observe legal London go by. Equally amazing is to sit in Temple Church where the sense of history is almost tangible. If you'd like to read while eating or having refreshment, try the Devereux Arms, just outside the Judges' entrance to Middle Temple. Here the very name evokes the past. It is the family name of the Earl of Essex, especially famous during the reign of Queen Elizabeth I when the Earl was a favourite. That Earl, though, was executed in the Tower of London!

Inner Temple and Middle Temple

High up on the wall of 6 Pump Court in legal London's Inner Temple the inscription of the sundial dated 1686 declaims, 'Shadows We Are And Like Shadows Depart'. Nothing could be more apposite. Everywhere in this place the shadows of history are there to surprise and astonish. By 1770, at 3 Pump Court Sir William Blackstone, a greatly gifted barrister, compiled his *Commentaries on the Laws of*

England in time, coincidentally, for them to be hugely used as one of the first widely printed legal references of the fledgling new America. Earlier, in 1749, at No. 4, Henry Fielding, who with his brother John introduced the independently paid police force known as the Bow Street Runners, wrote *Tom Jones*. Charles Lamb was born in 1775 at what is now a different Crown Office Row: 'Man would give something to be born in such places,' he decided.

In his play *Henry VI, Part 1* Shakespeare had the roses, symbolising the two royal houses in the fifteenth-century Wars of the Roses, picked in Temple Gardens. He must have known the place well and wrote *Twelfth Night* for Middle Temple. Milton was also commissioned by Middle Temple and Dickens, a frequent visitor, includes its then fountain in at least three works, especially *Martin Chuzzlewit*. To gain an insight into Temple life in the mid-nineteenth century read Thackeray's *Pendennis*. On what is now the site of Brick Court, Oliver Goldsmith rented rooms, behaved raucously and argued with his landlady about the rent. This incident was the apparent event that precipitated the arrival of his enormous friend Dr Samuel Johnson, who is reputed to have sold the manuscript of *The Vicar of Wakefield* to pay the overdue rent.

The nineteenth-century Dr Johnson's Buildings and Goldsmith's Buildings pay tribute to these two luminaries' Temple connections. At 1 Dr Johnson's Buildings, in the 1990s, John Mortimer, the inventor of the eccentric *Rumpole of the Bailey* (not to mention Rumpole's wife, 'she who must be obeyed') practised. And outside the main entrance to Goldsmith's Building, a name board lists the barristers from the books as if their Chambers were inside. In the churchyard beyond is buried Oliver Goldsmith, who died in Temple in 1774. To the last he never became especially wealthy. 'Here lies Oliver Goldsmith', it says on a modest grave, appearing the more modest when close by is the expensive weather-beaten effigy of a reclining merchant from the same century.

There really are multitudes of shadows, but for a while, at least, dismiss thoughts of lawyers and literature – even the fictitious tentacles of the characters from Dan Brown's *Da Vinci Code* that reach here. You see, the strongest shadow of history, still shaping the physical boundaries of the land, still here in the name Temple, still there with the benign presence of Temple Church, still emphatically omnipresent all around in fact, is the shadow cast by the Brethren of the Militia of Christ and the Temple of King Solomon. The name reputedly granted by King Baldwin of Jerusalem is more formally the *pauperis commilitones christi templique salommonici* and rather less formally and usually known as the Knights Templar or Templars.

It's a bizarre twist of history that this order of military monks, established by Hugh de Payens and Godferoi de Champagne in Languedoc, southern France and formalised in 1128, should by the 1150s have reached London, when their original purpose was to escort and protect pilgrims travelling in the opposite direction eastwards to the Holy Land and Jerusalem! It's surely an even more bizarre twist of fate, perhaps, that the Order was founded at all, since the vocation of monk was not expected to include military skills. However, the Templars are a spectacular example of an Order which at its height was utterly in tune with the times. Contemporarily to western medieval Christendom the fact that Christ's birthplace was in the hands of the Turks was a dire outrage that propelled it to embark on a series of faith-driven crusades to free the Holy Land and avenge the slight. Popes and Kings ostensibly wholeheartedly supported the Templars, showing them favour and giving privileges which set them apart, and the paradox of an Order of ferociously courageous soldier monks with a decidedly ascetic lifestyle just seemed to be entirely appropriate.

A curious mutuality between Pope, King and Templars (Pope Innocent III actually became a Templar) helped the Templars gain power and develop strongholds across Europe. In London the Order first used land to the north, closer to Holborn, and then on an unknown date occupied this land by the River Thames. Even this move was arguably strategic since the land is on the boundary between the trading wealth of the City of London and the monarch's principal palace at Westminster. The first known Master, Robert of Hastings, would have known the strategic importance of the location and the Templars would have worked with both City and monarch. For example, in common with all Templar strongholds, the property was guarded by soldiers day and night, who probably daily honed their military skills, including in London by jousting up the road at Lincoln's Inn Fields. Jousting was pretty well as close as you'd get to battle, with a reputation for injury and death. The Templars also held the right of Sanctuary. There were no better guardians of valuables and, whether merchant or monarch, it paid to deposit them here in the London Temple.

The development of the land included a forge, a river pier and two dining halls, one at each end. In hall the community dined in pairs to ensure that each knight actually ate enough food. Neither hall survives but when the lawyers later occupied the land, the presence of two halls encouraged the growth of two groups – hence Inner and Middle Temple. The lawyers turned the pier into Temple Stairs.

By far the greatest link to the Templars is their Round Church. Standing in front of the rarely open west door immediately gives a sense of its importance. This was the Templars' entrance. Here on an English winter's day, said to be 10 February 1185, Heraclius, Patriarch of Jerusalem and, it's thought, King Henry II arrived for the dedication of the church. Henry, strong-willed and strong-tempered, had been blamed for the brutal murder of Thomas Becket in 1179 but was

Up close – London Legal

Everywhere you look you'll see the influence of early times. It's there, obviously, in the names Inner Temple and Middle Temple. It's there too in the ciphers of each honourable society. In Inner Temple the flying horse or Pegasus is used – the buildings and even the drainpipes use this cipher. In Middle Temple the cipher is the Lamb and Flag. Both are said to derive from seals used by the Templars in London. The flying horse is said to have come about as a result of smudged printing of the earliest known London Templar seal that showed a Templar wearing armour on horseback carrying another Templar. The smudged Templars on horseback turned into Pegasus. Whether true or not, the seal itself was the inspiration of Inner Temple's 2000 'Millennium' sculpture on the pedestal outside the church. Albeit that the rear of the horse controversially faces Middle Temple, the symbolism of the sculpture continues to represent the Templar ideals of poverty, fraternity and military skill. Middle Temple's Lamb and Flag, the *Agnus Dei*, shows the lamb of innocence and white flag with a red cross. Originally sewn in leather on sleeves, it is famous to a modern world in film as denoting the (papal) authority of Templars. The flag is perhaps the lasting image of the Order down the centuries, albeit in effect hijacked as the flag of England, St George and the English football team!

nevertheless recognised as controlling an empire that stretched from Ireland on one side to much of France on the other. For his own part, Heraclius had, in tumultuous times, completed an extremely dangerous journey to be in London. He died during the visit and is said to have been buried in the church.

Both king and patriarch would have expected a Rotunda or Round Church – it was well known that the Order built churches in the round, modelled on the Church of the Holy Sepulchre in Jerusalem. In fact there had also been a round church on the earlier Holborn site. The first impact would have been to see the stunningly decorated stone Romanesque door arch. Terribly eroded, but nevertheless strangely haunting, carvings of both Henry II and Heraclius were added within ten years of the dedication. Taking in the majesty of the interior, much restored after damage in the Second World War and now with a modern roof, it is difficult not to be awestruck. The clusters of Purbeck columns that rise to support the triforium and clerestory create graceful pointed arches and the whole effect shows brilliantly the transition from Romanesque towards future Gothic. The sense of drama, too, is both exciting and breathtaking. The Round Church represents the very place where Christ's body lay in Jerusalem, remembered here by between 200 and 300 Templars. Some sixty-four carved decorative regal, religious, angelic and demented heads, suggested as being modelled on people alive in 1185, look towards where Templars would have celebrated mass.

The unique atmosphere is heightened by the rather excellently lit, restored, larger-than-life tomb effigies neatly laid out on the floor. There is no great crypt beneath the church and the effigies presumably come from long-lost graves. Every single person was fabulously rich and, as evident from the effigies, could afford to be protected by mail from head to foot, ready for horse combat with sword and broad shield. The important historic figure is the First Earl of Pembroke, who fought for and against King Henry II, was Marshal to King John – hence William (the) Marshal – and was a regent, by King John's express wish, to King John's young son Henry III. The earl would have given advice about Magna Carta, sealed by John in June 1215 but quickly repudiated, living up to John's nickname 'soft sword'. When re-affirmed by Henry III, the earl's seal was added to the document. No doubt he would have been fully aware of the boy king's respect for the Templar church and the plans that came to fruition to build a chancel to the east. Although buried in Westminster Abbey, Henry III's chancel provides the true early Gothic addition, later to be used, as it still is, by Inner and Middle Temple. The Master of the Temple Church could therefore be said to be the successor to Walter de la More, the last Templar Master who worshipped here. Having said that, life is now better – De la More died in the Tower of London.

The orchestrated destruction of the Order by the evil Philip IV of France – the 'Fair' – in collusion with the Pope, on Friday 13 October. 1307, also signalled the end of the Order in England. In fairness, King Edward II did not believe the monstrous charges laid against the Templars, but, with papal pressure having been exerted, 229 knights were arrested and the property seized by mid-January 1308. The land, after royal and legal wrangling, went to the Knights Hospitallers, the rival Order to the Templars.

Hospitallers already held land at Clerkenwell and had no practical use for this additional land – rather natural, then, to rent it out. Scarcely missing a heartbeat in history, the lawyers were here fast – by the 1320s, in fact. First paying to the Hospitallers and then, when that Order was suppressed by Henry VIII, paying the Tudors. The Crown, however, it seems found the outgoings, especially relating to the church, were a drain on royal coffers. The Stuarts, therefore, came to a curious agreement with Inner and Middle Temple. In 1608, 400 years ago, King James I granted the land to the two honourable societies and specifically transferred responsibility for Temple Church to them. Ironic that twice in the same century it was threatened by fire – first in 1666 when the Great Fire of London approached but was stopped just north at St Dunstan-in-the-West and then again later when fire broke out in the Temple. Water was frozen, beer didn't work, and buildings were pulled down to save the church.

The Blitz bombings of the Second World War, for 57 consecutive nights from 7 September 1940, plus daytime raids until the last major raid on 10/11 May 1941, took a catastrophic toll on both Inner and Middle Temple. In the courtyard outside Temple Church only the church itself has survived. Inner Temple lost chambers, its hall, treasury and library. Middle Temple also lost many chambers, its hall was damaged and it too lost its library – although, unlike Inner Temple, only one book was totally destroyed (on Rhodesia). Temple Church itself was also hit, really just leaving the walls standing. When an explosive bomb, dropped on 10 May 1941, went off inside the Round Church it's said the temperature must have reached 800 degrees Celsius.

Multitudes of crumbling coffins, skulls and bones were discovered during post-war excavations – it's estimated that up to 2,000 burials took place in the seventeenth and eighteenth centuries alone. They included the grave of jurist and academic John Selden, who died in 1654, now visible below a glass panel in the chancel. No one visiting would instantly realise the amount of sympathetic restoration needed – even the Purbeck marble columns cracked. Nor would they be aware that there had been a decidedly drastic previous restoration in the nineteenth century!

Standing or sitting in Temple Church, once central to Templar life, it is fascinating how what is seen here has been so relevant to the life of the nation and to the affairs of State. And the miracle is that the building has survived for 823 years. We owe a debt of gratitude to the Templars and, not least, to the generations of barristers who have richly fulfilled their commitment to care for this building. The stained glass at the east is post-war and includes a representation of how the Round Church once looked. The ciphers of both honourable societies are there, too. The 2008 stained-glass window on the south side celebrates the 400th anniversary of the granting of the land by Charter. And yes, the ciphers are present again, but there is also royal heraldry. Notice James I's Stuart lion for Scotland, the three lions, first used by King John, for England, and the harp for Ireland.

Before leaving the Church make time to look at Edmund Plowden's tomb. Plowden died in 1585 and his colourful, recumbent Tudor effigy looks entirely comfortable. So it should be. Here lies the brainchild responsible for the construction of Middle Temple Hall, the second outstanding building in Temple.

The route to Middle Temple Hall passes a number of buildings predominantly housing today's barristers in offices known as a Set of Chambers. This is the hub of legal activity in England and a look at the entrance boards gives a glimpse into the legal system. Names of those with accommodation in the building will be shown apart on the board. The main list of names will be those practising in the chambers. Typically the first name will be Head of Chambers, followed by other members in the order they joined. Every person is an individual business – a sole trader. Barristers in private practice cannot work as partnerships nor establish companies. Instead they come together for the common good, administered by the Clerk. The Clerk traditionally also acquires work, helps allocate it and negotiates fees. At one time Clerks received a percentage of each barrister's fees, but you can now expect a (good) salary to be paid. A good Clerk is a prerequisite for success. Large chambers may deal with general or common law, although there are other sizable chambers too, including those for commercial and family law. Every niche is covered one way or another. Women often keep their maiden name as their professional name and are increasingly represented in what was once an all-male domain. Some women would say they have to be better than the men to progress, though. Recent changes have even impacted on the way newer chambers list their members – for example, alphabetically. Clerks too have metamorphosed into practice managers and other modern functions. The two stalwarts of practice – advocacy and opinion/advice – remain essentially unchanged, however.

Middle Temple Hall is simply a remarkable Tudor building that's been used for its original purposes since it was completed in 1571. Edmund Plowden would be rather pleased and his bust just inside the hall itself still presides over proceedings. This hall has been the heart of the community for over 437 years. On entering through seventeenth-century screen doors the extraordinarily rare, fine oak double hammer-beam roof becomes fully visible. It gives an ambiance and it really is not difficult to imagine that Queen Elizabeth I was here in 1576 and that Shakespeare's *Twelfth Night* was premiered here in 1602. The story is told that the Virgin Queen banned the wearing of yellow stockings, which in turn gave rise to their inclusion in *Twelfth Night*. Actually Middle Temple appears to have had a notably good relationship with the Queen, who gave them a tree as a gift. The tree was in Windsor Great Park so it was cut down, floated along the Thames, brought to Middle Temple and turned into the 29-foot table still in use as the Benchers' dining table at the west end.

Elizabeth I's portrait is the earliest monarch's portrait in the hall. The others are Stuarts, beginning with the largest Van Dyke-esque portrait of the height-challenged King Charles I and ending with the last Stuart monarch, Queen Anne. The odd armour is also Stuart. Curiously, one of the rowdiest entertainments was a masque given for Charles I. Usually rowdiness was associated with Christmas Revels that lasted weeks. The Revels still occur – rather shorter, though, and tamer.

Benchers are the governing body of the honourable society (as they are at Inner Temple) and down the centuries they have steered the Inn, including dealing with rowdiness. They have kept the Inn true to its values and traditions. For example, while lunch is an informal and mainly self-service affair, dinners are a different matter and students of the Inn must normally still, as they always have done, eat in hall as a prerequisite to qualification as barrister. Most students realise that dining provides a valuable networking opportunity – and the wine cellar is very good! The Coats of Arms of Readers (Lectors) on the walls and in the older stained glass illustrate that Readers were appointed annually to take responsibility for training, and testify to the long tradition of learning. Jekyll and Hyde both appear in the glass. Following Bar examinations (and dining) students are nowadays called to the Bar at the 'Cupboard', which started life as the hatch cover of Francis Drake's famous ship, the *Golden Hind*.

Francis Drake was a Middle Templar, as was Sir Walter Raleigh and Sir Martin Frobisher. Albeit they possibly joined for the good entertainment, the Inn, in fact, had an abiding interest in navigation, discovery, colonisation and the New World. It is no coincidence that the library houses two rare late-Tudor terrestrial globes. Young Middle Templars often set off on voyages, some to settle in the new colonies. In 2008 it is quite possible for barristers to qualify at the English Bar, but also gain qualifications from other jurisdictions and work around the world.

For Middle Temple one of the greatest challenges came with American Independence. The 1776 Declaration of Independence, the Constitution and the Bill of Rights that followed have been dubbed models of drafting and statesmanship. The rub is that there already was a special relationship between the colonies and Middle Temple that continued with a new America, and Middle Templars were able to contribute their expertise to drafting. Middle Temple and the American Bar have never forgotten. When the east end of the hall was destroyed in the Second World War, including the so-called minstrels' gallery, the American and Canadian Bar Associations paid for the painstaking rebuild.

Overall Middle Temple Hall, Temple Church and the land that comprises Inner and Middle Temple cannot fail to make a mark on visitors in a positive way. They are places to enjoy and enjoy again. Long may they last for future generations to be able to journey back through the lawyers' occupation to the people who began it all – the Knights Templar.

Note: Temple is not always open to the public. Before visiting check the times Temple Church is open and be aware that Middle Temple is private and generally in use as a working hall every lunchtime. The hall is rarely accessible at weekends. Still-photography is allowed in Temple Church – but please give a donation. Staff there and at Middle Temple Hall are friendly and knowledgeable.

Fleet Street – 'Small Earthquake in Chile: Not Many Dead'*

ADAM SCOTT

Of all the Londons hidden along storied Fleet Street – the London of the pre-Reformation bishops, of the long-dissolved monasteries, Londons of half-forgotten battles, fire and riots, of mythical close shaves and cannibalism – the London most recently departed is the hardest to find. Our business – raking up the past – takes on a new twist here. In this neck of the woods, the past has long been a valuable commodity. Especially a sordid past. A scandalous past. An incriminating, shameful past. The kind of back story that shifts newspapers.

The past belonging to the newspapers themselves, however, is another matter. Perhaps Fleet Street hides its recent history because the biter seldom likes to be bitten. Maybe it's too early to be tossing plaques and platitudes around – it is, after all, only twenty and some years since the printing business's exodus from its home of five hundred years. The business of news exists entirely in the present. Who indeed,

---

*Winner of unofficial, in-house Most Boring Headline Competition at *The Times*, early 1950s

as Mick Jagger (himself a scarred veteran rider of the newspaper tiger) once asked, wants yesterday's papers? The answer to that is easy: we do. Unearthing the past is rewarding work, setting history in hot metal as opposed to pushing computerised pages across a silent screen.

WHERE TO READ THIS

London teems with enclaves that, just a few steps off the roaring highway, afford a peace and quiet greatly at odds with their noisy surroundings. These insider's hideaways spring up where one least expects them – and they come no better than at St Bride's churchyard.

All along Fleet Street

Like all wide-eyed, fledgling newspapermen we will start at the top, only to find ourselves sinking inexorably to the bottom. The devil has all the best tunes, they say: and all the circulation-boosting stories, too. The top in this case is the western extremity, where we get precious little help from a famous man of letters. Who, after all, would collude in the exhumation of ghosts that want to be left well alone? Certainly not Samuel Johnson, loitering behind St Clement Danes where The Strand meets Fleet Street.

In a statue by Percy Fitzgerald, the good doctor seems intent on minding his own business: knees bent in a sprightly walk, nose buried in a book, a 'Who sir? Me sir?' attitude surrounds him like the smoke of a surreptitious fag in the school toilet. He's even standing in The Strand, just shy of Fleet Street itself, trying to disguise a sidelong glance down that fabled thoroughfare. He couldn't look more guilty if he were self-consciously whistling a jaunty air. Cast as both gatekeeper and denouncer, this St Peter of Fleet Street seems set to surpass the fiery apostle's hat trick of denials and then some. 'Fleet Street? Me? A man of my standing?'

Don't you believe a word of it. Try as he might, Johnson will later give himself up. We know, as the old saying goes, where he lives. Better yet in Fleet Street: we know where he lunches.

Reuters has gone, the last of the big boys to leave, departing its Edwin Lutyens-designed building in 2005. D C Thomson is the last man standing, its London HQ guarding the western extremity of the Street. Unsuccessfully, as it turns out. The Scottish megalith publishes both the *Beano* and the *Sunday Post* (once the world's biggest sale, achieving the unique feat of having readership figures in excess of 9 million). The names of its stable – *People's Friend, Dundee Evening Telegraph* – are set into the very fabric of the building. In anticipation of a thousand-year Reich? Newspapermen should have known better.

Journalists come and go. Newspapers, likewise. The blank look in the eye of your news vendor when you ask for a copy of *Today* (dead since 1995) the *Sketch* (1971), the *Chronicle* (departed 1930, coincidentally in the same year as its most famous correspondent, Sir Arthur Conan Doyle) or even the *Post* (launched and folded within five weeks in 1985) is testimony to that. We'll not be sentimental, though: the Street would never have allowed it. That the nickname of the famous journo watering hole the White Hart was 'The Stab in the Back' suggests that sentimentality was never welcome here at the best of times.

That 'The Stab', like the papers and the presses, is also long gone brings us to a change in the Street, less well documented than the moving of Murdoch and his News International stable to Wapping in the mid-1980s.

The King and Keys, the old *Daily Telegraph* pub, closed recently without so much as a squeak. Forty years ago, the headline 'Pub Closes In Fleet Street – Drinkers Go Elsewhere' would have been a 'Man Bites Dog' sensation. In polite tourism circles the Street is known as 'The Street of Ink'. By those in the know, this has long been seen as a misprint, an error on the subs' desk. Of course, ink has been integral to the neighbourhood since the 1400s, but there has been another fluid just as vital to the folklore of the place. It's not ink. But it sounds like ink.

Sitting proud of Fleet Street over in the People's Republic of Soho, that enclave of non-conformity providing the perfect base from which to throw brickbats, the satirical magazine *Private Eye* still has fun with the antics of newspapermen and women, in its fictionalised old-timer Lunchtime O'Booze. Indeed, that magazine coined the popular euphemism for inebriation, 'tired and emotional', tailored for George Brown, the Labour politician of the 1960s whose thirst made even those on Fleet Street seem tame by comparison.

Up close – Fleet Street

The great editor of the *Daily Express* Arthur Christiansen (in the chair from 1932–56) always reminded his staff: 'Never forget the man in the backstreets of Wigan' – never, in short, lose touch with the Common Man. The common man in London terms was always 'The Man on the Clapham Omnibus', a description created by Fleet Street's bothersome, killjoy neighbours, the legal profession in the early twentieth century as a metaphor for the ordinary man in the street. The title was resurrected by the late Stewart Steven when editor of the *Evening Standard* as a byline for one of that paper's columns in the early 1990s. As for the omnibus itself, there are still a couple in service. The No. 15 Routemaster is one of only two 'heritage routes' (the other is the No. 9) that still trundle and growl their way through central London. Pick up the No. 15 at Trafalgar Square and it will take you clear to Tower Hill – via Fleet Street, of course. Aggressive in acceleration and growling noisily – a bus that behaves like a born Londoner – the Routemaster was only in production between 1954 and 1968 but was a good and faithful servant to the metropolis for a further thirty-seven years.

Despite recent closures, the Street still retains a retinue of fine pubs and bars – including the first Irish pub outside the Emerald Isle. A refreshing change from the chain homogeneity of those dismal Feck O'Donnell's Green Beer Emporia, the Tipperary at 66 Fleet Street was formerly the Boar's Head (from around 1700) and was renamed by the print workers returning to the Street after the end of the First World War (after the popular song 'It's a Long Way to Tipperary'). Built on the site of a monastery where the monks brewed ale, it was the first pub in London to sell both bottled and then later draught Guinness.

The Irish connection holds true at the bottom of the Street, too, in the shape of the journalists' church, St Bride's on St Bride's Avenue. St Bride is not, paradoxically, the patron saint of journalists – that difficult job belongs to St Francis de Sales. Neither does she particularly watch out for women on their wedding day – although Wren's tiered spire for her church was the inspiration for the traditional wedding cake. St Bride occupies an honoured place in the pantheon of Irish saints bettered only by St Patrick himself. Her miracle? She turned the water into . . . beer.

A walk along Fleet Street becomes a mere frivolous skip down memory lane if we do not acknowledge the mighty Irish contribution to English letters. It is best summed up in the words of a West End man who spent much of his professional life on Fleet Street: Kenneth Tynan, legendary drama critic of the *Observer* (the world's first Sunday newspaper, established in 1791). Of the great dramatist (and fierce drinker) Brendan Behan, he put it thus: 'The English hoard words like misers: the Irish spend them like sailors on leave.' How much poorer would our Fleet Street and literary culture be if they hadn't? Without T P O'Connor's title the *Star* (founded 1887), for example, we would lack some of the most vivid reporting on the Jack the Ripper case.

Words remain the currency here; even now the papers have gone.

We may live in the digital age but, as sure as Dogs' Home follows Battersea, Fleet Street is still wedded to journalism, even now that the lawyers have gleefully spilled in like so many cuckoos from their neighbouring enclave.

It is both an irony and a frustration that the Street always had the Law peeking over its shoulder, twirling the baton of libel like some overzealous policeman looking for trouble. With rich and scandalous pickings at either end of the Street, our old-school editors must have drooled all morning long. No wonder they needed a drink come lunchtime.

And what temptation: at the eastern extremity lies the City. And to turn that old northern capitalist's cliché upside down, where there's brass, there's muck. At the other end there's the City of Westminster, where the good people of London go to enjoy themselves. And where, on occasion, having enjoyed themselves a little too much, they turn from Jekylls into Hydes. Perfect fodder for the front page. Our politicians also work there. But surely that unimpeachable bunch wouldn't ever trouble our newspaper editors with their above-board endeavours and pastoral leisure pursuits. Would they?

Rather like the proverbial bad surgeon, Fleet Street buries its mistakes. Or rather, it spikes them, an act that also functions as a rather delicious allusion to London's gruesome past. And those who have published that which should have been spiked have been, if not quite damned, then certainly slapped on the wrist for libel. Sometimes slapped in irons.

The first Fleet Street libel case involved the publisher and editor John Walter. Walter founded the *Daily Universal Register* on New Year's Day 1785. As a third birthday present for his publication, he gave it a new name, the name by which it has been known these last 220 years: *The Times*. Eighteen months after that he was sentenced to a year in Newgate Prison for a libel on the Duke of York.

His publication gained the satirical epithet 'The Thunderer' in the

1840s. But the only building that thunders on Fleet Street – even today – is the former HQ of rival publication the *Daily Telegraph*. Elcock and Sutcliffe's Egyptian-inspired edifice at No. 135 was home to Britain's biggest-selling daily broadsheet from 1928 until 1987 when it followed the exodus east, ending up at 1 Canada Square at the horribly nicknamed 'Vertical Fleet Street' (it's since flitted back west to Victoria). Amid the timid Victoriana of the Street, this impressive 'newspaper palace' looks as if it has dropped directly from Batman's Gotham City. And if you look up high, just below the level of the old director's penthouse apartment, you can still see shadows of things that have gone before: the 3-D lettering is long gone, but the words 'Daily Telegraph' are still spelled out in sooty relief, looking for all the world like inky finger smears. London's dirt still makes the names of the newspapers here.

The *Telegraph*, that bastion of the establishment, has long enjoyed a reputation, amid all its austerity, for being a paper that rather enjoys writing about sex. So much so that many consider it to be the home of the Marmalade Dropper: a story so salacious, so downright filthy, a threat to the established order and, therefore, so riveting, that one's attention is taken utterly. The newspaper reader, sitting happily at breakfast, is suddenly gripped by a headline. With toast poised precariously halfway between plate and ever-gaping mouth, the tale consumes his interest. Reading on enraptured, he forgets the toast altogether – until, that is, the marmalade plops into the lap of his cavalry twills.

It is not, however, the proximity of scandal and skulduggery that brought the Press to this part of town. That distinction falls to Wynkyn de Worde, assistant to Joseph Caxton, father of the printing press. When de Worde inherited the business from Caxton in 1491, he simply moved it to where his customers were. In this case, just outside the City wall, to be near the educated and literate brothers at the Blackfriars monastery.

The church still enjoys a strong presence in this street so often concerned with lower matters. St Bride's has St Dunstan-in-the-West (186 Fleet Street) for company (its namesake in the east a bombed-out shell converted into the City's prettiest garden). Its location, on the north side of the Street, has accommodated a church for some thousand years. The current St Dunstan's is the work of John Shaw the Elder, completed by his son John the Younger and opened in 1883. It is dedicated to a popular British saint and former Archbishop of Canterbury who, legend has it, caught the devil by the nose and hammered horseshoes into his hooves. I wonder how he would have been immortalised by the subs desk of the *Sun*? Perhaps: 'Hoof Sorry Now?' 'Dunstan Casts Devil to the Land of Shod'? Or 'Dunstan and Dusted!'? Come to think of it, 'Gotcha!' would work equally well.

What Samuel Johnson would have made of the inclusion of the word 'gotcha' in his dictionary we can only speculate. Perhaps he would have tried to distance himself from such vulgarity. Had Johnson's home at nearby Gough Square not been turned into a wonderful museum, or if we couldn't find his cat Hodge (in statue form) waiting for his master, we would still have evidence to catch the Doc red-handed as a pillar of this inky community. For his spirit is still in Fleet Street – in liquid form at the bar at one of Johnson's favourite haunts: Ye Olde Cheshire Cheese (145 Fleet Street in Wine Office Court).

Ye Olde Cheshire Cheese has a board outside that reads like a who's who of Eng. Lit. Johnson tops the bill, alongside a roster of some fifteen monarchs who have reigned over us, happy (and miserable) and glorious (and ignominious). And one can ask for Johnson's spirit by name: it is brandy. 'Claret,' he said, 'is the liquor for boys; port for men; but he who aspires to be a hero must drink brandy.'

The most salacious item ever served on the menu at this historic pub was a very cold dish indeed: Dead Man's Letters. During the days of the death penalty (abolished finally in 1971), informants keen to make a few bob from the insatiable papers could strike up correspondence with condemned men. Doomed to dance at the end of a rope, the miscreant would often be found on fine confessional form. The correspondence would turn into a friendship and the memories and confessions would pour forth like water. On the day of the hanging, the dead man's new best friend would hot-foot it to the Cheshire Cheese where he would sell the story to the highest bidder. These latter-day Resurrection Men profited not from the contents of dead bodies, but the more ephemeral cargo of departed memories.

Nearing the bottom of the Street, the elegant No. 128 glints into view – arguably the Street's most famous building. Just as the *Telegraph* was still preening in all its Citizen Kane-ish glory, along came Ludgate House a mere four years later. It remains one of the most outstanding modernist structures in London. Perhaps it is even a mark of our reticence to embrace the architectural new that it still stands out as outré some eighty years after its creation. Nicknamed the Black Lubyanka (again by *Private Eye*, a nod to the Moscow HQ of the KGB) it boasts London's first ever curtain wall. Behind this architectural first, the beautiful Art-Deco foyer captures *Express* proprietor Lord Beaverbrook's vision of his beloved British Empire. One wall is a fresco of scenes and riches from the former colonies, the other of the might and splendour of England. Linking the two across the tiled floor, a series of wavy lines, undulating from wall to wall representing those waves ruled, of course, by Britannia.

One Fleet Street legend from the newspaper days remains unexplored – El Vino's. And it's still there, back up the hill at No. 47.

The closest this bunch of rogues and footpads ever had to a

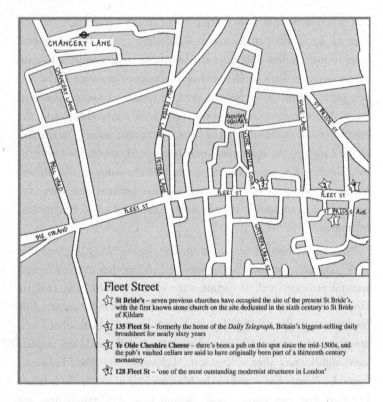

Fleet Street

⭐ **St Bride's** – seven previous churches have occupied the site of the present St Bride's, with the first known stone church on the site dedicated in the sixth century to St Bride of Kildare

⭐ **135 Fleet St** – formerly the home of the *Daily Telegraph*, Britain's biggest-selling daily broadsheet for nearly sixty years

⭐ **Ye Olde Cheshire Cheese** – there's been a pub on this spot since the mid-1500s, and the pub's vaulted cellars are said to have originally been part of a thirteenth century monastery

⭐ **128 Fleet St** – 'one of the most outstanding modernist structures in London'

gentlemen's club (once upon a time, not so very long ago, women were forbidden from ordering at the bar), El Vino's was a great favourite haunt of my late father-in-law, Commonwealth Press Union supremo Terence Pierce-Goulding, who loved its unassuming atmosphere cloaked in coat-and-tie formality. Robert Edwards, editor of four national papers including the *Express* at the height of its powers (when it sold 4 million copies a day in the 1960s) records it wistfully in his autobiography, *Goodbye Fleet Street*. The distance between the *Express* and El Vino, he bemoans, was just too great to cover if Beaverbrook called on the phone. From many another hostelry, one could be back at one's desk in a matter of mere minutes, pretending to have been in a meeting with the chapel (as the printers' unions were known). Not so El Vino's, making it out-of-bounds for Edwards of a lunchtime. A good thing, if you ask me: the ample charms of this great Fleet Street institution are too great to be interrupted by anything – even a call from Lord Beaverbrook.

Now that the Fleet Street era of newspapers is over, it is perhaps appropriate that we end our tale with that most forbidden of old Fleet Street lunchtime fluids: water. The Street, after all, takes its name from the shadowy Fleet River that rises on Hampstead Heath and runs beneath its eastern extremity before making its final watery genuflection at the hem of the Thames beneath Blackfriars Bridge. Traces of the old newspapers are almost as hard to find, twenty years after they went east, as the elusive Fleet River itself. But while the Street these days chains together the two great beasts of City and Westminster, its very name remains soaked in ink. No Londoner in the twenty-first century thinks cabbages and carnations at the mention of Covent Garden. But the words Fleet Street still set the presses thundering and the headlines spinning in the Moviola of the popular imagination.

Sinister
London

JACK THE RIPPER

DONALD RUMBELOW

Whitechapel is the name that most people associate with the Jack the Ripper murders. Weeks before he was identified by the newspapers by his brand name, a stroke of genius by some enterprising journalist if the name was not the murderer's choice, he was popularly referred to as the Whitechapel murderer or the East End murderer. Logically any walk should start in Whitechapel, but wartime bombing and post-war redevelopment mean that a tighter circumference of the killing ground is necessary.

Two police forces

A good place to start your walk is at Tower Hill underground station. There are two reasons for this. The first is the old Roman and medieval city wall which for centuries enclosed the one square mile of the original City of London. The second is the Tower of London. London in 1888, the year of the murders, had (and still has today) two police forces. The City of London police for the one square mile with St Paul's Cathedral as its centre, and the Metropolitan police force based at Scotland Yard for the rest of London. Inside the wall was the original London. Over the centuries the City expanded just a short way beyond this wall – we are talking in yards not miles – and so the wall is a boundary line for the two police forces. In 1888 the police powers of both forces stopped at this boundary. On their own territory the policemen had full police powers; on the other side of the wall, they were no more than men in fancy dress with only an ordinary citizen's powers of arrest. Modern police powers now extend to both sides of the boundary. Zigzagging backwards and forwards across the old boundary, as the Ripper did, would play havoc with the investigation. His behaviour suggests that he deliberately did this to buy time and this, in turn, suggests more than a degree of local knowledge. Geographical profiling, which is used in modern murder investigations today, has him living within two hundred yards of two of the killings.

'How many victims were there?' is the question most frequently asked. Well, that depends on which expert you consult. Some will say three, others five and stretching the imagination may go as high as fourteen, but that particular expert only reached such a mind-boggling total by counting one of the supposed victims twice. The generally accepted canonical number is five but even this number was challenged by some of the original detectives, who believed there were only four Jack the Ripper murders. Most people today think the number of victims was much higher than it actually was and are surprised at such a low body count. What often is not taken into account is how compact the killing ground was. The modern serial killer with a car can commit murders hundreds of miles apart. At its widest point, the Jack the Ripper killing ground is a walk of no more than fifteen minutes across.

WHERE TO READ THIS CHAPTER

The Ten Bells pub on the corner of Commercial and Fournier Streets, or a seat in the sun somewhere at Tower Hill.

The number of murders in the East End had increased over the previous three years from eight in 1886, to thirteen in 1887 and twenty-eight in 1888. The generally accepted number of Ripper victims is five, one of them in the City and only four of them being in the East End. They were Mary Ann 'Polly' Nichols, Annie Chapman, Elizabeth 'Long Liz' Stride, Catherine Eddowes and Mary Kelly. Another murder victim, not one of the canonical five, was Emma Smith who was attacked on the night of Easter Monday, 3 April 1888 by two or three men, robbed and then had something rammed up inside her. With difficulty she was helped to the London Hospital where she died of peritonitis several hours later. The number of men involved suggests this was not a Ripper murder but down to one of the gangs in the area, possibly preying on these helpless women.

The Walk

In a walk of two hours, it is impossible to cover all the murder sites, most of which have changed beyond recognition. This means that the murders cannot be done in sequence. If, however, you do have time, take the fifteen minute walk from Aldgate down to the Royal London Hospital.

On the way you will go past Altab Ali Park. Notice the metalwork shaped like the onion domes of a mosque and now straddling the remains of the nineteenth-century gateway that once led to St Mary's church. This church was badly damaged during the Second World War and had to be demolished but the outline of the church, which is clearly visible, was marked in stone. These markers enclose the site of the original medieval chapel that gave the area its name. The chapel was painted in lime wash to protect it from the weather and so in appearance was a white chapel.

Opposite the Royal London Hospital is Whitechapel underground station. Immediately to the right of it is a Victorian building with large first-floor picture windows. This was the Working Lads Institute where inquests were held on some of the Ripper's victims.

One of those was the first Ripper victim, Mary Ann 'Polly' Nichols, who was murdered on 31 August 1888. Behind Whitechapel underground station is Durward Street. In 1888 it was known as Buck's Row. Dominating the street is the only Victorian survivor, the schoolhouse, now converted into fourteen apartments. To one side there is a wall leading to a car space and some modern housing. The car space is where Polly Nichols' body was found. Earlier that night she had been looking for a fourth customer. She was confident of getting one because she was wearing a new hat. 'I'll soon get my doss money. See what a jolly bonnet I've got now,' she had boasted to the lodging keeper who had turned her away because she had not got the money for a bed. By 'doss money' she meant her rent money or bed money. When found later at 3.30 a.m. the bonnet was lying by her side, but her throat was cut and she had several brutal cuts in her breast and abdomen; the vagina had been stabbed twice.

Jewry Street

Starting at Jewry Street, take up position opposite the Church of St Botolph's Aldgate, in the Ripper's time known locally as the prostitute's church. It was the pick-up point by the prostitutes for customers mostly travelling to and from nearby Spitalfields market. If they did not keep walking about then the prostitutes could be arrested by the police for soliciting and so they kept moving by using the church like a traffic roundabout, hurrying up when at the back where they were unlikely to get a customer and slowing down at the front of the church where there was every chance of a pick-up.

The night of 30 September 1888 is known as the night of the 'double event'. Our killer, still known only as the 'East End murderer' or the 'Whitechapel murderer' killed twice that night, once on Metropolitan Police territory and once on City of London Police territory.

Earlier that day, a woman in her forties named Catherine Eddowes had been running up and down the road in front of St Botolph's church, in and out of the horse-drawn traffic, imitating a fire engine. Eventually, she became so exhausted by this that she sat down against a shop wall and fell asleep. She was picked up by two City of London policemen and taken away to nearby Bishopsgate police station where she was put in a cell to sleep off the drink. By about 1 a.m. she had sobered up sufficiently to be released. With a cheery 'Night, old cock, my husband will give me hell', she returned to St Botolph's church looking for another customer. She found one. She picked up Jack the Ripper, fresh from his first killing of that night in Berner Street (now Henriques Street), a ten- to fifteen-minute walk away, across the boundary on Metropolitan Police territory. Unless you are a real enthusiast there is little point in going to Henriques Street. The 1888 street has long gone and a school playground now covers the murder site.

Cross now to Mitre Square. The space in front of the garden bench – there is only one – is the spot known locally as 'Ripper's Corner'. This is where the body of Catherine Eddowes was found.

Forty minutes only separated the two murders. The body of the first victim, a Swedish prostitute named Elizabeth Stride, nicknamed 'Long Liz', had been found at 1 a.m. in Berner Street by a travelling salesman coming home late from work. His pony shied away from the object lying inside the gateway and, reaching over with his whip, the salesman prodded it. He said later that he thought it was his wife. Leaving the body there, he parked his pony and trap before returning with a light. Stride's throat had been cut but there were no other mutilations and it is possible that the murderer was hiding behind the gate when the salesman came home and escaped when he went to get a light. Heading west, the murderer crossed the boundary between the two police forces and picked up or was picked up by Catherine Eddowes.

Only the cobblestones of Mitre Square are original but they give you the shape and size of this tiny square, which was patrolled every fifteen minutes by a City of London policeman. A policeman and his family were sleeping in a house directly opposite the murder scene. A man was working behind a part-open door on the other side of the square. Eddowes was seen talking to her killer at the entrance to what is now St James's Passage. He is described as a man of shabby appearance, about thirty years of age, with a fair moustache and a peaked cap. That was at 1.35 a.m. Ten minutes later she was dead. Her face had been slashed down both cheeks, there may have been an attempt to cut off one of her ears. The throat had been cut back to the spine. She had been cut open from the vagina to the breastbone, her insides dropped over her right shoulder and a kidney removed and taken away by the killer.

Up close – Jack the Ripper

London has several police forces. Scotland Yard – i.e. the Metropolitan Police – the City of London Police, British Transport Police, the Thames Police. OK, the Thames Police are now part of the Met, but historically they're so important. The Thames police force is the oldest police force in the world, founded in 1798. So they predate Scotland Yard by some thirty years. All of that also underlines the importance of the River Thames to London. Now look at the helmets. Scotland Yard Police have a silver badge on the front of their helmet. City of London Police have a black and gold helmet plate. And the shapes of the two police forces' helmets are also different. The City of London Police helmet has a ridge or crest running along the top of it, said to be a visual echo of the crest on a Roman legionnaire's helmet. In which case the topper of a twenty-first-century City of London policeman is a further reminder of London's 2,000-year-old origins.

From Mitre Square, following the murderer's escape route, head east once more back on to Metropolitan Police territory, crossing Middlesex Street, on Sundays the street market 'Petticoat Lane' and the boundary between the two police forces, to Goulston Street.

Making this crossing in 1888 would have meant leaving the City of London, the richest square mile in the world, to a part of London known as 'outcast London', an area of slums, poverty and crime. Overcrowding was rife with people sleeping seven, eight, nine persons in one room. Children were the biggest sufferers – more than half would be dead before the age of five. One in ten would be born a mental defective. The age of consent was thirteen years old.

From Middlesex Street, walk through New Goulston Street – the Market Trader pub is on the corner – and this will bring you out directly opposite a block of apartments four storeys high. In 1888 it was a model dwelling. In the centre is the Happy Days restaurant, the main door of which has now replaced the original entranceway into the block. It was in the original doorway that the killer wrote a message on the wall and below it dropped a piece of Eddowes apron, which he had cut from her clothing and used to wipe his knife. The message, in chalk, said, 'The Juews are the men that will not be blamed for nothing'. No satisfactory explanation has ever been given for its meaning. No photograph of the message was taken as Sir Charles Warren, the Metropolitan Police commissioner, who attended the scene, had it removed. The area was home to a large Jewish population and it was thought that retaining the message until daylight could lead to anti-Semitic riots.

The murderer was now no longer the anonymous 'Whitechapel murderer' or the 'East End murderer' as he had been for several weeks. The press and public now had a name. A letter posted to the Central News Agency on 25 September 1888 and published on the eve of the 'double event' gave the name 'Jack the Ripper'. The letter was almost certainly a hoax but the name has stuck and ever since then the murderer has been Jack the Ripper. A more sensational item sent on 16 October to Mr Lusk, head of the Whitechapel Vigilance Committee, was a parcel containing what was claimed to be a part of Catherine Eddowes' kidney and a letter addressed 'From Hell'. It read:

Mr Lusk Sir I send you half the kidne I took from one women prasarved it for you tother piece I fried and ate it was very nise I may send you the bloody knif that took it out if you only wate a while longer, signed Catch me when You can Mishter Lusk.

Looking north along Goulston Street can be seen the former Providence Row Refuge, now a student hostel, at the corner of Crispin Street and Artillery Row. The word 'WOMEN' is still visible on the lintel above the former doorway. Built by the Catholic Church in the mid-nineteenth century, this is where Mary Kelly, the last victim, is said to have stayed before moving to a house nearby.

Brushfield Street

The next street is Brushfield Street, where the old Spitalfields fruit and vegetable market has undergone a transformation. Built in 1887, one year before the murders, it was a prime spot for the prostitutes to come and pick up customers. At the far end of the street is Hawksmoor's Christchurch Spitalfields, which has had a £10 million face-lift. On the opposite corner of Commercial Street and Fournier Street is the Ten Bells, better known locally as the 'Jack the Ripper pub' or the 'prostitutes pub'. This pub was known to and used by all the Ripper victims.

Walk through Puma Court, a gloomy alleyway of small houses, to the left of the pub and follow it round to Hanbury Street, the location of the second Ripper murder. Only one side of the street is contemporary with the murders. The murder site, a shabby terraced house opposite Nos 28 and 30, was pulled down when the present building was constructed in the 1960s. The body of Annie Chapman was found at 5.30 a.m. on 8 September 1888 in the backyard, her throat cut, the body disembowelled and horribly mutilated. Earlier she had been seen talking to a man of foreign appearance wearing a brown deerstalker hat.

Return to the Ten Bells at the corner of Fournier Street. The houses in this street were part of the killing ground and the overcrowded slums of 1888. Slums in 1888, desirable residences today. Almost directly opposite Christchurch Spitalfields is White's Row multi-storey car park. The open parking space was once Dorset Street, one of the most infamous streets in London. 13 Miller's Court was a partitioned-off room of 26 Dorset Street where lodged 25-year-old Mary Kelly, the final victim. The location would have been about fifty yards in from Commercial Street. She was murdered on the night of 8/9 November. A faint cry of 'Murder'

Jack the Ripper

☆ The first victim, **Mary Ann 'Polly' Nichols** was killed here on the night of 8 September 1888

☆ **Annie Chapman**, the Ripper's second murder

☆ **Elizabeth 'Long Liz' Stride**, the first of two murders the night of 30 September 1888

☆ **Catherine Eddowes** murdered here, the second victim of the night of the 'double event'

☆ **Mary Kelly**, the last-known of the Ripper's murders

was heard coming from her room at about 3.30 a.m. but such cries were commonplace and everyone ignored it. When her body was found in the morning the face had been skinned down to the skull, flesh had been stripped from her body and stacked up on the table beside her, other body parts such as her breasts, kidneys and liver were found under her feet and neck. Her heart was missing.

With her death, the Jack the Ripper murders came to an end.

Ever since there has been the great guessing game. Who did it? Did he commit suicide? Who was the Ripper?

At present the list of suspects totals more than two hundred. Far-fetched, ridiculous and total nonsense are most of them: a Royal grandson, a bohemian artist, mad doctor, policeman, abortionist, Liverpool diarist, and the author of *Alice in Wonderland* are just a few of the named suspects that have been put forward. The brutal reality is that there is not a shred of evidence to convict anyone. As far as identity is concerned this can best be left to a verse popular in the area for many years after the murders:

> *I'm not a butcher, I'm not a Yid,*
> *Nor yet a foreign skipper.*
> *I'm just your own light-hearted friend.*
> *Yours truly, Jack the Ripper.*

HAUNTED LONDON

SHAUGHAN SEYMOUR

A Man in Black

There are ghosts abroad in London. Only natural when you think of the millions who have lived and died here . . . St Paul's cathedral, for instance, the remnants of past times buried beneath its floor. Underneath, the foundations of the old St Paul's, destroyed in 1666, and below those ruins, the palimpsest of a Roman temple. The dust of so much activity and human endeavour compacted in one place. No surprise that some souls may still remain . . .

18 March 1927

I, Gerald Walker, Verger at St Paul's, feel it incumbent upon me to record what happened this evening at St Paul's. It was after evensong – about five minutes to seven – and I had just completed my duties in the Kitchener Chapel. The altar cloth needed to be renewed, and candlesticks trimmed of wax and polished. Some of the clergy would have been in the cathedral, but at the choir end. As I folded the old altar cloth I had a sense of someone close to me, and as I turned around to face the north wall I saw someone dressed in black robes walking towards me with determined strides. My instinct was to step aside as the person was so close, but there appeared to be no lessening of pace. The figure moved past me, and I had the impression of a bearded grinning face with teeth bared. As the person passed me I could hear a curious tuneless whistle and – there is no other way to explain this – the figure melted into the southeast corner of the chapel. I stood rooted to the spot with astonishment – no door, no window, no recess could have received this shape. It made such a strong impression on me that I decided to speak to the Dean straight away. I called upon him at his lodging in Amen Corner, and he showed me into his study. After I had spoken, he looked at me thoughtfully, his eyes wide with interest. 'Tomorrow you must show me where this shape disappeared.'

19 March 1927

I met the Dean this morning in the chapel, and I indicated the corner. He walked up to the spot, felt around the stonework.

'The mortar here is loose,' he said, 'and as it happens, we are due to do some restoration next week. But what you witnessed yesterday, others have seen over many years. My predecessors have left accounts in diaries and, in one instance, in the minutes of a Chapter meeting. Now that the Keeper of the Fabric has been given instructions to remove the stones, perhaps we will find an answer.'

28 March 1927

This morning I was called into the chapel by the Dean, and found him standing by a large pile of bricks and Portland stone. Where the stones had been was a wooden door which when opened revealed a spiral staircase winding upwards.

'It goes to the top of the bell tower,' he said 'and no one knew of its existence. It must have been blocked off sometime in the last century.'

'And the gentleman in black?' I enquired.

'Nothing.'

Supping with the Devil

If you walk a short distance from St Paul's Cathedral to the west, crossing Ave Maria Lane you arrive at Amen Corner. These seventeenth-century houses are the grace-and-favour homes of the Dean and other clergy. In their garden is a long brick wall, all that is left of Newgate Prison, the place of much suffering and degradation, but none so strange as that described by Richard Thomas . . .

11 November 1609

Lord God give me strength to survive this night. Called this morning to Newgate to witness the confession of a prisoner, I was taken by the Gaoler to a large room on the second floor of the prison. I have over the years, as clerk and scrivener, visited this sad repository many times, and am almost used to the stench and misery. Today I was tried to the utmost. At the door to the cell, a turnkey sat, a cudgel by him. When we came near, he rose and opened the cell. The light being bad, I asked for a candle as I would have need to write. I entered and could dimly see the form of a man in a corner, thin and ragged, as so many are, his complexion grey and wasted. He stared, it seemed, at nothing, and his lips moved as if in prayer. I spoke his name – John Partridge – and he turned his head to mine.

'I have come to hear you bear witness to your crimes,' said I, 'and I will write what you tell, and you will sign.'

He moved his head. 'I will tell all I have done and seen, and may Christ have mercy on me.'

I called for fresh water to be brought for the prisoner, and set parchment and ink on a joined-stool, and prepared myself.

The prisoner began: 'I, John Partridge, wish to freely confess my offence of forgery. I knowingly forged a deed of property belonging to William Hart and sold it for twenty pounds. This I confess, and am truly sorry for the offence.

'What I also wish to confess concerns another matter, of which no Judgement of Man can save me.

'Three days ago, I, with twelve others was in a room on the lower floor. We had had no easement of irons or any kind of food for two weeks save one loaf of stale bread. We cried out for food, but none was brought. We had even started to eat our garments in the hope of sustenance. One night the door opened and another prisoner was brought in. He fell down on the ground, a man of substance, large, dressed in black. He lay in pain, calling for mercy – he had been under torture. Through his pain, as he laboured for breath, he told me that he had been a doctor, but that he was also a practitioner of the Dark Arts – necromancy – and had fallen in with those who supped with the Devil. He knew his fate was sealed, and he would suffer yet more under the Court. He therefore begged us, weak as we were, to dispatch him – "My life is worth nothing but the Vengeance of the Bishops – take it and do with my body as you will."

'We fell into a conclave the other prisoners and me and talked the matter over. We could reach no agreement, and spoke of leaving him to die. But then one of our number, Hugh Downing, crazed with lack of food, shouted, "From the Devil to the Devil," and taking his length of chain, passed it around the Doctor's neck and pulled the man against the wall, breaking his spine. He was dead, certain sure, and his body lay by the wall. But the next moment – how can I tell you?! We could see and smell food, meats and cheese and strong wine – starving as we were, we all fell to, and filled our bellies well.

'This feasting made us sleep, but the next savour that awoke us all was not for Christian appetites. The smells of sulphur and death forced us awake. For where the doctor had lain was blood and bones. Our hands were covered in blood, and our beards stiff with blood also. From the ruins of the body there appeared as in a vision, the shape of a creature; eyes red, chains on its paws, and on its head a writhing mass of snakes. It raised itself on hind legs and walked towards us. We were frozen with fear, and had the sense of lowering spirit, as if our very souls were being taken. I called, "Jesu, have mercy!" and prayed for deliverance. The creature then sank down into the ground. Two of my fellow prisoners were found against the wall, their eyes open with terror, teeth bared, both stone dead. Another was in the corner, stark mad. I understood what had occurred. The doctor had persuaded us, by what magic I know not, to eat his flesh. And so consumed, his spirit returned to take us to Satan. May God have mercy on me, I fear he will return to torment those who doubt and fear and have not made their peace with God.'

Distressed as he was in having told me this terrible story, the prisoner John Partridge signed my record of the conversation and I witnessed it. A few days later he had been sentenced by court and hung, taking his fearful story to the grave.

The Dark Sisters

In our somewhat cynical and scientific age, it is easy to think that the city's ghosts and other apparitions are only in the long ago past. Not so . . .

Up close – Haunted London

At night, at the back of Dean's Yard, in Great College Street, the lamps are alight, some of the 2,000 or so gas lamps that are still working in London. The mantles are incandescent – usually there are three or four in a cluster – and are made using a treatment of cerium and thorium oxide, and are slightly radioactive in fact. They give a romantic gentlemanly glow to the stock brick and flint walls of the Inns of Court, Westminster and Covent Garden. The last lamplighter retired some twenty years ago, though many of the lamps still require their automatic timers to be wound up every few weeks. If you walk down Great College Street, towards Westminster School, there are some ladders chained to a lamppost – these are for the 'lamp-winder'. The very first gas lights were quite primitive, large tubes that still flare occasionally outside the Reform Club and the Athenaeum on Pall Mall. Later came the 'fish tail' or 'fantail' lights – like those at the front of the National Gallery.

Wardrobe Court
City of London EC2
13 October 2002

Dear Erica,

Thanks for your letter to the Bank. They have managed to get me a really central set of rooms here in London. I walk to work!! It's just to the south of St Paul's, a courtyard of eighteenth-century houses around a yard with trees, divided up into apartments. Real Purty & Olde Worldy! It's quiet here, especially at weekends. That is, until the ghost walkers come in! Yes, I kid you not, every Saturday night, a group of about twenty or so people come in to the central yard and some guide tells them about its history. Last week I had the window open, and the tour leader was saying that King James I would attend private parties here. He said that as result of the King's experience here, he became interested in witchcraft. I half-listened to this hokum, and shut the window. That night, I got to bed at about 1.30, but must have woken up an hour or so later, and I could hear some kind of singing in the yard. I thought it might be drunks or soccer fans or something, but it sounded like women. I opened the window real slow, and through the branches, I could see women moving in a circle.

They were wearing quite flimsy clothes, like half a sheet draped round them, and were chanting a song of some kind. I could make out 'take me, take me'. I have to say I was rooted to the spot, it was so strange. I thought it may be some kind of student prank, or perhaps they were doing a movie; but there were no lights other than what came from my window. I turned my light off, and went back to the window, but now could see nothing and no one.

The next day, I spoke to two other lodgers about it, but they had heard nothing. But now I have learned that the yard was known hundreds of years ago as a place where witches would convene. And that they gathered clad in only shifts, near naked. Further that they move about by means of the effect of a potion they took, one consisting of aconite, soot, the blood of a flitter-mouse (bat), and the blood and flesh of a young child!

What I may have witnessed was a haunting of the Dark Sisters, preparing for sacrifice. Do come and visit soon, I could use the company!

All the best,
Mark

Hog Face

Documentary evidence is sometimes hard to obtain when one investigates tales of hauntings in the City. But in this next case there exists a dossier and press cutting saved from bomb damage in 1940, a file taken from the cellars of the Daily Telegraph *building in Fleet Street. The file had the singular title, 'HOG FACE'* . . .

Playhouse Yard
London EC
30 September 1856

Sir,

I hope you will forgive my imposition on your time, but circumstances compel me to write to you. As the Freeholder of this property, I feel you should know of what occurred last Friday night. My wife and I were about to take to our bed, when we could both hear heavy footsteps upstairs. In alarm I called out 'Who's there?' but there was no reply. Thinking the noise was just settlement of the boards, we started to ascend. As we did so, the footsteps increased in pace and volume. We were frozen to the spot with terror, and saw, at the top of the stairs, a large shape of a woman, dressed in black. We could only see her body at first, her face was obscured, but as she descended, her features came into view. Now I have seen persons we would consider ill favoured in appearance, but this was ugliness beyond imagining. It was as though a hog or swine had spawned with a human. Around the figure was light, an emanation of light, suffused with blue. My wife Jane cried out, and fell into a swoon. As she fell into my arms, the figure disappeared, leaving my wife unconscious and myself shaken to the core. It was several days before we could bring ourselves to our bed without fear. What have we seen? And have any others witnessed this?

Please reply at your earliest convenience.

I remain, Sir,
Joseph Barret

Chancery House
Gray's Inn Road
WC
3 October 1856

My dear Mr Barret,
I received your letter on Tuesday last, and was somewhat surprised by its content. I have never received reports of the occurrence you describe. I am what you might call something of a skeptic in matters of religion & etc, but as the freeholder, I felt it necessary to enquire about a matter that has disturbed a tenant of mine. I therefore had words with Mr Trinder, the gentleman responsible for the yard outside, and someone entrusted with the keys from time to time. He said that there had been odd noises coming from the house, but when he entered, no one was present. I will enquire further and inform you if anything unusual comes to my attention. I apologise for the disturbance, and hope Mrs Barret is fully recovered.

Yours,
Edward Dowd

Playhouse Yard
London EC
2 November 1856

Sir,
I have to tell you that my wife and I no longer wish to live at these premises. Last night we had another visitation; the noises from the upper rooms were so loud that our dog, Nelson, was frantically yelping and was trying to escape from the front door, hurling himself against the wood. The figure appeared at the top of the stairs once more, and

when I called out 'Who are you?' it seemed that odd coughing, grating sounds emanated from it. My wife screamed in terror, and it vanished, just as before.

Sir, this is not a house for Christian souls to live in. We have informed Mr Trinder, and will move out tomorrow. We did not agree to share the house with other tenants. Please send the money owed to us to Child's Bank, Fleet Street.

Yours,
Joseph Barret

From the *London Chronicle*:
18 November 1856

We must report that the House in Playhouse Yard, Blackfriars, is vacant once more; tenancies there do seem to be somewhat short-lived. Several residents have complained over many years to the landlord, of strange noises and odd visitations – whether of burglars, bats, or over-zealous chimney sweeps is not clear. However, upon looking through some old accounts at the Guildhall, it seems there is a permanent incumbent. A Parish Letter (St Anne's) of 1698 states that: 'The House in Playhouse Yard, built after the Fire, received a Visitor of strange appearance – a woman, large in stature, wrapt in a cloak, was seen upon the upper storey. It may have been that of Tamasin Skinker, late of Saxony, resident here some seventy years ago, refused by her English lovers. Horrid in appearance, hog-faced and unable to speak, but being rich, expected a suitor. Being refused, returned to Germany in anger. Incapable of sensible talk, she is able to grunt and squeak only.'

On Duty Still

On the northern edge of the City is the oldest hospital in the British Isles – St Bartholomews, first founded in 1123 by Rahere, an Augustinian prior. Regarded as a beneficent figure, he started a trade fair at Smithfield to raise revenues for his hospital. It appears he is still on duty . . .

St Bartholomews Hospital
London EC
12 June 1962

Dear Mr Andrews,

As the Historian of St Bart's, I thought you might be interested in one or two stories that came to light fairly recently. I was approached by one of the probationers, who said that she had witnessed something rather strange. As she was wheeling her trolley along the first-floor corridor, she sensed a movement to her right, and thought she had seen a rat, or some kind of animal, following her alongside. It was brown, and round, but pale in the centre. She stopped, and the 'thing' stopped also. Then it continued slowly, and turned across the corridor. It was, she said, someone's head! She could see the eyes, nose and ears, and it vanished into a wall. She was a little shaken by this, as you can imagine, but to cap it all at the same time in the ward below a patient saw feet on the ceiling! He called out to the ward sister, and said he had seen sandalled feet walk along the ceiling and disappear. I spoke about this with a couple of the older members of staff, and John Grantham, who has been porter here for over thirty years, said, 'That's Rahere'. It would seem that our founder, Rahere, is still around – eight hundred years later, and checking up on us!

Yours Faithfully
Angela Wilson
Matron

No Rest for the Wicked

Another for whom there is no rest . . .

Snow Hill
City of London Police
London EC 1
3 December 1957

<u>Incident at Newgate Street EC1</u>
PC 625 John Carr

At 0615 on 19 October, a Mr Harold Sweet, working at King Edward St Post Office, having finished his shift, was walking through the bomb site by Newgate Street, reported seeing a woman walk towards him, dressed in a grey blanket, clutching at her chest in some distress. She seemed to him to be in pain, or disturbed in some way, but when he asked her if she was all right, appeared not to hear, and then seemed to vanish into the tower of the ruined church. He called at the station, and asked us about it. I passed by the bomb site on my beat, and decided to investigate. I could see nothing unusual, and no door or sheltering place in the church tower, so thought little more about the matter. However, on 29 October I was on night shift, and patrolling Newgate Street at 04.30, when I noticed movement in the bomb site area. The site is in fact the remains of Christchurch Newgate, a Wren church badly damaged in 1940.

As I stepped over the wire that protects the site, I saw a person dressed in a grey cloak move through the rubble. I called for the person to stop, but they appeared not to notice. I called again, 'Stop! Police!' but whoever it was walked towards the church tower and disappeared. I got round to the other side of the tower and vestry, but there was no sign. Back at Snow Hill station I spoke to the Desk Sergeant, Sgt Ryder, and over a cup of tea, he told me about the ruined church.

It turns out that where the church stood, was a monastery in the thirteenth century. The Franciscans or Greyfriars had it until Henry VIII's time and two queens of England are buried there – Margaret, wife of Edward I, and Isabella, wife to Edward II. Isabella, an attractive French princess, was married to Edward when he was Prince of Wales. But he had a boyfriend favourite, Piers Gaveston, and another lover, Despenser. This didn't go well with her. She plotted her husband's downfall and had him murdered 'by passing a red hot poker through his privy parts'. Her son, Edward III, kept her under house arrest until her death. She had asked to be buried in the monastery in a Greyfriar's habit, believing that this would get her through the gates of Heaven, no matter how sinful her life had been.

However, when she was eventually interred, they placed the embalmed heart of Edward II in a box on her breast, and it is said that as a result Isabella is unable to enter Heaven, and walks in torment round the church. History knows her as the She-Wolf of France. I wrote my log for the beat later, but didn't mention any queens or wolves, just 'woman in grey cloak'. Maybe others will file similar reports in future.

Dickens's London

Charles Dickens's
A Christmas Carol

JEAN HAYNES

This is a walk for the wintertime. 'It is required of every man,' quoth the ghost of Jacob Marley, 'that the spirit within him should walk abroad among his fellow men . . . and if that spirit goes not forth in life, it is condemned to do so after death, to wander through the world and witness what it cannot share but might have shared and turned to happiness.'

Let us go forth and wander, as Dickens often did, the streets in search of *A Christmas Carol* and the transformation of Ebenezer Scrooge, 'hard and sharp as flint and solitary as an oyster'. Dickens's story was written with the purpose to act as a 'sledge hammer' to rouse the public spirit on behalf of the poor and destitute. It has never been out of print! The Christmas book, and it moves us still.

The ghosts of London past

Intertwining the story are the festive decorations, the myths and customs which celebrate the season as we walk the City streets. Scrooge knew his city well. His counting house was here and his dwelling nearby. It's a gloomy house and the very large knocker on the front door is described in the story as taking on the appearance of Scrooge's dead partner – who died 'seven years ago, this very Christmas Eve'– with 'a dismal light about it, like a bad lobster in a dark cellar'. (There's a similar door-knocker on the Hung, Drawn & Quartered pub in Great Tower Street.) St Dunstan's Hill may have been the location for Scrooge's house, as Dickens makes reference to the saint who, with his red-hot tongs, tweaked the Devil's nose: 'Foggier yet and colder . . . if the Good St Dunstan had nipped the evil spirit's nose with a touch of such weather as that, then indeed he would have roared to lusty purpose.'

WHERE TO READ THIS

Trinity Gardens on Tower Hill has seats and is pleasant in fine weather. The walk starts there. Or try one of the pubs/eateries in Leadenhall Market, or the Crypt at St Paul's.

261

Travelling westward along Eastcheap, we come to an elaborate building over the way which stands near the site of the tavern where Falstaff, Prince Hal and their crew used to carouse – the Boar's Head. If you look up, beneath the central arch, there is a representation of the beast emerging from some rushes, which evokes an ancient yuletide song, 'The Boar's Head Carol'. Its origins are in a Scandinavian yule feast, in praise of a dish sacred to the heroes in Valhalla. It is celebrated still. On 16 December each year at the Cutlers' Feast in London, St Paul's Choir sings 'The Boar's Head in hand I bear, Adorned with bay and rosemary' as the boar's head is carried in procession, the traditional apple in its mouth.

Carols were not religious to begin with but grew out of round dances at feastings. Suppressed in the seventeenth century, these songs were revived and rightly should not be sung until Christmas Day. In London, carols were sung by the official band of 'City Waits' and this is the name of the tune of the carol most associated with Dickens's tale. A boy comes to Scrooge's door and begins 'God Rest Ye Merry, Gentlemen', but is soon chased off. The Waits were very jealous of their official standing and if an opposition choir set up, would resort to fisticuffs.

We now cross the road to Philpot Lane. An Italianate building stands at the eastern corner. If you look carefully you'll see two little mice set on the join between this building and the next. They are a reminder of the mice that stole the builders' bread and cheese while the shop was being erected. Forward now to Leadenhall Market. Although built after Dickens's time, in 1881, Leadenhall has all of the Victorian exuberance he wrote about and a link with Dickens's description of the streets through which the Ghost of Christmas Present passes:

The fruiterers were radiant in their glory. There were great round-bellied baskets of chestnuts, shaped like the waistcoats of jolly old gentlemen lolling at the doors and tumbling out into the street in their apoplectic opulence: there were pears and apples clustered high in blooming pyramids . . . piles of filberts, mossy and brown . . . bunches of grapes . . . Norfolk Biffins [a kind of apple] squat and swarthy, setting off the yellow of the oranges and lemons . . . The scales descending on the counter made such a merry sound . . . the canisters were rattled up and down like juggling tricks . . . the candied fruits so caked and spotted with molten sugar . . . the figs were moist and pulpy . . . the French plums blushed from their highly decorated boxes . . . everything was good to eat and in its Christmas dress . . . but the customers were all so hurried and eager in the hopeful promise of the day that they tumbled up against each other – clashing their wicker baskets wildly, and left their purchases upon the counter and came running back for them – in the best humour possible.

Crossing the Central Hall is Whittington Avenue, named after the famous Lord Mayor of London who is celebrated as that poor boy-cum-entrepreneur, 'Dick', in pantomime. The topsy-turvydom of pantomime has its roots in the old Roman Saturnalia and Whittington Avenue is as happens on the site of the Roman Forum and Basilica. At such festive times merriment and anarchy prevailed. Roles were reversed: masters served their servants. 'Disguising' or masking took place, which later occurred also in the old Mumming Plays of St George and the Dragon. The metamorphosis of pantomime continued in Britain as an import from Italy, the Commedia del Arte with its Harlequin and Columbine and Pantaloon. The London pantomimes date from the time of John Rich, a famous eighteenth-century Harlequin. Transformation scenes and cross-dressing remain today in our modern 'Panto' shows.

There is usually a large Christmas tree set up in Leadenhall, an evergreen symbol of Eternity, as is the greenery of the florists. Holly to remind us of the blood on the Crown of Thorns; ivy to keep out the witches; and mistletoe, the 'Golden Bough' with its white berries, a kiss for each under the Kissing Bunch. *Viscum album* it is named – 'all heal' – and is good against hypertension, but poisonous. It is the wood with which the evil Norse spirit Loki killed Balder the Beautiful, a pagan connotation and so not used in church decorations.

One special piece of greenery is the Glastonbury Thorn. Legend says the tree sprang from the staff of Joseph of Arimathea when he stuck it in the ground of Wearyall Hill in Somerset while escorting the young Jesus here ('And did those feet in ancient time, Walk upon England's mountains green?'). The Queen is sent slips of this tree, which is said to flower on Christmas Eve, for her table display.

Now cross Gracechurch Street and head down St Peter's Alley, where the pub is called the Counting House. Very appropriate, as we are in the vicinity of Scrooge's office in St Michael's Churchyard:

> The ancient tower of a church whose gruff old bell was always peeping slyly down at Scrooge out of a Gothic window, became invisible, and struck the hours and quarters in the clouds with tremulous vibrations, afterwards, as if its teeth were chattering in its frozen head, up there. It was cold, bleak, biting weather . . . and the fog came pouring in at every chink and keyhole so that, although the court was of the narrowest, the houses opposite became mere phantoms.

When seven o'clock came that Christmas Eve, Scrooge grudgingly allowed Bob Cratchit to go home and take Christmas Day off – 'Be here all the earlier next day!' Grudgingly, for until 1870 bank holidays were unknown: 'The office was closed in a twinkling and the clerk went down a slide on Cornhill at the end of a lane of boys, twenty times in honour of its being Christmas Eve.' We, too, will go out into Cornhill, past the George and Vulture, where Mr Pickwick was 'suspended' prior to the breach-of-promise trial, past Simpsons, another old chop-house, both looking very much as they did in Dickens's day and where, at the former, his descendants still meet to toast his memory.

Up close – A Christmas Carol

In St Martin-le-Grand, there is a statue, that of Sir Rowland Hill, outside what was the main Post Office. It was he who in 1840 instituted the Universal Penny Postage, encouraging communication which, a few years later, included the first Christmas card. The stamp on these letters and cards was the 'Penny Black' with an image of the young Queen Victoria. It was her consort, Prince Albert, who made popular that 'pretty German Toy' – the Christmas tree.

We have reached the Royal Exchange where, when Scrooge was being shown by the Spirit of a Christmas Yet to Come, 'He saw no likeness of himself among the multitudes that poured in through the porch', and his heart was full of dread that his 'place knew him no more'. At Bank Junction is the home of the Lord Mayor of London, during his year of office: 'The Lord Mayor in the stronghold of the mighty Mansion House gave orders to his fifty cooks and butlers to keep Christmas as a Lord Mayor's household should.' Leftovers from such festivities were handed out through the side windows to the poor, who lined up for such treats.

Christmas pudding for the day was traditionally made on the Sunday before Advent, 'Stir up Sunday'. The church Collect for that day runs: 'Stir up, O Lord, the wills of thy faithful people that they, plenteously bringing forth the fruit of Thy good works, may of Thee be plenteously rewarded.' In *A Christmas Carol*, Mrs Cratchit's pudding was a source of anxiety for them all; she over its consistency; the young ones that someone might have got over the back wall and stolen it:

Hello! A great deal of steam. The pudding was out of the copper. A smell like washing day – that was the cloth; a smell like an eating house and a pastry cooks next door . . . Mrs Cratchit entered with the pudding like a speckled cannon ball . . . blazing in half of half a quartern of ignited brandy and bedight with Christmas holly stuck in the top.

The Cratchits were slightly better off than the tailor and his wife who would have dined off beef. No goose for them, though even the Cratchits' was a small one, 'eked out by the apple sauce and mashed potato, it was a sufficient dinner for the whole family'.

People used to save up all the year round in Goose Clubs and when Christmas came their names were drawn out of a hat. If lucky, their goose was large; if not, the difference in money for a small goose was made up in ale – pleasing the men, but not their wives with mouths to feed. The fowl would be taken to the baker's to be cooked, along with many others, in his big oven at the cost of a few pence. The young Cratchits claimed they had identified their own by the aroma as they came home. Later, after his reformation, Scrooge sent them an enormous turkey: 'What, the one as big as me?' exclaimed the boy he dispatched to order it; and if we look across Poultry, we can see a cherub, struggling with a similar-sized goose.

Moving westwards we come to the site of the Temple of Mithras, a Persian God of Light whose '*Dies Nationalis Invicta Solis*' – Birthday of the Invincible Sun – was celebrated on 25 December, a pagan date taken over by the Christians in the fourth century. The cult of Mithras was very popular with the Roman military in this country, so we might like to fancy that Christmas in London began here.

Along Bow Lane now, which during the festive time is decorated with lights, towards the Olde Watling, a pub built by Christopher Wren for his workmen. At this time of year taverns would serve 'Lambs Wool', warmed ale containing roasted crab apples, sugar, spices, eggs, thick cream and sippets of bread. Mulled wine and punch were also popular. Dickens always mixed the punch himself. He was a good host, writing out the menus in his own hand and seeing that his guests had a good time. The word 'punch' is derived from the Indian word *panch* or 'five', the number of ingredients in a good punch.

After Scrooge's conversion, he offers Bob Cratchit a bowl of 'Smoking Bishop'. This was made by baking six Seville oranges, each stuck with five cloves, then placing them in a warmed earthenware bowl, adding sugar, a bottle of Portuguese red wine and leaving the oranges warm for a day. Then the oranges are squeezed, a bottle of port added and the whole heated and served. The colour is then that of a Bishop's vest.

St Mary-le-Bow is world famous for its bells. Born within the sound you will be a true Cockney. Scrooge delighted in the City's carillon when he realised he had not missed Christmas Day after all: 'The churches ringing out the lustiest peal he had ever heard . . . ding, dong, bell, hammer, clang, clash . . . glorious, glorious.'

We come out on Cheapside, the old medieval marketplace, and cross to the site of St Peter Cheap, under the tree at the corner of Wood Street. Here we find: 'A churchyard. Here, then, the wretched man whose name Scrooge was yet to learn, lay . . . walled in by houses, choked up with too much burying, fat with repleted appetite. A worthy place.' Discovering his own name there, Scrooge, unmourned and unloved, has his life changed: 'I will honour Christmas in my heart and try to keep it all the year.'

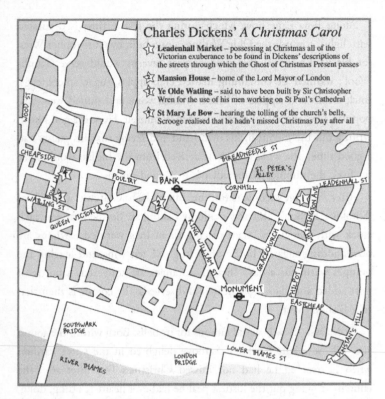

Charles Dickens' *A Christmas Carol*

⭐ **Leadenhall Market** – possessing at Christmas all of the Victorian exuberance to be found in Dickens' descriptions of the streets through which the Ghost of Christmas Present passes

⭐ **Mansion House** – home of the Lord Mayor of London

⭐ **Ye Olde Watling** – said to have been built by Sir Christopher Wren for the use of his men working on St Paul's Cathedral

⭐ **St Mary Le Bow** – hearing the tolling of the church's bells, Scrooge realised that he hadn't missed Christmas Day after all

Crossing St Martin-le-Grand, we see a statue, that of Sir Rowland Hill, outside what was the main Post Office. It was he who in 1840 instituted the Universal Penny Postage, encouraging communication which, a few years later, included the first Christmas card. The stamp on these letters and cards was the 'Penny Black' with an image of the young Queen Victoria. It was her consort, Prince Albert, who made popular that 'pretty German Toy' – the Christmas tree.

In 1843, Dickens was writing his 'little book', as he described it and of which it has been said that it 'fostered more kind feelings, prompted more positive acts of benevolence.' *A Christmas Carol* is forever associated with the season it may, it could be said, have reinvented. True to his own dictum that 'We should all be children, sometime, and what better time than at Christmas when its Mighty Founder was a child Himself,' Dickens would enter wholeheartedly into the spirit of the time. He was an expert conjurer; he rehearsed his sons when they came home from school in the plays they would put on for family and friends; and his parties were as joyous as that at the Fezziwigs, with dancing and blind man's bluff and snapdragon.

Influenced by *A Christmas Carol*, Victorian philanthropy began to flow into many channels where 'want is keenly felt' for, like Scrooge after the visits of the Spirits, Dickens 'knew how to keep Christmas well', if any man in the Good Old City of London knew.

AUTHOR BIOGRAPHIES

Nick Day

is an actor who has successfully divided his time between theatre, film and television. He has worked extensively at the National Theatre and the Royal Shakespeare Company where he appeared most recently in the Complete Works Festival. In London he has appeared in plays at the Almeida, Donmar Warehouse and Royal Court theatres and several times in the West End. In pantomime, more years ago than he cares to count, he fought a nightly linguistic duel with Mary Tucker in improvised rhyming couplets. They became firm friends and Nick became one more of Mary's fellow actors that she has pressed into service over the years.

Angela Down

was born and brought up in London. When not walking the streets, she is an actress. No change there, then.

Kevin Flude

is a museum curator and lecturer. He runs the Old Operating Theatre Museum near London Bridge, and lectures for the University of the Arts, London and for Elderhostel. He has a lifelong interest in the history and archaeology of London. He is a member of the Institute of Field Archaeologists and a former archaeologist at the Museum of London.

Peter Glancy

like those other great Londoners Shakespeare, Dr Johnson and Dickens, does not hail from the metropolis. He was bred and born in Nelson, Lancashire, but came to London in 1974 to study at the Drama Centre. After an intermittently average acting career he has fallen literally on his feet with the wonderful London Walks®. Guiding the public through the streets of London combines his three great loves: architecture, history and showing off.

Ed Glinert

was born in Dalston, London, and read Classical Hebrew at Manchester University. He set up the Manchester's listings magazine *City Life* in 1983 and has since worked as a journalist for *Radio Times, Mojo* and *Private Eye*. His books include *The Literary Guide to London* (2000), *The London Compendium* (2003), *East End Chronicles* (2005), *West End Chronicles* (2007), *London's Dead* (2008) and *The Manchester Compendium* (2008). He has also edited *The Diary of a Nobody* by George and Weedon Grossmith, and collections of the Sherlock Holmes stories and the Gilbert & Sullivan operettas for Penguin Classics.

Jean Haynes

is a Londoner born and bred. A qualified teacher, having taught for over thirty-five years, she joined London Walks® as a City of London Guide with a wide range of tours, some in costume. As an actor, her leading roles have ranged from Greek drama and Shakespeare to music hall and pantomime. She lectures and writes on London, history, genealogy and literature, is a member of the Society of Genealogists and the Dickens Fellowship, and is on the committee of the Friends of Keats House.

Jean's chapter is dedicated to the memory of June Street, a great guide and a good friend.

Brian Hicks

trained as a lawyer, became office manager for a courier company, was director of an art gallery, and in between was an assistant surveyor, catering manager and motorcycle courier. He has lectured on everything from the Anglo-Saxons to the English legal system, has served on the Executive Council of the Guild of Registered Tourist Guides and on the Board of the Institute of Tourist Guiding, and has been involved in guide training in various capacities. He won a guiding prize for his 'On Site' guiding. He has also written various articles and pieces on London. His chief pleasure is motorcycling and he relaxes with gardening and travel.

Tom Hooper

is a barrister, Fellow of the Royal Geographical Society, Examiner for the Blue Badge Guides Course, travel writer and a professionally qualified Blue Badge Guide (he's the Chairman of the Guild of Guides Association). Follically challenged but motorcyclingly virile, his graceful wit, classic elegance of mind, infectious giggle, and gentle and generous heart make him the delight of all who know him.

Sue Jackson

has a background in publishing but had been taking guided walks alongside her full-time job for a very long time before deciding, ten years ago, to make guiding her priority. She completed the Blue Badge qualification, and today guides, takes tours all over the country and gives lectures. These are mainly delivered to the National Trust or the National Association of Decorative and Fine Arts Societies, but she also runs courses for the City Literary Institute on aspects of power and politics and the development of London.

John Mahoney

was born in South London and bred in North London, and has lived the great majority of his life in the metropolis. He worked for a number of years as a London Walks® guide following his retirement from forty years in journalism, working mainly as Foreign Editor for Independent Television News and later at BBC News and *Newsnight*. In between ITN and the BBC, he was for a time News Editor at London's commercial local news programme *Thames News*. In the recent past he has been concentrating on voluntary press work for two national charities.

Judy Pulley

was born in Warwickshire but has lived in London for thirty years, working as a teacher and in the media before becoming a full-time guide in 1995. Judy is a London Blue Badge guide and a City of London guide, conducting tours in all areas of London, with particular interest in East London where she lives. She has written a book on the City of London – *Streets of the City* – which was published in 2006. Her interests include photography, industrial heritage, architecture and stone carving.

Hilary Ratcliffe

read history at Bristol University and taught in high schools before training as a City of London guide in 1991. She trained as a Blue Badge guide in 1998 and now works full-time as a tourist guide. She recently completed the St Albans city-guide course. In addition Hilary is a Soroptimist – a member of an international business and professional women's service organisation which works to improve the lives of women and girls worldwide. In her spare time she enjoys theatre, walking, reading and travelling.

Richard Roques

trained as an actor at the Central School of Speech and Drama. He works full-time as a guide with London Walks® with a repertoire of over forty different walks. He has written seven full-length plays for the stage and a number of short stories and radio plays. Of his first play, *Looks Like Freedom*, Bonnie Greer wrote in *Time Out*: 'His insights . . . are compassionate and often hilarious . . . this play, with its honesty and willingness to engage the world, is worth all the well-crafted, directed to death but essentially tiny plays currently in fashion.' Richard won the 2006 Windsor Fringe Festival award for his short play *Don't Open the Door*. His comedy *The History of London Until it Got Burnt Down* had a successful run in the West End in 2008 and is set to return. His latest play *Get Rich Quick* will also be premiering in 2009.

Donald Rumbelow

is internationally recognised as the leading authority on Jack the Ripper. Britain's most distinguished crime historian, he is the author of the pre-eminent book on the Ripper, the bestselling *The Complete Jack the Ripper*. A former Curator of the City of London Police Crime Museum and a two-time Chairman of the Crime Writers Association, he is a Freeman of the City of London and a professionally qualified Blue Badge and City of London Guide.

Adam Scott

is an author, columnist, critic and blogger who moved to London from his native Edinburgh 'just to see what all the fuss was about'. That was eighteen years ago. He's still here. He has covered theatre for the *Independent*, bars for *Time Out* and has written about London from every angle, from the Button Queen shop in Marylebone to Dulwich Hamlet Football Club. He counts it a privilege to shout his head off in the street about the world's greatest city and dedicates his chapters to his wife Karen (a former Blue Badge Guide of the Year) and his baby daughter Isobella.

Shaughan Seymour

has worked as a London Walks® guide for eighteen years and has trained as a City of London and Blue Badge Guide. He has followed other London tale-tellers and scribbled in their wake, picking up what scraps he can, rummaging in the archives, and visiting as many second-hand bookshops as possible. He also works as an actor, mostly in television and film, and occasionally serenades his groups with a song or two.

David Tucker

is the seigneur of this favoured realm (London Walks), broods over words, breeds enthusiasms, and is generally 'unmanageable'. A balterer, literary historian, university lecturer and lifelong thanatophobe, he's also the London Walks® 'pen' – he writes the leaflet and website.

INDEX